HANDWRITTEN

HANDWRITTEN

REMARKABLE PEOPLE ON THE PAGE

Lesley Smith

BODLEIAN
LIBRARY
PUBLISHING

I am fully Senceible of the great Fatigue you m
Suffer from the Weighty affairs of your high Off
Multiplycity of Applications Continually rolling in upon y
reason I refrain as much as possible from giving a
n by approaching you Yet cannot Conceal my Con
if the affair of Well settling Catt Island be wholy Neg
Measures Concerted relating thereto until the Parliament
moved to buy out the Lords Proprietors, there will
uch other business on foot as will postpone this; I m
glad of opertunety to say something to you upon it in
n by the foretop, and also perticularly to acquaint you, and you only
a good Sum of Money wch has laid Many years unapply
derable larger Sum than what the Parliament have lat
Settling Foreign & other Protestants in Georgia; a
rswaded you may with ease (but I cannot) get for ma
t & Defenceible Settlement on Catt Island
knowledge of this Money until within a few Months,
now of a Close designe to apply to the Parliament for
ng of Next Sessions, But I conceive you can lay anoth
rd of them and get that Money appropriated for the
ttling Catt Island, if you shall think fit to take it in
ers can endeavour for it.
lution of acquainting none but your hon^r wch this matter

CONTENTS

Composers

Writers for Children

Spies and Detectives

Families

Scribes and Calligraphers

Postscript

ACKNOWLEDGEMENTS

This book is a love letter to a great library, its remarkable collections and remarkable staff. Even under pandemic conditions, those in the Rare Books and Manuscripts Reading Room at the Weston Library of the Bodleian kept the boxes coming. Their good humour about the number and variety of my manuscript orders made each day a (masked) pleasure, as was their willingness to enter into the game of finding even more. Thank you, Ernesto, Gillian, Hannah, Neil, Nicola and Oliver.

The Library's curators and conservators offered their expertise with typical generosity. Thanks to Stuart Acland, Debbie Hall, Martin Holmes, Andrew Honey, Rachael Marsay, César Merchan-Hamann, Nick Millea, Alasdair Watson and Mike Webb, not just for knowing so much, but for being so eager to share it.

Michael Kauffmann and Henrike Laehnemann rescued me from the clutches of German script, and Henrike shared her knowledge of Luther's hand. Alexander Peplow generously offered his master's thesis on the Bodleian's Luther autograph.

Sometimes one is lucky enough to gain not just a graduate student, but also their spouse. Thanks to Karl Kinsella, but especially to Jane Carroll for sharing her knowledge of children's literature.

Everyone should have a friend who is an archivist-palaeographer, and I am lucky to count Clare Hopkins (still a 'by hand' correspondent) as mine.

Martin Kauffmann, Head of Early and Rare Collections, has once again made everything so much better. His contribution is outshone only by that of the anonymous reader from Bodleian Library Publishing, who saved me from many a slip and found a place for Pepys.

And, finally, this book should have been for my mother, whose daily letters and awful handwriting unwittingly provided my first lessons in palaeography.

LS

Oxford, 2021

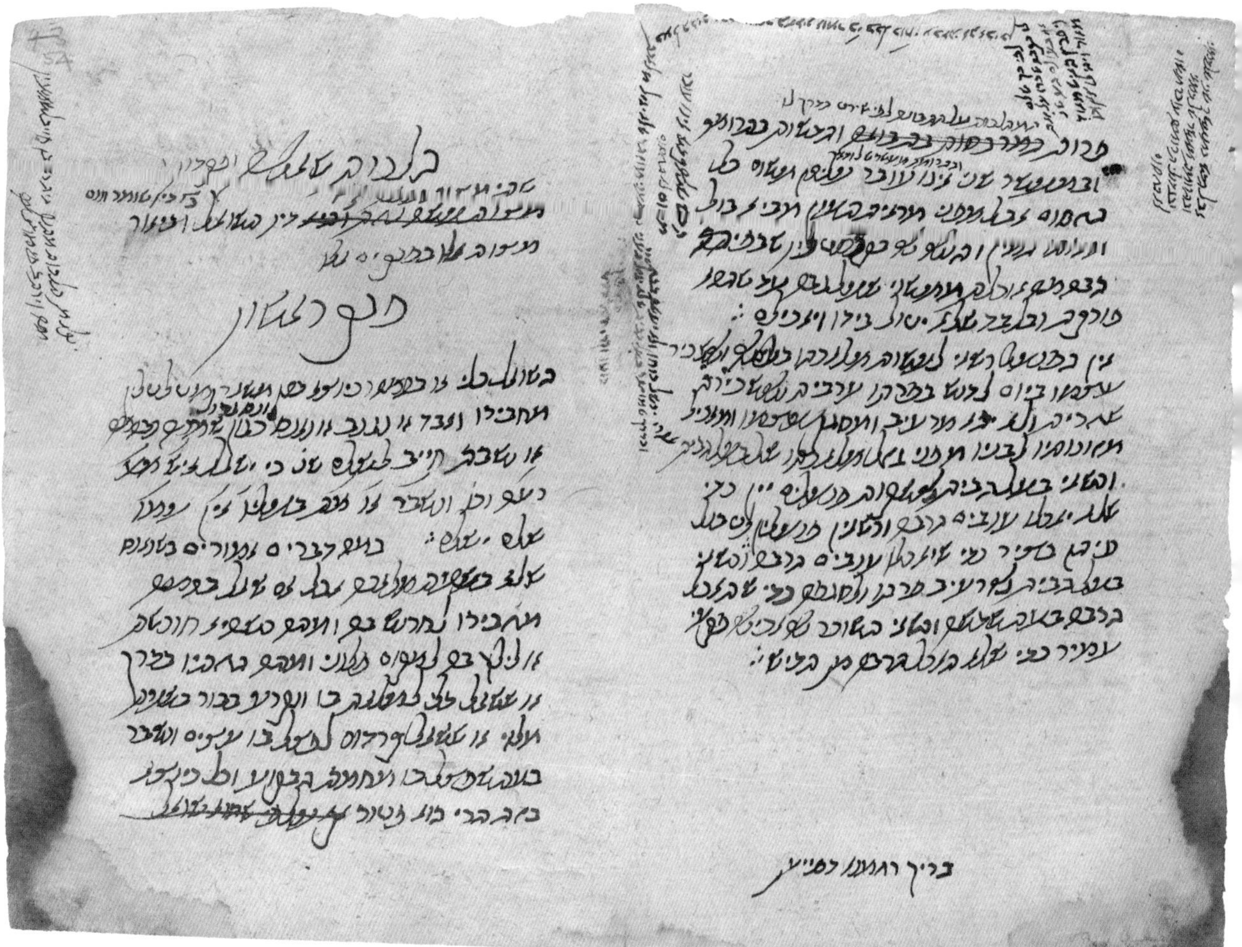

1 Maimonides, *Mishneh Torah*, c.1180

By My Own Hand ...

[R]emarkable people are made present to me in a magical way, through their handwriting.

Goethe, letter to Friedrich Jacobi, 10 May 1812

The less it is part of everyday life, the more the appeal of the handwritten grows. Perhaps that won't be so for the born-digital generations, but for those of us who remember when not all writing was typing, texting or social media, the pleasure – or not – of recognizing a familiar script is deep and immediate. The close relation of the script to its writer provides a particular thrill. Once upon a time, I could recognize the handwriting of each of my students; now, I'm lucky if I spot their customary font in an email or a printed essay. Easier for legibility, perhaps, but still a feeling of something missing: it's not just remarkable people who are magically present through their handwriting, but everyone we can see making their mark. Fans who use their phones to take selfies with the players as they leave the Wimbledon Centre Court also hold out giant tennis balls or paper programmes for those same players to scrawl an unreadable autograph.

In 1936 the critic Walter Benjamin published a famous essay, 'The Work of Art in the Age of Mechanical Reproduction', in which he argued that new technology for making high-quality copies would render originals obsolete. When an excellent copy was cheap and easy to get, the 'real thing' would lose its interest; no one would care about the artist's original because everyone could have their own. Benjamin was absolutely right in recognizing the importance of the new technology, but equally wrong in his analysis of its effects. The easier it becomes to reproduce the *Mona Lisa*, the longer grow the queues to see her in person in the Louvre. Rather than decreasing the value of the artist's own handiwork, our ability to reproduce it has sent interest in and prices for the original soaring – an interest parodied by the street artist Banksy and his picture, which was meant to be shredded by a device embedded in its own frame as soon as it had been sold. Ironically, the semi-shredded picture, *Girl with Balloon*, now called *Love is in the Bin*, was sold again for even more money only three years later.

Why might we be drawn to the hand-produced? Surely, first of all, because it seems to bring us close to the writer by uniting a thought and an action, following the clues as they leave a trail on a page. It's one thing to know that Elizabeth I, the daughter of King Henry VIII of England, had a succession of new stepmothers, but quite another to hold the devotional book she wrote out for Katherine Parr as a propitiatory New Year's gift. Indeed, with our modern knowledge of DNA, it's been hard, as I've worked with these documents, not to imagine the closeness in those terms – that some minute particle of the DNA of the writer, and perhaps of subsequent readers, might pass from what's in front of me on the desk to my own fingers as they carefully turn the leaves. The written page becomes a kind of relic of the person who wrote it. This is true, for instance, with the Bodleian's precious copy of parts of the *Mishneh Torah*, or *Repetition of the Law*, by the greatest Jewish scholar of the Middle Ages, Moses ben Maimon, known as Maimonides (d.1204), drafted around 1180 in his own hand.

Maimonides was born in Cordoba in Spain, but spent most of his working life in Fustat (Old Cairo), where he was the head of its important Jewish community, a practising physician, and a philosopher and biblical and legal authority. This autograph draft, read from right to left, written in Judaeo-Arabic – Arabic language in Hebrew characters – gives a vivid sense of Maimonides's working method. We know from his letters that he began with a draft made mostly from memory, followed by additions and alterations after he had checked his sources. Here we can see his bold central text in Sephardic script, with interlinear revisions and marginal notes – which he sometimes complained were misplaced by copying scribes. A Bodleian curator told me how a visiting rabbi reacted to being shown pages in Maimonides's own hand: it was, he said, the greatest day of his life. The handwritten text is the closest we can get to meeting the author (p. 8).

Maimonides's stained and nibbled paper pages also bear witness to the serendipity of survival. The fragment is one of those discovered in the *genizah* of the Cairo synagogue in the 1890s. The *genizah* was a storeroom specially made to house discarded pages of texts that contained the name of God. The Cairo *genizah* was only rediscovered during rebuilding work on the Ben Ezra Synagogue – its treasures, dating back to the tenth century, had been preserved in the dry Egyptian climate. The Maimonides fragment (among others) would probably have been left there when a fair copy – most likely by a professional scribe – had been made from his autograph draft. It was common practice for copyists or, later, printers to throw away the drafts when they had served their purpose. Only a series of lucky chances has left us this handwritten messenger, eight centuries old.

And of course, there is closeness simply in the idea of writing – the desire and ability of cultures to record something beyond the boundaries of personal memory, to put it out so it can be read. Among the Bodleian's treasures is a letter from a boy, who gives his name as Theon (θεων: p. 13, first word), to his father in the ancient Egyptian city of Oxyrhynchus. Written on papyrus in Greek, in the second or third century CE, it reads (in part):

> If you won't take me with you to Alexandria I won't write you a letter or speak to you or greet you ... Send for me, I implore you. If you don't, I won't eat, I won't drink; so there!

Across time and geography, Theon's letter still speaks.

There is also a long-held belief that writing betrays character. We would like to think we can see personal traits, virtues and vices in the angle of writing, the loops and spaces on the page – spacious script signals a generous character and uncrossed *t*'s a slapdash mind. Even sober scholars fall prey to this chimaera at times. The works of the ninth-century Irish theologian John Scot Eriugena are preserved in a very few contemporary manuscripts, parts of which were written by Irish scribes. The possibility of spotting the hand of the master at work in one of these copies has led normally cautious academics (tactfully left anonymous here) to lose their heads:

> If it were not a duty to refrain as far as possible from subjective opinion … it would be tempting to recognize more specious characteristics of an Irish-cosmopolitan intellectual [Eriugena] in the rapid, nervous, dispersed, sometimes rather disorderly hand which is designated I–1

A ninth-century Irishman, it seems, follows the stereotype of an Irishman of 1977 (when this comment was written) – quick, nervy, unfocused and sometimes rather (drunk and?) disorderly – traits discerned from marginal notes in a very old book!

A letter in the Library wittily gives the lie to this idea. From 1948 to 1968, American writer Elizabeth Smith conducted a transatlantic correspondence with Oxford author and composer Bruce Montgomery. In one typewritten 'P.P.S.' from 1950 she notes:

> you asked the reason for my having several handwritings (two, forsooth, I have dozens!) and that is because, having acquired a typewriter at the age of five, I never really learned how to write. I can imitate anybody's handwriting and can forge like mad, although I don't have any friends with enough substance in the bank to make chicanery on my part worth while.

She continues to make the point by hand on the same document (see p. 14). As well as illustrating the Palmer Method of penmanship taught in US schools, she can produce the script of

> the introvert who writes short, secretive letters backhand. My t's always show firmness of character, but this is a false impression I have conscientiously endeavoured to establish after reading a book on graphology.

Just read the book, it seems, and you can copy the tricks of the character-reading trade.

The link between writing and individuality is not one that would have appealed for much of history. Writing was seen as a menial task, delegated to secretaries who were trained to write in regular, uniform script, whether

ΘΕΩΝ ΘΕΩΝΙ ΤΩ ΠΑΤΡΙ ΧΑΙΡΕΙΝ

2 Letter from a boy named Theon (θεων) to his father, 2nd–3rd century CE

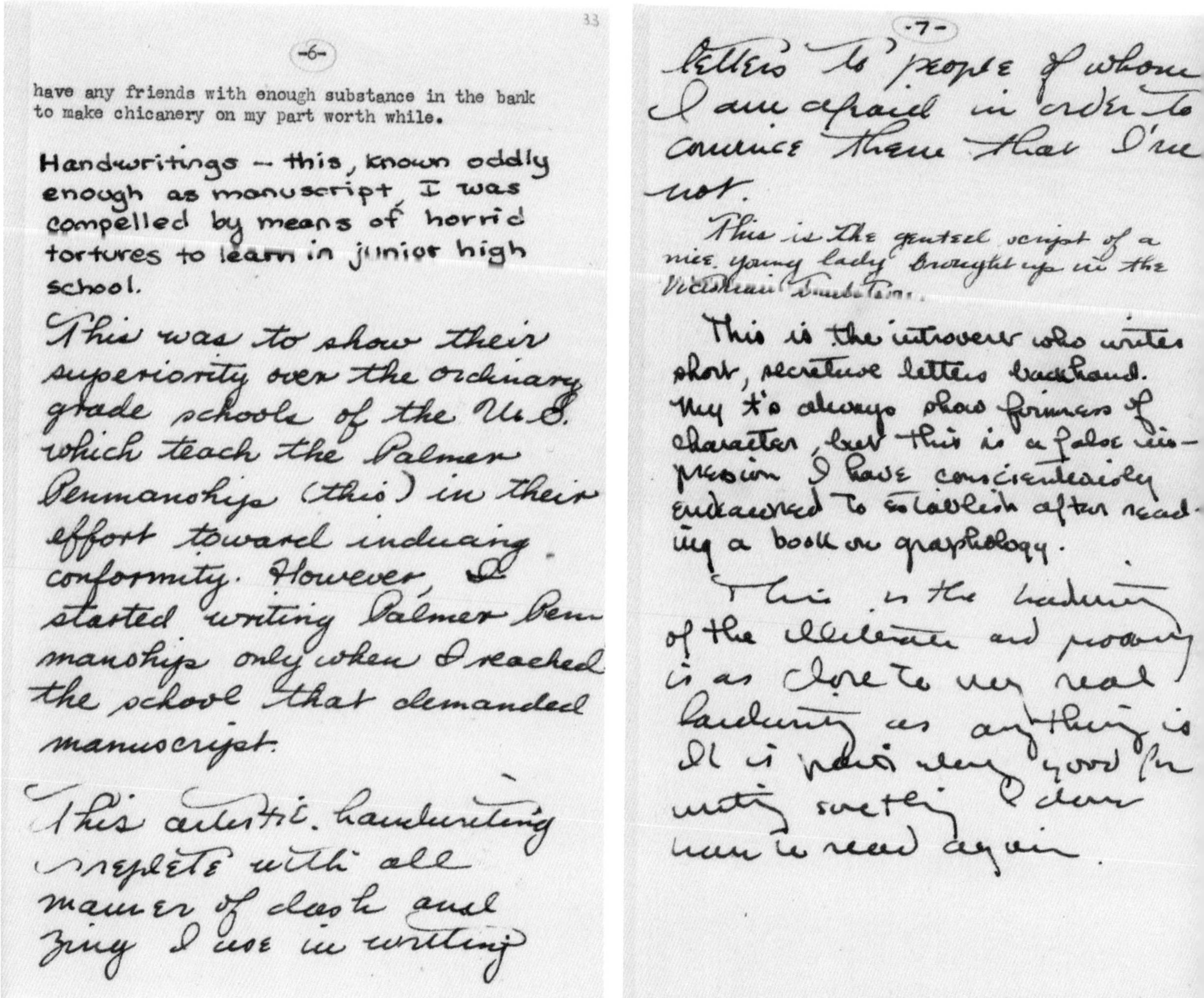

33

-6-

have any friends with enough substance in the bank to make chicanery on my part worth while.

Handwritings – this, known oddly enough as manuscript, I was compelled by means of horrid tortures to learn in junior high school.

This was to show their superiority over the ordinary grade schools of the U.S. which teach the Palmer Penmanship (this) in their effort toward inducing conformity. However, I started writing Palmer Penmanship only when I reached the school that demanded manuscript.

This artistic handwriting replete with all manner of dash and zing I use in writing

-7-

letters to people of whom I am afraid in order to convince them that I'm not.

This is the genteel script of a nice young lady brought up in the Victorian tradition.

This is the introvert who writes short, secretive letters backhand. My t's always show firmness of character, but this is a false impression I have conscientiously endeavored to establish after reading a book on graphology.

This is the handwriting of the illiterate and probably is as close to my real handwriting as anything is. It is plainly very good for writing something I don't mean to read again.

3 Letter of Elizabeth Smith to Bruce Montgomery, 1950

copying or taking dictation from the author. The famous Roman lawyer and author, Marcus Tullius Cicero, had an almost equally famous slave, Tiro, who acted as his secretary, but on occasion he would also have used professional scribes. Sometimes he adds a postscript in his own hand to assure the recipient of his friendship, to assert the authenticity of the rest of the text or to record a secret:

> But here I go back to my own hand, for what follows is confidential.
> (Cicero, letter to Atticus, 6 August 47 BCE)

Cicero is typical of a literate class who could write, but who saw the mechanical business of writing as a chore. The same thought is expressed by Peter the Venerable, twelfth-century abbot of the great monastery at Cluny in France, who declared that writing is the work of the hand but composition the work of the heart. In English, the verb 'to write' has come to express both – very different – activities.

These historical professional scribes took the form of a living typewriter or word processor, and like those modern inventions, the best scribes and scriptoria – places in monasteries where books were copied – aimed not for individuality but for identity. Scribes were taught to write in the same way, making the same letter forms and employing the same page layout. Some could write a variety of scripts to order, depending on the context they were working in. Headers, main text and marginal notes might all be written by the same person, but in different styles. In the Middle Ages, a large work might be copied by more than one scribe, but ideally the reader should barely be able to notice the changes on the page. Reading medieval manuscripts today, there are times when the change of scribe is evident not from the look of the page, but only when tiny changes appear in the text – slightly different abbreviations for words, for example. At the level of the page, the house style is preserved.

We can see something similar in the national characteristics of handwriting today, although these are less common than they were. No one could confuse the script of someone who went to school in twentieth-century America with that of someone trained in twentieth-century France. Handwriting was seen as an accomplishment: in the nineteenth century, a clear and accurate hand might lift a working-class lad from a life of manual labour to that of an office clerk. And, as an accomplishment, it had a considerable history. The young Tudor princess Elizabeth and her half-brother Edward shared a writing tutor – a man called, for obvious reasons, Jean Belmain – and as queen Elizabeth was proud of her elegant script. As this book shows, she was a woman for whom literacy was important, and many examples of her writing are still preserved. We can chart the development of her handwriting over her life, as she became more skilled, as the pressure of business forced her to write a speedier scrawl, and then as, plagued by rheumatism and poor eyesight, her pen control declined. She herself complained that her writing was not what it had been; and one historian of her handwriting, Henry Woudhuysen, reckons that the changes were so great over her lifetime that it is sometimes hard to credit that it was produced by the same person – even though we know this to be the case.

The Bodleian has been the caretaker of handwriting for centuries. Much of what it holds was written by anonymous professional scribes or those known only by characteristics of their script – such as the thirteenth-century annotator dubbed 'the tremulous hand of Worcester'. As we come closer to the present day, we reach the boxes and boxes of personal papers and correspondence, and these have been invaluable for this book. In some, we may be lucky enough to catch a whole life. The first preserved writing of the nineteenth-century mathematician and computer theorist Ada Lovelace dates from a letter to her mother when she was perhaps three or four years old (p. 17).

Reading through the box of her correspondence with her mother, Lady Noel-Byron (as the letters are addressed), we follow Ada as she grows up, excitedly records her early education, her marriage and children, her continuing love of mathematics, her mathematical progress with Charles Babbage and Augustus De Morgan, her persistent illness and her own sure knowledge, despite the assurances of her doctor, that her health was not improving. Finally, after her early death at the age of thirty-six,

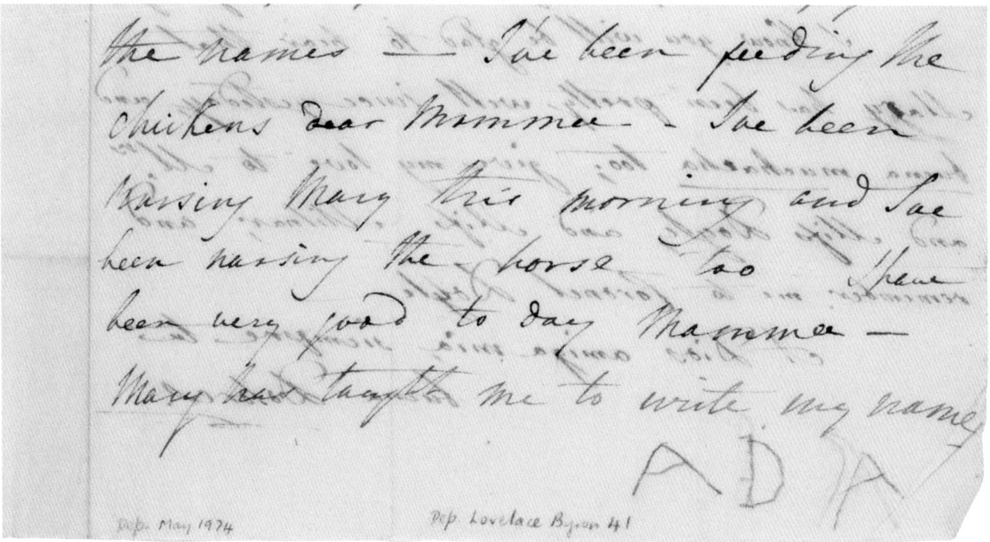
the names — I've been feeding the
Chickens dear Mamma — I've been
kissing Mary this morning and I've
been kissing the horse too I have
been very good to day Mamma —
Mary has taught me to write my name
ADA

Dep. May 1974 Dep. Lovelace Byron 41

4 Letter to her mother 'signed' by Ada Lovelace as a child

we reach the letters of condolence to her mother. Ada's written pages fizz with energy and fun. The modern reader turning the pages is given an extraordinary glimpse of her life – all the more to be struck by the poignancy of her death.

Although there is evidence for autograph collections in antiquity, and the cult of the author's own hand seems never to have died out, the fashion for large collections of signatures and letters probably began in earnest in the seventeenth century; the German writer Goethe, for instance, had a collection numbering 1,862 items, with the earliest dating from 1552. The Bodleian holds a number of autograph collections from the nineteenth century – treasure troves and snapshots of particular points in time. Some are elaborately organized either alphabetically or by profession – royalty, politicians, novelists and music hall artists. Collectors sometimes add (in their own hand) short biographies of the writers of the documents stuck onto the pages, with newspaper cuttings or publicity photos to illustrate the subject. Hosts of now little-known judges and churchmen crowd into these pages, which are a vivid reminder of the transience of fame and celebrity. Men are much more likely to be represented than women; and even those women who *were* reckoned to be worth collecting are often in less 'permanent' professions than men – singers, actors and society hostesses, for example. One collection in several volumes, bound in leather and gold-stamped with his name, belonged to Prince Leopold, the youngest son of Queen Victoria, who was in the lucky position of being able to waylay the famous and the powerful at his family's various homes. At Balmoral Castle, the artist Landseer – best known now for the great bronze lions around the fountains in Trafalgar Square in London – draws a charming dog (below). In the same collection, at Osborne House on the Isle of Wight, the politician Disraeli exclaims that he can't think of anything to write (p. 20). The prince even collected Abraham Lincoln's modest signature, on the same page as that of the *Hiawatha* poet, Henry Longfellow (p. 21).

The premise of this book, then, is that handwriting is inherently interesting for anyone who can read. In seventy-six entries, divided into

5 Signed drawing of a dog by Edwin Landseer, 1867

eleven sections and a postscript, it presents the writing of ninety-nine people, from the ninth century to the present day. With each entry, I have tried to tell a pocket-sized story: who is this writing, to whom, when, where and why. Choosing who to include was difficult: the Bodleian's collections are vast, and the *salon des refusés* contains an equally distinguished gathering of writers. It's my hope that most of the people presented here will be known to most of my readers, and that the stories of those who aren't – although famous in their own day – will prove interesting enough to convince you that they should still be remembered. I soon decided against a section of politicians, although the Library has an enormous collection of their papers, and I similarly ignored churchmen, few of whom have survived in modern memory. In contrast, the section on poets and novelists could have been expanded to take over the whole book. The Library has the signature of every US president and a huge variety of non-British royalty but, apart from a Tudor or two, a mere signature – the modern definition of 'autograph' – is not enough in itself for inclusion. In a very few cases I have included a personally signed typescript, but only where the document has itself been typed by the writer. The short final section of scribes and calligraphers records the hands of eight of those who wrote professionally, charting a mini-history of the development of script over time.

Everyone who works in the Manuscripts Reading Rooms at the Bodleian knows the excitement of receiving the grey boxes of precious materials – and indeed will recognize on many of those boxes a distinctive italic script, recording the shelfmarks, warning of the state of preservation or explaining how the material was conserved. The librarian who wrote that elegant hand is now retired but, even for those who will never meet him, his handwriting will afford a glimpse of his presence in the Library for years to come. Similarly, working with the documents in this book, I have found myself moved to admiration, laughter and even occasional tears by the remarkable people whose handwritten texts are presented here. It's been a pleasure and a privilege to try to tell their stories and bring them to life again, in their own show of hands.

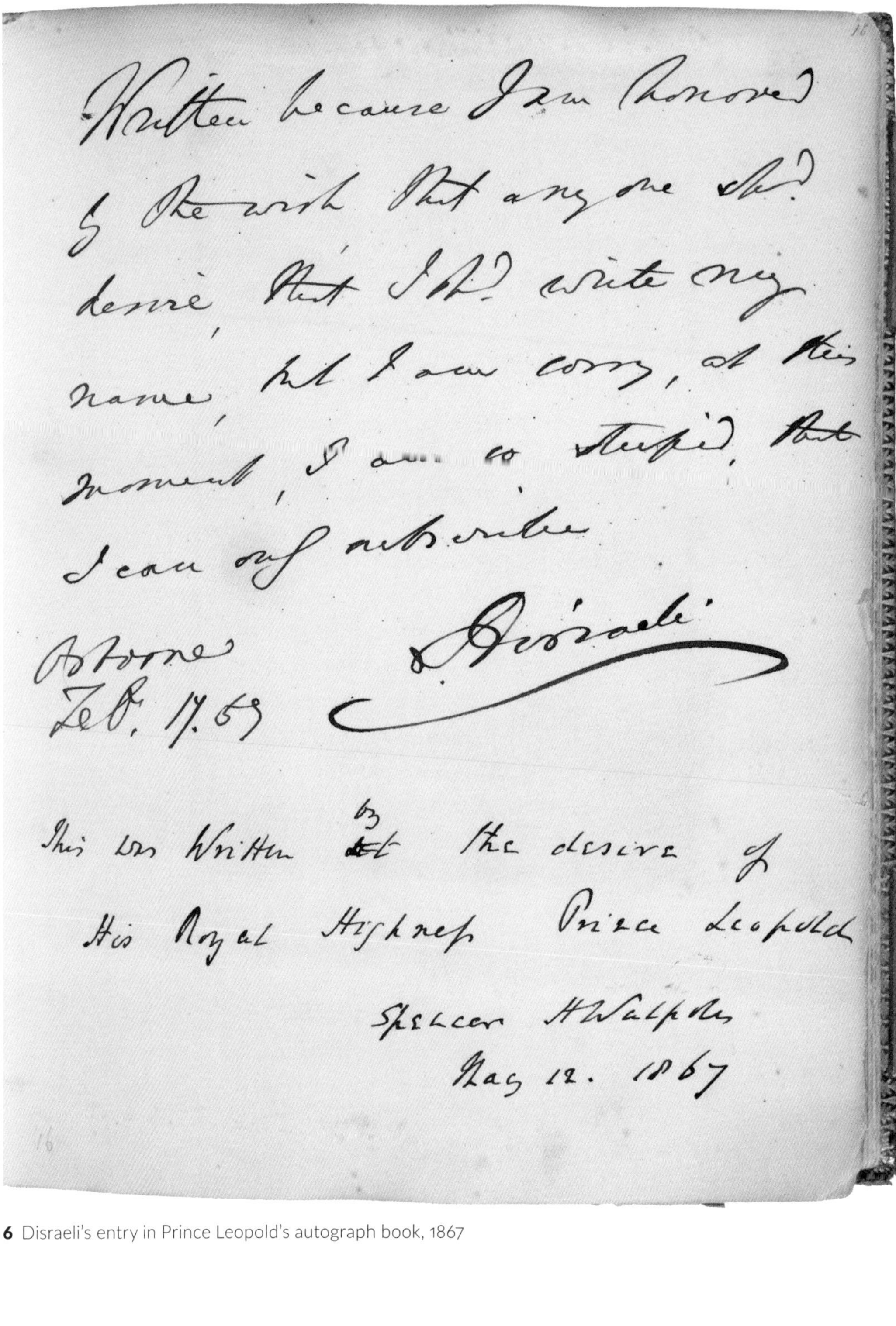

Written because I am honored
by the wish that anyone shd.
desire, that I shd. write my
name; but I am sorry, at this
moment, I am so stupid, that
I can only subscribe

Osborne
Feb. 17. 67

B. Disraeli

This was Written ~~at~~ by the desire of
His Royal Highness Prince Leopold

Spencer H Walpole
May 12. 1867

6 Disraeli's entry in Prince Leopold's autograph book, 1867

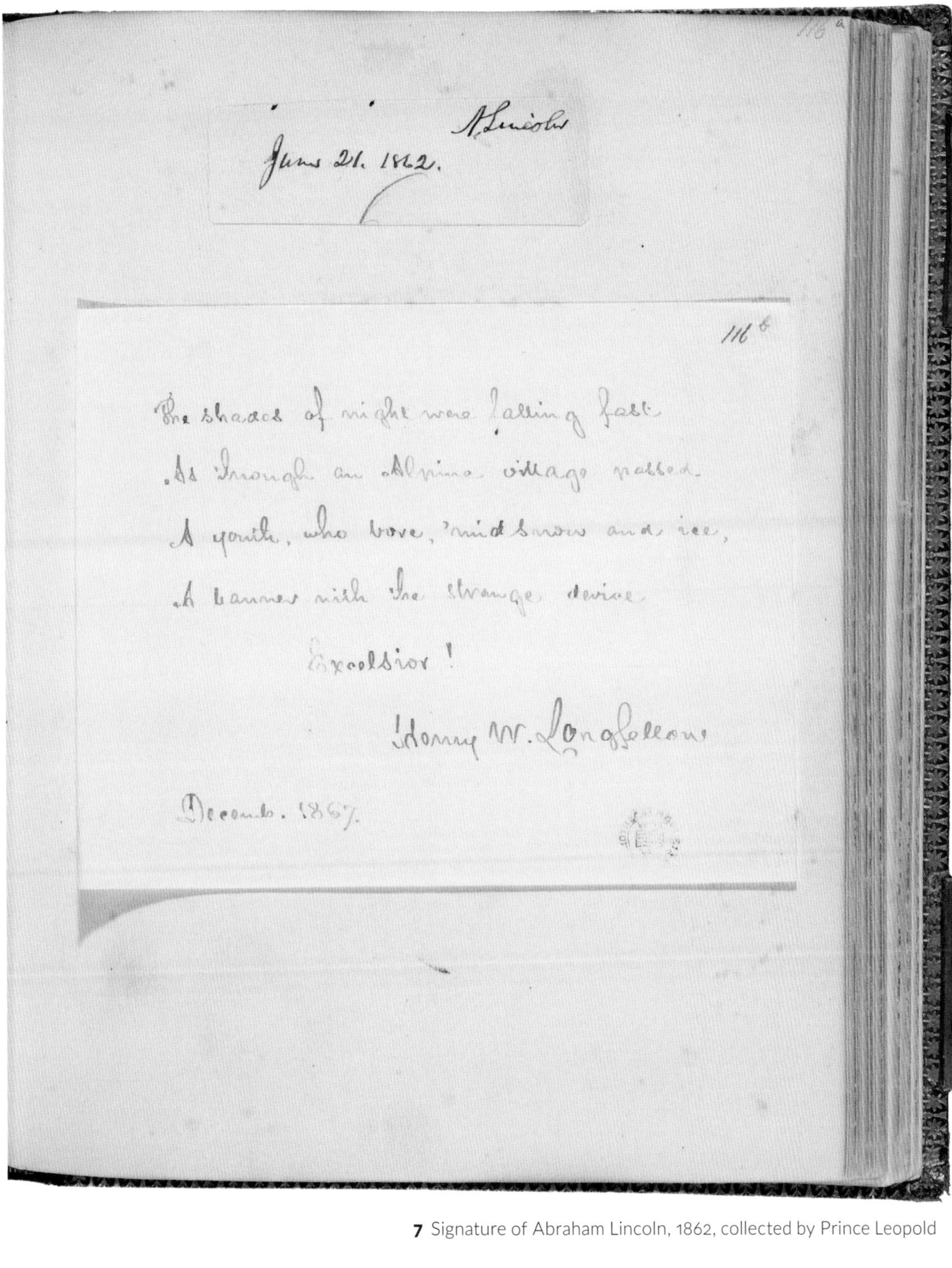

A Lincoln
June 21. 1862.
116 b
The shades of night were falling fast,
As through an Alpine village passed
A youth, who bore, 'mid snow and ice,
A banner with the strange device
Excelsior!
Henry W. Longfellow
Decemb. 1867.

7 Signature of Abraham Lincoln, 1862, collected by Prince Leopold

THE TUDOR COURT

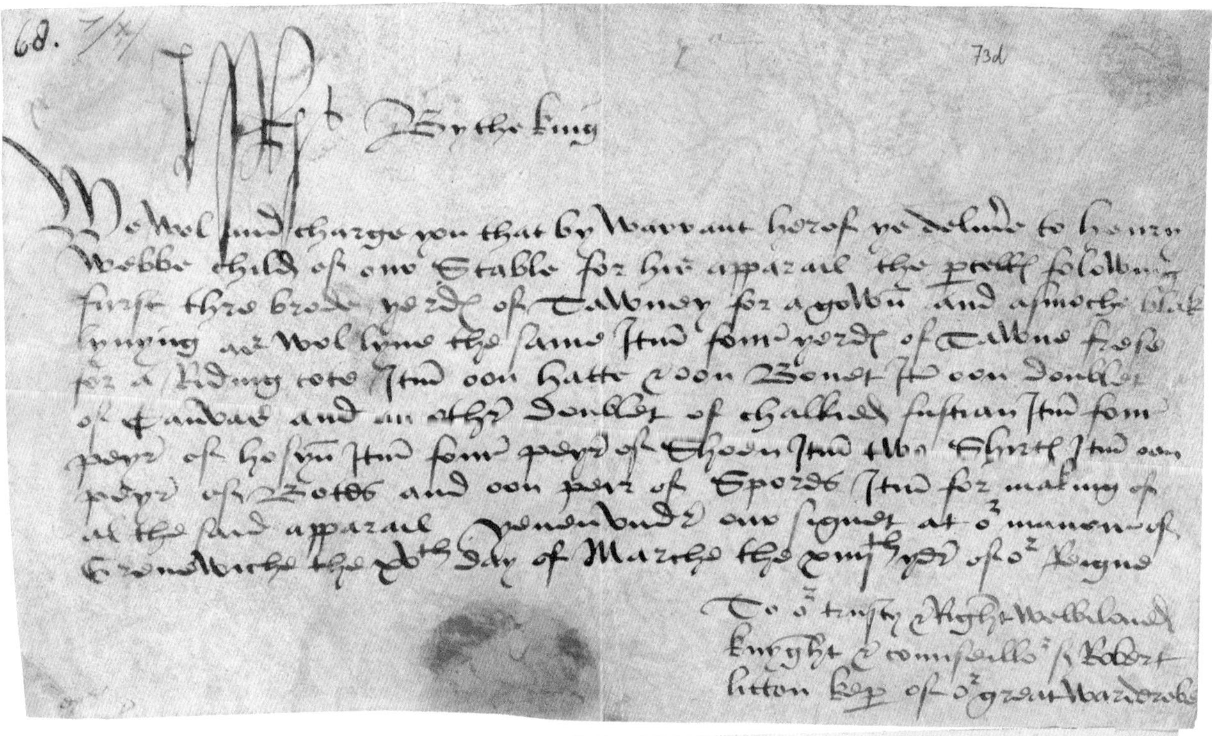

Henry. By the King.

We wel and charge you that by Warrant hereof you deliver to Henry Webbe child of our Stable for her (his) apparail the parcels following first three brode yards of tawney for a gown, item (and) as much (moche) black lyning or wollane the same item four yards of tawne frieze for a riding cote, item, oon hatte and oon Bonet item oon doublet of canvass, and another doublet of *chalkied fustian, item four payr of Hosen, item four payr of shoes, item two shirts, item oon payr of botts and oon payr of spords (spurs) item for making of all the said apparail given under our signet at our manor of Greenwiche the 15 day of March the XIIIj (14th) of our Regne.

To the trusty and welbeloved Knight and Counsellor, Sir Robert Litton Keper of our great-Wordrobe.

*This means bleached

Henry VII ('HR') approves expenditure, 1499

Henry VII 1457–1509

The founder of the Tudor dynasty is less famous now than his son or his granddaughter, and yet his own particular talents laid the foundations for the success of their line. When he was crowned in 1485, Henry's claim to the English throne was far from clear, but his wily statecraft, rather than either his legal right or his military successes, eventually assured his position. Realizing that security would follow money, the king set about putting his realm on a solid financial and administrative footing. He appointed trained and reliable men – often lawyers – to his royal household to discover, calculate, organize and collect all monies, taxes and revenues due to the Crown, and he took a personal and detailed interest in their work. This was a king as CEO – and triumphantly so: having begun with a kingdom in debt, Henry died with investments worth more than a million pounds.

His secret was keeping his eye on the ball. Here, at Greenwich on 15 March 1499, the king approves an order written by a clerk to supply livery for a new groom, Henry Webbe. Sir Robert Litton, the Keeper of the Wardrobe – that part of the royal household supplying the king and his servants with clothing and furnishings – is authorized to dispense material for a lined gown, riding coat, hat, bonnet, two doublets, four pairs of stockings and four pairs of shoes, two shirts, a pair of boots and a pair of spurs: this is Webbe's uniform as a royal servant. Such a small matter doesn't warrant a complete signature, and the king's 'HR' (Henricus Rex) at top left, is the equivalent of initialling a document today.

Henry Webbe, described here as 'child of our stable', seems to have spent his life among the royal horses: in 1520 he was a 'yeoman of the stirrup' for Henry VIII, and in 1544 he (or perhaps his son) was still working as a groom for Queen Katherine Parr.

profyte of their neighbours. All and synguler which gyftes and graces I knowlege, and professe that they procede from this holy spirite, and that they be gyuen, conferred, & distributed vnto vs mortall men here in erthe, at his owne godly wyll, arbitre, and dyspensation, and that no man can purchase or obteyne, ne yet receyue reteyne or vse any one of them, without the speciall operation of this holy spirite. And although he geueth not, nor dispenseth the same equally and vnto euery man in lyke: yet he gyueth alwayes some portion therof vnto all persones, whiche be accepted in the syght of god, and that not onely frely, and without all theyr deseruinges, but allso in suche plentie, and measure, as vnto his godly knowlege is thoughte to be moste beneficiall and expedient.

And I beleue that this holy spirite of god is of his owne nature, autour of charitie and holy loue, or rather that he is charitie it selfe. Fyrst bycause that he is that ineffable and incomprehensyble loue or concord, wherwith the father & the sonne be conioyned inseparably the one with the other. Seconde, bycause he is the bonde and knotte, wherwith our sauiour Jesu Christe, and his moste dere beloued espouse the churche (which is allso his very mystical body) & al and singuler the veray membres of the same churche and body, be vnited, knytte, and conioyned to gyther in suche perfyte and euerlastynge loue and charitie, that the same can not be dissolued or separated. Thyrdely, bycause he is allso the verye bonde and knotte, wherby all and euery one of the membres of Christis sayde churche and body, be vnited, coupled, and conioyned the one of them with the other, in perfite mutuall loue and charitie. For I beleue assuredly, that lyke as the membres of our mortall bodyes be, by the spirituall operation and vertue of our soules, not onely preserued holly togyther, in one body, and be endewed with lyfe, and power to exercyse suche naturall functions, and offyces, as be deputed vnto them, but allso be conteyned in mutuall affection

and

whyche wyll not [illegible] was lefte to us therfore to remember us of our Duty yff we wyll [illegible] the same hys illumynations and good motions. And yet he gyveth not nor dispensith the same equally and unto evry man in lyke but he devydeth them perticulerly and specyally to evry member of his mystycall bodye the churche as is most necessary for the hole body, and in suche plentie and measure as unto his godlie will and knowledge is thought to be most benefycyall and expedyent for the same all which thinges he doth of his mere mercy and goodnes frely and wout all our deservings

Henry VIII 1491–1547
Thomas Cranmer 1489–1556

Tall, cultured and athletic, King Henry VIII of England stood, literally and figuratively, head and shoulders above his subjects. His youthful promise was only later overshadowed by his marital history, considerable girth and propensity to behead those who stood in his way.

Henry was his father's second son, but his elder brother Arthur's sudden death in 1502 left him as the heir to the throne. The sixteen-year-old Arthur had been married the year before to Katherine of Aragon, as part of a diplomatic deal with the Spanish against the French. The alliance was too good to be derailed by Arthur's death: one of Henry's first acts when he became king in 1509, aged eighteen, was to follow his father's last wish and marry Katherine. When the marriage failed to produce a male heir, and having fallen heavily for Anne Boleyn, Henry used the uncertain legality of a marriage to his brother's widow as grounds to sue for an annulment. When that proved unsuccessful, he began to seek more radical means that would allow him to break his ties with Katherine – 'the King's Great Matter', as the question of divorce began to be known. If the Roman Catholic Church would not suit his purpose, then perhaps the Church, rather than the king, would have to move.

In fact, matrimony aside, there were other reasons for Henry to be interested in church reform. The Protestant reform movement in northern Europe was not without sympathizers in England. Economically, the land and wealth of monastic foundations was tantalizingly attractive to a king always on the lookout for money. And we should not forget that Henry was educated; he owned a considerable library of manuscripts and printed books, often bound in his signature black velvet. Theologically literate, he was genuinely interested in the issues at stake in the Catholic–Protestant controversy, involving himself personally in the development of the new Church of England, of which, after the final break with Rome, he was declared 'supreme head'.

Henry VIII (upper) and Thomas Cranmer (lower) comment on *The Bishops' Book*

Setting aside the doctrines of Rome required an alternative code of beliefs and practices, and in July 1536 the bishop of Hereford, Edward Fox, produced a set of Ten Articles of religion, which Henry had approved. When the Articles did not receive general approval, Thomas Cromwell, in spiritual as in temporal affairs the king's fixer, convened a group of forty-six clerics and theologians under the leadership of the archbishop of Canterbury, Thomas Cranmer, to try again. The result was *The Institution* [Instruction] *of a Cristen* [Christian] *Man*, published in London in October 1537. Commonly known as *The Bishops' Book*, it provided an exposition of the Creed, the Sacraments, the Ten Commandments, the Hail Mary, the Lord's Prayer, the question of justification by faith and the nature of Purgatory

The remarkable copy shown here is Henry's own, with passages deleted, amended and added in his own hand. Inside the front cover is a note in the book's own voice: 'The King's commandment is that I should not be had out of the privy chamber.' Henry wanted his copy to be handy.

On this page, on the eighth article of faith, Henry is attempting to revise the complex and contested theology about 'the speciall operation of this holy spirite':

> Whyche wyll not lett and was leffte with us therfore to remember us of our Duty yff we willyngly and wylfullye rejecte nott the same hys illumynations and good motions.

Below Henry's bold and spiky writing, however, the neat and practised hand of Archbishop Thomas Cranmer has added a note of his own. Henry leans more to the traditional Catholic interpretation of the workings of the Holy Spirit, while Cranmer champions the Lutheran or Protestant view. On this extraordinary page, the king and his archbishop are in dialogue over the right interpretation of the Christian faith.

The book came to the Library in 1755 as part of the bequest of the collector Richard Rawlinson, one of its most important benefactors.

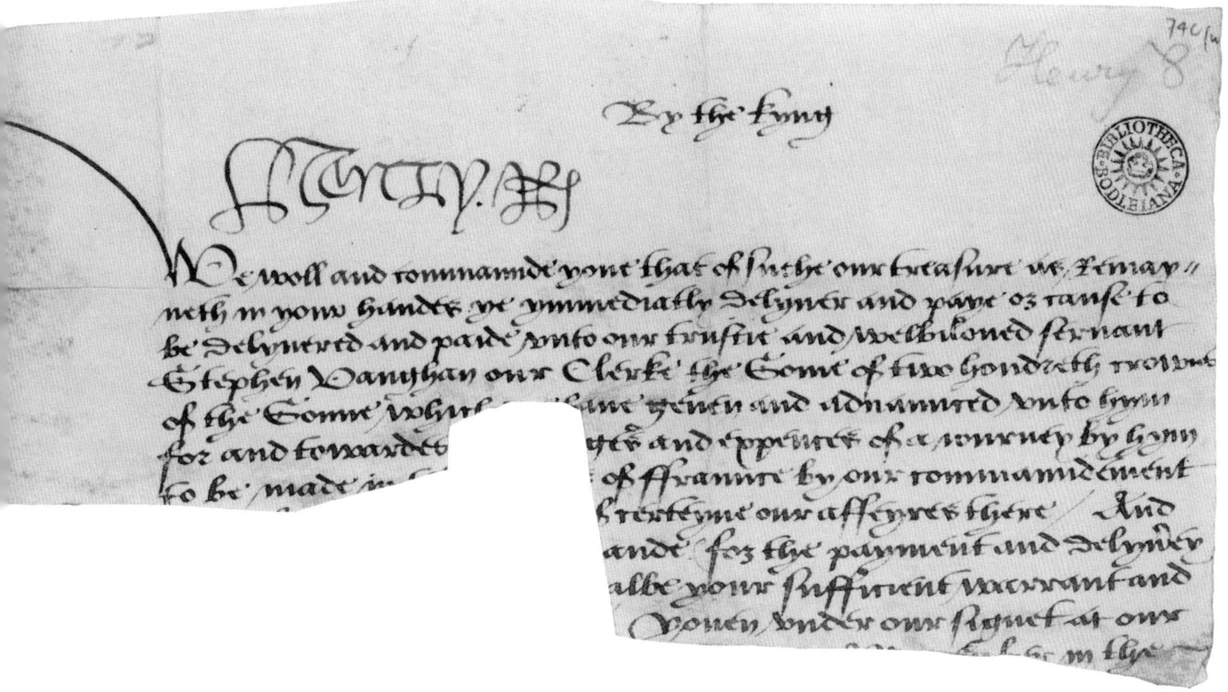
740(w
Henry 8
BIBLIOTHECA BODLEIANA
By the kyng
Henry R
We woll and commaunde you that of suche our treasure as remay-
neth in your handes ye immediatly delyuer and paye or cause to
be delyuered and paide unto our trustie and welbiloued seruant
Stephen Vaughan our Clerke the Somme of two hundreth crownes
of the Somme which … haue geuen and admitted unto hym
for and towardes … and expences of a iourney by hym
to be made in … of ffraunce by our commaundement
… concernyng our affaires there And
… maunde for the payment and delyuery
… shalbe your sufficient warrant and
… Yeuen under our signet at our
… in the

Signature of Henry VIII

ent is there ... be ... ticularly
and expoundyth

s permittyd to suche brethern of
above theage of xxiij the yeres and
the same, to contynue in the
ans iniunction to the cotrarye no
t causes of the sayd monastery stan
of the more pte of thys brethern in
arte or shall as shall thought
te to the tyme convenient
ghant man may resorte and come to
e sale of clothe and other merc
that all suspicious resorte be avoided
of dispensacion appoyntyd in the iniun
take place onlye in suche case
me is violatyd and brokyn wittyn
and none other wysse

Thomas Crumwell

Thomas Cromwell 1485–1540

Henry VIII surely regretted his rash decision to behead Thomas Cromwell, his chief troubleshooter and right-hand man. Cromwell's misstep in promoting the marriage to Anne of Cleves was minor in comparison to his brilliant activity on the king's behalf in a decade of service. He had the gift of seeing creative and radical new ways out of difficult situations, but he was also a details man, always on top of the minutiae, whatever the issue.

After time spent on the continent, where he acquired some sort of legal training, Cromwell started work for Henry's Lord Chancellor, the archbishop of York, Thomas Wolsey. After Wolsey's fall from grace, Cromwell cannily managed to hold on to the king's favour, rising to become Lord Privy Seal in 1536. He is perhaps best known now for his part in the dissolution of the monasteries – the closure of all religious houses and the seizure of their land, goods and money, to be redistributed to the Crown and its supporters. An administrator's administrator, Cromwell began in January 1535 by making a complete valuation of ecclesiastical property in England, the Valor Ecclesiasticus, sending 'visitors' across the country to investigate. The heading of the document opposite and overleaf, from 1536, records Cromwell's agreement to 'The Relaxacion off certane particules off the injunctions gyven off late in the monastery off sanct mare off yorke By the visiters for the kynges hyghnes ther'. St Mary's was the largest and richest monastery in the north of England, with a valuation of over £2,000 – a fortune at the time. The visitors recorded that the Benedictine monks at the abbey had become rather lax in following their Rule, and insisted on a greater strictness. The monks appealed to Cromwell, who here (by his signature) agrees to a degree of leniency. It was soon not to matter: the abbey was dissolved in 1539.

Notice that, as was common in medieval Latin documents, to save time and space, the clerk writing the document has used abbreviated forms of some words, signalled by a line or hook to show that letters are missing.

Thomas Cromwell signs an agreement with St Mary's, York, 1536 *(detail from pp.32–3)*

The Relaxacon off certane articles off the iniuncions gyven
off late in the monastrye off Seint mare off York by
the visiters for the kynges hyghnes ther

In primis that thabbott may go forthe off hys monastrye as well unto
1 hys maners and other places as also for any other honest cause and
that he beyng forthe may ther tarye for lyke causes and to take
wt hym thre or more off hys brether at hys discrecon so that
thay resort not to any suspect places or infamyd company

Item that the table for straungers may be understond and observyd
2 wher thabbot shalbe abydyng by cause the most resorte ys at all
tymes to hym and suche places wher he abydythe

Item in brethren beyng officers off the sayd may wt licens off
3 thabbott go abrode for the executyng off ther offyces at suche
tymes as yt shalbe thought convenient by the discrecon off thabbott so that thay avoid the company off suspect
and infamyd persons

Item that thabbot may licence certane brethren off the sayd
into meadows or (Medys) feilds — house or monastrye to walke forthe in to medows or feylds
4 adioynyng to the sayd mon and thare to use honest
recreacon at suche tymes as it shalbe thought convenient by the discrecon off thabbott so that thay be at the lest
foure all tymes in company and retorne to thare mon
agane in dew houres avoydyng also the conversacon wt
all suspect and infamyd persons

Item that the almons accustomyd to be gyven to the
scolers off the cite may be distributyd as yt hathe ben
usyd and that suche gates off the monastrye as in tyme
5 past hathe ben usyd for any necessarye carriage may
for lyke causes be opened in tyme to come so that
at all other tymes thay be surely lokyd accordyng
to thiniunction gyven in that behalfe

Vid ye following
Articles fol 117

vid fol 114.b for ye 5 foregoing articles

6 Item that one brother of the monasterye or other lernyd in the scriptures may supplie the place of thabbot in preachynge ons in a monethe so that the brother so deputyd be of honest conversacion and declare the worde of God purelye and sincerelye

7 Item that a lecture in scripture sincerelye and diligentlye redd iij tymes weeklye may suffise and that the brethren beynge of the graduate and lernyd in scripture and approvid by the bisshope of the diocese may with licence of thabbot go abrode and preache the worde of God so that thay the same purelye and sincerelye and also that it may be permyttyd to suche brethren to lye in chambres to be assignyd by the discrecion of thabbot for thare more quiet studye and also for so myche as the brethren of the sayd monasterye be well instructyd in the latin [illegible] sufficient so that it be diligentlye and sincerelye taught and expoundyd

8 Item that it may permittyd to suche brethren of the sayd house beynge above the age of xxiiij yeres and wo voluntarelye desyre the same to contynue in the habit of thare religion any injunctions gyven to the contrarye notwithstondyng

9 Item that for urgent causes of the sayd monasterye stondyng thabbot with consent of the more parte of hys brethren may emplege suche plate or jewells as shall be thought for that parte necessarye to the tyme convenient

10 Item that honest wemen may resorte and come to the sayd monasterye for the sale of clothe and other necessaries for the brethren so that all suspicious resorte be avoided

11 Item that the payne of deprivacion appointyd in the injunctions may be declared to take place onlye in suche cases where any of thame is violatyd and broken wittyngelye and of contempt and none otherwyse

Thomas Cromwell

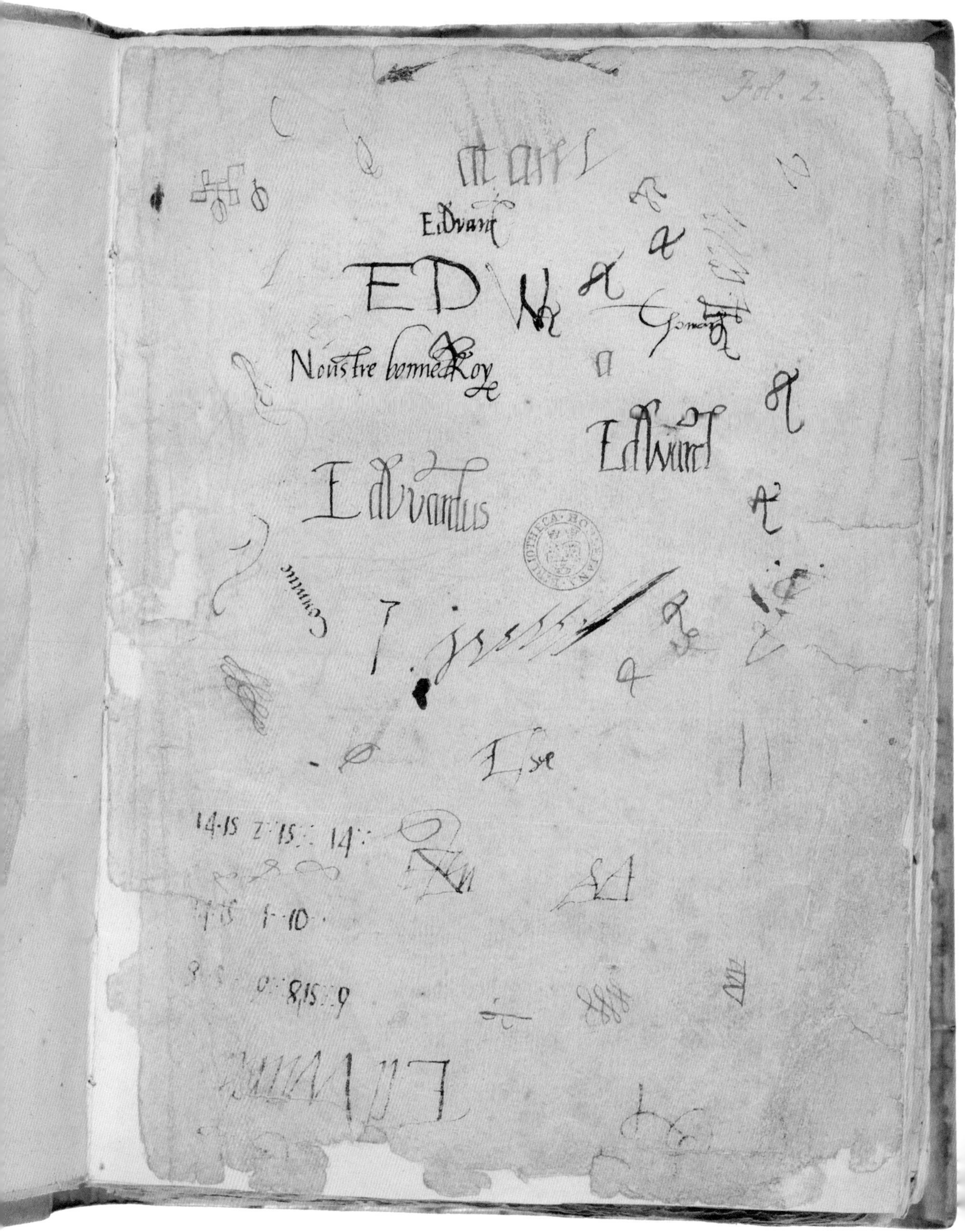

Fol. 2
Edvvart
ED
Nous tre bonne Roy
Edward
Edvvardus
14·15 2·15 14
1·10

Edward VI 1537–1553

'Naturally haughty and arrogant, like all the Tudors', was historian Geoffrey Elton's verdict on Henry's son, who became king at the age of nine, in 1547. Character aside, Edward also shared in a serious Tudor education. The exercise book shown here, one of two of Edward's schoolbooks the Bodleian owns, dates from 1548. By then, Edward was also, at least nominally, king of England, although his realm was actually governed by a privy council appointed by Henry VIII before his death. King he might be, but one who still had to learn his Latin.

The pages overleaf show Edward's 'title page' and the first of his daily exercises for learning the second book of Cicero's treatise *De officiis* – On Duties – a suitable work for a king, we might think, but also a classical text popular from the Middle Ages onward. Edward dates his pages of work, so we can see that he is beginning here on '5th April [March has been crossed out], Thursday [die Iovis]'. The dates show he was expected to work six days a week, with Sunday off. His task for the day includes five sentences to translate, with six 'verbal phrases' and six 'noun phrases' of vocabulary to learn. Sentence number two reads, 'Wisdom is the knowledge of both divine and human things.'

The single page opposite comes from the very front of the notebook. The boy Edward, like thousands before and after him, practises writing his name in different forms, along with the phrase 'Noustre bonne Roy': 'Our good king'.

The end of the book has two shorter sets of similar exercises in two other hands, one of which has been likened to the early handwriting of Elizabeth I, who would have been fourteen at the time: brother and sister, perhaps, thriftily using the same notebook. We know that at times they shared the same tutors at court, including the Protestant scholars Roger Ascham and Jean Belmain who, as his name suggests, was famed for his penmanship.

left The young Edward VI practises signing his name, 1548
pp. 36–7 Edward VI's schoolbook, 1548

RECITATIO SECUNDI LIBRI CICCRONIS DE officijs.

Sententiae 5° ~~Martij~~ Aprilis die Iouis

1. Nihil est aliud philosophia nisi studium prudentiae.
2. Sapientia est scientia rerum diuinarū & humanarū.
3. Nihil est utile quod non iustum sit idem.
4. Temeritas maxime dissidet a sapientia.
5. Nihil est optabilius sapientia nihil melius nihil homini clarius, nec homine dignius.

Phrases uerborū.

1. Mandare literis.
2. Ponere curam.
3. Orbari muneribus reipublicae
4. Traducere opinionē.
5. Cogitatione distinguere.
6. Deponere molestias

Phrases Nominū.

1. Studium sapientiae
2. Munus reipublicae.
3. Oblectatio animi.
4. Requies curarum.
5. Valetudinis curatio.
6. Frugum pceptio.

Digna patre tanto salutatione premissa, agnosco plurimum debere me reverendissime sanctitati
vestre, cum inmundis de literis mihi a vobis ad Ampthille regiam traditis, tum (vel maxime) quod
summo meo oblectamento regis regineque parentum (quorum utriusque salutem regnum ille supre-
mus quam diutissima felicitate dignetur) ministerio communi vestro dudum beneficio mihi frui licuerit, una
vero me interim (alioqui felicissimam) torquebat visende sanctissime paternitatis vestre negata occasio
que si vobis respondisset meis cum sancta vestra benedictione humillime petita, merita in me vestre
munifice frequentia (quibus licuisset) gratiis rependissem; id quoniam mihi quantumvis desyde-
ranti assequi tum temporis non obtigit, quod mei iam officii superest, vestram istam benedictionem
non nisi omni cum observantia mihi nominandam instantissima implorans, celsitudinem vestram maio-
rem in modum obtestor, ut cepto erga me animi candore perpetuo sit, ita (quod multis aliis nominibus
debeo) obnixius mihi orandum erit, ut incolumitate vestram Britannie rei publice nedum mihi
deus optimus maximus longissime protrahat. Hartlebury

Tua spiritualis filia

Maria princeps

Mary I 1516–1558

Aged ten, Princess Mary, daughter of Henry VIII and his first wife Katherine of Aragon, writes in Latin to her godfather Thomas Wolsey, Lord Chancellor and archbishop of York, to thank him. She was grateful for the letters he'd written to her at Ampthill Castle, but even more so for persuading her parents that she might spend time with them: 'through your intervention, I shall have been allowed for a month to enjoy, to my greatest pleasure, the company of the king and queen my parents' ('summo meo oblectamento regis regineque parentum … menstruo convictu vestro dudum beneficio mihi frui licuerit') (lines 3–4). By the following year, Henry had decided that Katherine must go, but for now at least they were together, and Mary with them.

As his only child, Mary was her father's heir and already a pawn in his (and Wolsey's) diplomacy. When she wrote the letter, in October 1526, she had been travelling with her own household and council for more than a year in the English and Welsh borderlands (or Marches), representing the king and making a show of royal authority.

This letter, entirely in her hand, is her earliest known writing. She writes a clear and even, abbreviated script, although her age is perhaps betrayed by the number of words used in their Latin superlative forms – 'most reverend', 'most holy', 'happiest', 'meekest', 'longest' – suggestive of childish exuberance. Writing from Hartlebury ('Hertleburye') Castle, the bishop of Worcester's country residence, she signs herself 'Your spiritual daughter, Mary, prince' ('Tua spiritualis filia, Marya princeps'). Her use of the male form *princeps*, rather than the more usual style for a princess, *regis filia*, shows her awareness of her position and her future expectations. Although both were derailed by her parents' divorce and the birth of her half-brother, Edward, Mary did eventually become queen for five short years, after his early death in 1553.

Mary I, aged ten, writes to Thomas Wolsey, 1526

Elizabeth I 1533–1603

Even at the age of eleven, Princess Elizabeth, daughter of Henry VIII and his second wife Anne Boleyn, already knew that it was vital to make friends with your stepmother. Henry was by then married to his sixth wife Katherine Parr, chronically ill, irascible and disappointed that his many marriages had produced only one unsatisfactory male heir. Henry had hoped that Anne would produce the boy his royal succession needed, and the birth of another daughter had been a serious disappointment. Relations between the king and his children were never straightforward: in 1543 Henry banished Elizabeth from court; she must have feared for her future.

In the summer of 1544, however, Henry was in Boulogne, and Elizabeth heard that Queen Katherine had remembered her stepdaughter fondly to the king each time she had written to him. Elizabeth wrote – in Italian, one of her several languages – to thank Katherine for her kindness and to ask for her blessing. Katherine's good offices on her behalf bore fruit, so that by September, Henry had forgiven Elizabeth and allowed her to return to court.

MS. Cherry 36 is Elizabeth's thank you gift to Katherine for her kindness. She began by translating from the French a long spiritual poem written in 1531 by Queen Marguerite of Navarre, *The Mirror of the Sinful Soul* (*Le miroir de l'âme pécheresse*). She then wrote out the text and Marguerite's preface, 'To the reader', in a large, clear hand, adding her own dedicatory letter to Katherine. Not yet content, she embroidered a personal cover for the finished book, in gold and silver thread on a blue silk background. Both back and front show a complicated knotted design, with a pansy in each corner and Katherine's initials, 'KP', in the centre. The edges are bound with gold braid, with a line of red silk at the top and bottom. In the sophisticated world of Tudor semiotics, the pansies –

Book binding in silk and silver thread embroidered by Elizabeth I named from the French *pensées* (thoughts) – also known as heart's ease or the humble violet, sent a message in themselves.

Elizabeth's dedication to Katherine, shown here, begins:

> TO OUR MOST NOBLE AND
> vertuous quene KATHERIN, Eliza-
> beth her humble daughter wisheth
> perpetuall felicitie and everlasting joye
>
> NOT ONELY knowing the affectuous wille, and fervent zeale the wich your highnes hath towardes all godly lerning as also my duetie towardes you (most gracious and souverayne princes) but knowing also that pusillanimite and ydlenes are most repugnante unto a reasonable creature: and that (as the philosopher sayeth) even as an instrument of yron or of other metayle waxeth soone rusty onles it be continualy occupied, Even so shall the witte of a man or woman waxe dull and unapte to do or understand any thing perfittely onles it be alwayes occupied upon some maner of study. Wiche thinges consydered hath moved so small a portion as god hath lente me to prove what i could do. And therfore have i as for aseye or beginninge (following the right notable saying of the proverbe aforesayd) translated this lytell boke out of frenche ryme in to englishe prose, joyning the sentences together as well as the capacitie of my symple witte and small lerning coulde extende themselves. The wich booke is intytled or named the miroir, or glasse, of the synnefull soule.

She ends:

> Prayenge god almighty the maker and creatoure of alle thinges to garaunte unto youre highnes the sam newe yeres daye a lucky and a prosperous yere, with prosperous yssue, and continuance of many yeres in good helhte and contynuall joye and all to his honnoure, praise, and glory. Frome asherige, the laste daye of the yeare of our lord god, 1544.

Elizabeth I, aged eleven, writes a book of prayers for Katherine Parr

TO OVR MOSTE NOBLE AND
vertuous quene KATHERIN, Eliza
beth her humble daughter wisheth
perpetuall felicitie and everlasting ioye

NOT ONELY knowing the affe
ctuous wille, and feruent zeale the
which your highnes hath towardes
all godly lerning as also my duetie
towardes you (most gracious and
souerayne princes) but knowing also that
pusillanimite and ydlenes are most
repugnante vnto a reasonable crea
ture and that (as the philosopher
sayeth) euen as an instrument of yron

Anne Boleyn had worked for Marguerite of Navarre for a short time while Marguerite was still Duchesse d'Alençon. After Anne married Henry in 1533, Marguerite got in touch again, this time as queen to queen, and sent her a copy of her work. It is likely that Elizabeth translated *Le miroir* from a copy in her mother's collection. Katherine was clearly pleased with Elizabeth's gift, arranging for her translation to be printed; it was published in Germany in 1548, with an introduction and conclusion by the noted scholar John Bale. The text went through several editions in Elizabeth's lifetime.

The gift highlights Elizabeth's lifelong interest in language, in writing and in the Protestant religion. She translated a number of spiritual texts, including John Calvin's *Institutes* and, as a New Year's gift in 1545 for her father, a trilingual translation, from English into Latin, French and Italian, of Katherine's own *Prayers and Meditations*. The considerable quantity of Elizabeth's own handwriting that still survives allows us to chart its changes from childhood to her death. From the clear and regular – but undoubtedly juvenile – script of Cherry 36, it developed into an elegant and efficient instrument for the expression of her thoughts and will. As she got older, with rheumaticky fingers and possibly failing sight, she complained that her handwriting was getting worse; certainly her signature became bigger and less controlled.

All her life she was aware of the power of the handwritten word to make and keep alliances. In the letter opposite, from her late teens, she writes to her younger brother, Edward, who was already king, ending 'Maiestatis tuae humilima soror et serva Elizabeth': 'Elizabeth, most humble sister and servant of your Majesty'. Her elaborate signature includes the looping knot her father and grandfather had also employed, and which she embroidered on the cover of Katherine's gift.

MS. Cherry 36 is a book that links four queens in a shifting pattern of fortunes. In a library full of extraordinary and poignant things, it must surely rank amongst its most affecting.

Princess Elizabeth signs a letter to her brother, Edward VI

Amoris erga me tui argumenta nulla vel plura, vel illustriora dari potuerunt Rex sereniss: & Illustriss: quàm cum proximè fructu iucundissimæ consuetudinis tuæ perfruerer. Cuius sanè cum recordor (quotidie autem recordor) quasi tecum esse & collocutionem tuarum humanitate præsens ipsa frui planè videor. Cæterum cum in mentem veniunt innumerabilia tua illa in me ~~officia~~ beneficia, quibus isthuc advenientem excepisti, discedentemque abs te dimisisti, non facile habeo commemorare quantopere in diversas partes distrahatur animus, ancipitemque cogitandi curam afferat. Nam ut ex beneficiorum erga me tuorum magnitudine amorem in me tuum propensum maximeque fraternum perspiciens non parum inde gaudij lætitiæque concepi, ita rursus meritorum erga me tuorum multitudinem æqua instar lance expendens doleo, quod intelligam me eorum vim ne cogitando quidem nedum referenda gratia ullo unquam tempore consequi posse. Ne tamen tua Maiestas tot tantaque in me benefacta aut male locata, aut potius (ut Ciceronis ex Ennio sumptis utar verbis) malefacta esse arbitraretur, aut denique parum me memorem gratamque esse iudicaret, volui nunc saltem, cum re non possem, verbis tuæ Maiestati gratias agere. Quod quidem ipsum citius à me vel literis vel nuncio misso factum fuisset, nisi opusculum quoddam, quod etiam ad tuam Maiestatem mittere cupiebam, propositum meum intervertisset. Id quod cum propter angustiam temporis, quod mihi vel aqua citius effluxisse video, ad calcem (uti me facturam opinabar) a me ipsa perduci minime potuerit, spero nunc hasce literas quantumuis rudes meam absentis causam apud tuam Maiestatem acturas esse, simulque animum erga te meum quomodocunque saltem declaraturas. Nam ut id plenè abundèque satis vel mutis vocibus a me fiat, minime fieri posse existimo. præsertim cum (ut tua non ignorat Maiestas) meæ naturæ quasi sit proprium, nō modo non tantum verbis dicere, quantum mente cogitare, verumetiam nō plus dicere quā cogitare. Quorum posterius (plus dicere puto) quemadmodum pauci detestantur, ita multi ubique usurpant, maxime verò in aulis principum & Regum: quibus id unice cavendum est, ne plures intra cubicula sua κόλακας quàm extra aulam suā κόρακας habere videantur. Qua quidem de re hoc loco satis. Illud tantum precor ut Deus conservet tuam Maiestatē quā diutiss: incolumem ad nominis sui gloriam regnique utilitatē. Hatfildiæ 2° februarij

Maiestatis tuæ humillima soror
& serva Elizabeth

Madame, Jestoy comme resolue de ne vous importuner plus de mes lettres voyant quelles vous estoient si peu aggreables mais lextremite ou Je suis reduicte par vos commandement me contraint vous faire ceste cy pour vous prier vouloir escouter mons.r de la Mothe fenelon Ambassadeur du Roy treschrestien monsieur mon bon frere et lord Levingston present porteur sur ce quils vous diront de ma part ne faisant doubte quils ne vous satisfacent et mettent hors de souspecons que vous ont este donnez a grand tort contre moy Sur lesquels me remettant Je ne vous ennuyray de plus longue lettre que pour vous dire que si le traictement que Jay receu continue mes forces ne sont suffisantes pour le porter / Je commence ressentir ma maladie de lannee passee de vous doubter que Je ne suis pour la faire longue en cest estat / Je suis entre voz mains vous en ferez a vostre volonte Mais cependant Je seray veue devant dieu et a vous et a tout le monde que Je ne vous ay donne occasion de me traicter ainsi et seroy bien marrye lavoir pense Pardonnez moy si Je ne vous escry presentement de ma main car Jay ung si grand mal de teste quil nest pas en ma puissance / Et tant Je prye dieu vous donner madame tresbonne et longue vie Escript au chasteau de Sheffeild le viij.me iour de Septembre 1571

Madame vencant selon le commendement donnay que tons ceulx non compris en vng certeing memoyre deussent aller ou leur affayres les conduisoit, Iauoys choisi monssieur de Leuingston pour estre porteur de la presente ce que m'estant refusay et luy retenu jay estay contraynte n'ayant aultre libertay mettre la presente aux meyns de monssieur de Schrewsberi de la quele & de celle siendoses je vons suplie aumoingns par pitie me fayre quelque responce car si je demeure en cest estast il ne spererai jamais vous donner plus de peyne

Vostre affligee bonne seur et cousine
MARIE

Mary, Queen of Scots 1542–1587

'Vottre afflisgee bonne soeur et cousine, Marie R' – 'your afflicted good sister and cousin, Mary, Queen' – is how Mary Stuart ends this note to Elizabeth I, squeezing the valediction and signature sideways into the margin of a busy page. The language chosen by the Queen of Scots is telling and canny: she emphasizes her equality with the English queen – she too can write R after her name; she reminds her of their blood relationship – Mary's grandmother was Elizabeth's aunt; and she makes the point that both are rare women – sisters – in a man's world. The tone is interesting, too: Mary is 'afflicted'; and so, too, must Elizabeth have felt herself by the problem of Mary Stuart.

After many hesitations and retractions, Elizabeth had Mary put to death at Fotheringhay Castle on 7 May 1587. She had avoided the decision for years, but circumstances, exacerbated by Mary as her own worst enemy, had finally left her no choice. Elizabeth was furious at having to give the order and blamed everyone around her but herself. The neat, professional hand of the clerk who has written the bulk of this letter has dated it from Sheffield ('Cheefeild'), 8 September 1571, long before the final scenes of Mary's story would play out, but her life was already a whirlwind of intrigue and controversy. She had been compelled to abdicate her throne in favour of her son, whose legitimacy was in doubt; she had been forced out of Scotland; she had been twice married to utterly unsuitable men and implicated, at least by rumour, in murder and adultery. Her fellow Catholics in Spain and France, who might have taken her side, were appalled and repelled by what they heard.

For nineteen years, Elizabeth allowed Mary a form of sanctuary in England, but under very strict terms. In effect, she lived the rest of her life under house arrest – in the comfort of castles, it's true, but without the possibility of freedom. Elizabeth respected Mary's heritage as a queen but feared her involvement, even if unwitting, in a variety of plots against Elizabeth herself.

Mary, Queen of Scots writes (lower) to Elizabeth I, 1571

Elizabeth moved Mary from castle to castle, and by 1571 she was housed in Sheffield, which was to be her home and prison for fourteen years. She writes, in French as befitted one cultured European monarch to another, to bemoan her situation. At the end of the first part of this letter, she asks Elizabeth's forgiveness for not writing in her own hand: she has such a 'grand mal de teste' – a bad headache – that she simply can't manage it. Nonetheless, when the time came for her to sign what the clerk had written, she was unable to resist adding a codicil in her own large, clear hand, beginning 'Madame'. She explains that she will have to rely on Lord 'Schreusberi' (Shrewsbury), the owner of Sheffield Castle and responsible for her confinement from 1568 to 1585, to forward the letter to Elizabeth, as she had been prevented from using her preferred messenger, Lord 'Levingston'. The Livingston family were part of Mary's separate household in the castle – which at times numbered forty people – comprising a cook, doctor, apothecary and various other servants and companions. Mary appears to claim that she is close to death, ending her note to her cousin, 'Je vous suplie aumoingns par pitie me fayre quelque responce car si je demeure en cest estast je nespere jamais vous donner plus de poyne': 'I pray you, for pity's sake, at least to give me some answer, for if I remain in this state, I shall not hope to give you more trouble.'

On the reverse, the letter is addressed 'To the Queen of England, Madam, my good sister' and is sealed with Mary's small signet seal of a lion rampant flanked by the letters M.R.

Mary, Queen of Scots: letter addressed to Elizabeth I with Mary's seal (right)

A la Royne dangleterre
Madame ma bonne seur

POETS AND NOVELISTS

Hence comes yt that yor Beauty wounds not harts
As others, wth prophane and Sensuall darts
But as an Influence vertuous thoughts imparts.
But if such frinds by the honor of yor sight
Grow capable of thys so great a light,
As to partake yor vertues and theyr might,
what must I thinke that Influence must doe
where yt finds Simpathy and Matter too
vertu, and Beauty, of the same stuffe, as you.
wch ys, yor noble worthy Sister; shee
Of whom if what in thys my extasye ~~I see~~,
And Revelation of you both, I see,
I should write here, As in short Galleryes
The Master at the end large glasses tyes,
So to present the roome twice to or eyes,
So I should give thys letter length, and say
That wch I sayd of you, There ys no way
from eyther, but by th'other, not to stray.
May therfore thys bee 'nough to testify
My true Devotion free from flattery.
He that beleeves himselfe, doth never ly.

127

To ~~the Honorable lady~~
the lady Carew.

John Donne 1572–1631

This is Donne's only English poem surviving in his own handwriting and it is something of an oddity – an exercise in gentle flattery or appreciation for two young women whom he had never met. Lettice and Essex Rich were the daughters of Robert Rich, first earl of Warwick. It seems likely that it was written at the request of their brother, Sir Robert Rich, whom Donne met in Amiens in 1612, while staying with his patron and friend Sir Robert Drury. Rich, rather than Donne, would have been the giver of this gift.

The poem is written out on a single folio of elegant gilt-edged paper and folded horizontally to form a thin strip about an inch (23 mm) wide. It is addressed on the verso side (shown here): *To the Honorable lady/the lady Carew* which was the married name of Lettice Rich, the wife of Sir George Carey (an alternative spelling for Carew).

The text begins, 'Madame', and most of the poem is an encomium to Lettice, comparing her virtues to the fixed stars of the heavenly firmament, in contrast to the changeable nature of human behaviour. Only near the end of the piece does Donne refer to Essex Rich, who appears as rather an afterthought, an echo of her sister's goodness, her virtue and beauty the result almost of Lettice's influence:

> what must I thinke that Influence must doe,
> when yt finds Simpathy, and Matter too,
> Vertu, and Beauty, of the same Stuffe, as you
> which ys, your noble worthy Sister.

The poem's last three lines are quietly ironical: whatever the truth of the matter, they imply, if the speaker believes what he is saying, then he is no liar:

> May therfore thys bee inough to testify
> My true Devotion free from flattery.
> He that beleevs himselfe, doth never ly.

John Donne, poem addressed to Lettice Rich, Lady Carey

The beautifull Cassandra.

a novel, in twelve Chapters.

Chapter the first

Cassandra was the Daughter and the only Daughter of a celebrated Millener in Bond Street. Her father was of noble Birth, being the near relation of the Dutchess of —'s Butler.

Chapter the 2d

When Cassandra had attained her 16th year, she was lovely & amiable & chancing to fall in love with an elegant Bonnet, her Mother had just compleated bespoke by the Countess of — she placed it on her gentle Head & walked from her Mother's shop to make her Fortune.

Chapter the 3d

The first person she met, was the Viscount

Jane Austen 1775–1817

After her death at the age of forty-one, Jane Austen's nephew Edward Austen-Leigh wrote the first *Memoir* of his aunt, with the help of his sister Caroline and half-sister Anna Austen Lefroy. Edward was very conscious of the Austen family image, so, although it is full of fascinating detail, the *Memoir* also takes a somewhat po-faced line on his literary aunt. He was clearly unwilling, for instance, to give his readers more than a brief glimpse of her extensive early writings, of which the Bodleian holds 'Volume the First'. Written between the ages of twelve and fifteen, but copied out into a single notebook in 1792–3, the materials that make up this, the first of three volumes of her so-called 'juvenilia', paint a picture of family fun and home entertainment, with Austen's fluent pen creating parodic versions of the literary and dramatic genres of the day.

Austen dedicates 'Volume the First' to her youngest brother (of six), Charles, although a number of the fourteen individual pieces she lists on a contents page have their own dedication. Titles include 'Frederic and Elfrida, a novel', 'Sir William Mountague, an unfinished performance', 'The Visit, a comedy in 2 Acts' and 'The Adventures of Mr Harley, a short but interesting Tale … inscribed to Mr Francis William Austen Midshipman on board His Majesty's ship the Perseverance by his Obedient Servant The Author'. Austen's only and beloved elder sister, Cassandra, is represented by the page shown opposite:

> The beautifull Cassandra.
> a novel, in twelve Chapters.
> Chapter the first
> Cassandra was the Daughter and the only Daughter of a celebrated Millener in Bond Street. Her father was of noble Birth, being the near relation of the Dutchess of ——s' Butler.

Jane Austen, *The beautifull Cassandra*

The Library acquired 'Volume the First' in 1933, at the urging of its first editor, R.W. Chapman. He arranged the purchase of the manuscript (for a bargain £75) with the aid of the Friends of the Bodleian, at a time when the collection of such 'early scraps', as he apologetically termed them, had only just begun to be of interest. In fact, the Library had not bothered to claim Austen's books when they were first published, which as a copyright library it was entitled to do, because it was thought at the time that novels were not the sort of thing a serious library should collect. In consequence, it was not until the twentieth century that the Bodleian completed its set of Austen first editions.

No such opinions about the value of novels were voiced in 2011, when the Library bought thirty-four leaves from the manuscript of Austen's unfinished work, 'The Watsons', shown opposite. The other six leaves had been purchased by the Morgan Library in New York in 1925, and together they make up around 17,500 words, about a sixth of the size of her finished books. According to Edward Austen-Leigh (who gave the fragment its customary title), it is likely that his aunt had begun the book while she was living in Bath and had abandoned it before she left in 1805. The plot concerns one Emma Watson, who has been brought up by a wealthy aunt. Circumstances contrive that Emma's prospects are ruined by her aunt's foolish remarriage, so that she must return to live with her widowed father and three elder sisters, whom she now outstrips in education and refinement. Added interest is provided by the Watsons' titled neighbours, the Osbornes. Slowly, Emma comes to value her eldest sister, Elizabeth – who returns her regard:

> A week or ten days rolled quietly away after this visit, before any new bustle arose to interrupt even for half a day, the tranquil and affectionate intercourse of the two Sisters, whose mutual regard was increasing with the intimate knowledge of each other which such intercourse produced.

Scholars have enjoyed speculating on why Austen left 'The Watsons' incomplete. Many of the novel's themes are worked out elsewhere, but the Austen expert Professor Kathryn Sutherland has noted that, even

Jane Austen, 'The Watsons'

A week or ten days rolled quietly away ~~the~~ after this visit,
~~this visit at Stanton Parsonage~~ before any
new bustle arose to interrupt even for half a
day, the tranquil & affectionate intercourse of the
two Sisters, whose mutual regard ~~for each other~~ was in:
:creasing with the intimate knowledge of each other which
such intercourse produced. — The first circum:
:stance to break in on this serenity, was the receipt
of a letter from Croydon to announce the speedy
return of Margaret, & a visit of two or three days
from Mr & Mrs Robert Watson, who undertook
to bring her home & wished to see their Sister Emma. — It was an expectation to
fill the thoughts of the Sisters at ~~Stan~~ Stanton, &
to busy ~~employ~~ the hours ~~corporeal powers~~ of one of them
at least — for as Jane had been a woman of
fortune, the preparations for her entertain:
:ment were considerable, & as Eliz: had at all
times more good will than method in her
guidance of the house, she could make no change
without a Bustle. — An absence of 14 years ~~Emma had not heard~~
had made all her Brothers & Sisters ~~anything of Margaret's character~~ Strangers to
Emma, but in her expectation of Margaret
there was more than the awkwardness of such

though unfinished, the handling of the text marks an important staging post in her development as a writer. The unfinished text gives readers the opportunity to observe Austen at work, with crossings out and insertions, hasty spelling and punctuation, and inconsistencies in her plot – a world away from the smooth running of her published prose.

Austen did not begin to publish until relatively late in life, although she had composed – precociously so – the initial drafts of a number of works in the 1790s. *Sense and Sensibility* was the first to appear in 1811, followed by *Pride and Prejudice* in 1813. *Mansfield Park* was begun at Chawton sometime before 1811, finished in 1813 and published in May 1814. It had sold out by 14 November, and made her more money than any of the others. Nevertheless, on 22 November 1814, she finishes the letter shown here to her niece, Anna Austen Lefroy, 'Make everybody at Hendon admire Mansfield Park.'

Anna Austen – the daughter of Austen's eldest brother, James – was something of a favourite niece, sharing her aunt's love of fiction. At the time of this letter, she had been married to Benjamin Lefroy for only a fortnight, and the couple were living in Hendon with his brother. Benjamin was a cousin of the Tom Lefroy with whom the young Jane carried on an extended flirtation – though with what degree of seriousness we shall probably never know. The letter begins with Austen passing on the congratulations ('and there they are') of Harriet Benn on Anna's marriage, and it carries on with a swift roundup of family and local news. It is clear from the lack of her own congratulations that the pair have exchanged several letters since the wedding and Anna has already sent a description of the countryside around Hendon, which her aunt rather damns with faint praise: 'It must be very pretty in Summer.'

Jane Austen, letter to her niece Anna Lefroy

My dear Anna

I met Harriet Benn yesterday, she gave her congratulations & desired they might be forwarded to you, and there they are. — Your Father returned to dinner, Mr. Wm. Digweed who had business with your Uncle, rode with him. — The chief news from their Country is the death of old Mrs. Dormer. — Your Cousin Edward goes to Winchester today to see his Brother & Cousins, & returns tomorrow. Mrs. Clement walks about in a new Black velvet Pelisse lined with Yellow, & a white Bobbin-net-veil, & looks remarkably well in them. — I think I understand the Country about Hendon from your description. It must be very pretty in Summer. — Should you [illegible] that you were within a dozen miles of [illegible] the atmosphere? — I shall break my heart if y[illegible] not go to Hadley. —
Make everybody at Hendon admire Mansfield Park. —

Your affec: Aunt
J. A.

Tuesday Nov: 22. 1814

I say it? / all your friends
knew you so well deserved; therefore the little paragraph gave us
the shock of a joyful surprise;-
and you must let us Gaskells
congratulate you on the splendid
Scarlet gown they hope to see you
wearing with all the dignity of
a Head the next time they go
to St Marys.
Seriously dear Mr. Pattison you
must kindly accept the sincere
congratulations of my daughter
Mr. Gaskell. and of

Yours most truly

E. C. Gaskell.

I am half afraid of putting
'Rector of Lincoln' on the
address of my letter, for fear
it should not be true.

Elizabeth Gaskell 1810–1865

The Bodleian's only catalogued autograph of the celebrated novelist 'Mrs Gaskell' is this letter, written in 1861 to congratulate the Revd Mark Pattison on his election as rector of Lincoln College, Oxford. She writes on behalf of all 'us Gaskells', expressing the hope of seeing him wearing a 'splendid Scarlet gown ... with all the dignity of a Head' of the college, the next time they go to St Mary's, Oxford's University Church.

The Gaskells were a prominent Manchester Unitarian family and Pattison was a High Church Anglican, influenced by John Henry Newman and the Tractarian movement; at first glance, theirs would seem an unlikely acquaintance. But the openness and warmth of her language here helps explain Elizabeth Gaskell's wide and varied circle of friends and correspondents, which included Florence Nightingale and Charlotte Brontë. She had met Pattison during her first visit to Oxford in 1857, when she had also heard the future archbishop of Canterbury, Frederick Temple, preach in St Mary's.

Gaskell expresses some trepidation that the report of Pattison's election might not be accurate, since he had failed to win the rectorship ten years earlier. Shortly afterwards, disappointed with Oxford life, he had resigned his fellowship and gone to work on the radical *Westminster Review*, where Mary Anne Evans (George Eliot) had recently been editor, with a stable of writers that included the prominent Unitarian reformer Harriet Martineau. Their sympathy as social progressives outweighed their differences in religion.

Gaskell's fiction is remarkable for its depiction of the hardships of working-class life and especially the position of many of the poorest women. Alongside her husband, William, minister of Cross Street Chapel, Manchester, she distributed food and clothing and visited the homes of some of the destitute victims of the Industrial Revolution. Her novels *Mary Barton*, *Ruth* and *North and South* tackle the grim position of those left behind by the meeting of new economic forces and traditional social values.

Elizabeth Gaskell, letter to the Revd Mark Pattison, 1861

185

To W. S. Williams Esqr—

Novbr 22nd—

Dear Sir

Will you have the goodness to post the enclosed letter for Mr Lewes.

I have received "Howitt's Journal" "The Literary Circular" "The Manchester Examiner" and to-day the "Nottingham Mercury".

I am dear Sir

Yrs respectfully C Bell.

Charlotte Brontë 1816–1855

The two letters shown opposite and overleaf mark the progression of a friendship and of a literary career. Both are to W.S. Williams, publisher's reader for the relatively new firm of Smith, Elder and Co. The first, of 22 November 1847, is from one Currer Bell, an unknown writer whose debut novel, *Jane Eyre: An Autobiography*, Smith, Elder had just published. 'Yrs respectfully CBell' reports the arrival of reviews of the book from *Howitt's Journal*, *The Literary Circular*, *The Manchester Examiner* and the *Nottingham Mercury*, and asks if Mr Williams will forward on a letter to a certain Mr Lewes.

George Henry Lewes, who would later become the life partner of another novelist, Mary Anne Evans, was also at an early stage in his career. He had been sent a complimentary copy of *Jane Eyre*, and had admired the book so much that he had sent off a review to *Fraser's Magazine* and written to Currer Bell to congratulate the author. Brontë and her sisters, Anne and Emily, had chosen their literary pseudonyms, Acton, Ellis and Currer Bell, to disguise their gender, while giving the impression of being male; but Lewes was quite convinced that the skilful depiction of character and the realism of the narrative could only be the work of a woman. After his initial approach, Brontë and Lewes continued a correspondence, and the letter she here asks Williams to forward is her second reply to him.

Lewes's appreciation was not the opinion of every reviewer. Many thought that the novel was coarse, tasteless and even revolutionary in its depiction of the harsh life of a single woman making her way as a governess and finding, even on marriage, that she had got more than she bargained for. But the public approved and the book was a success. The reverse of this letter notes its sender as 'Currer Bell, Haworth', the location of the parsonage in Yorkshire that Charlotte shared with her father, sisters and brother, Branwell. *Jane Eyre*'s success, however, gave her access to a different society. Although cripplingly shy and uncertain of herself, she

Charlotte Brontë (Currer Bell), letter to W.S. Williams, 1847 travelled to London and elsewhere, and began to meet and even make friends with other writers and literary lions. Staying with her publisher, George Smith, she met Lewes, as well as her hero Thackeray, went to exhibitions and theatres, and even agreed to have a portrait painted. She stayed at Ambleside with that ubiquitous woman of letters Harriet Martineau, and became close to Elizabeth Gaskell, whom she visited in Manchester. After her friend's early death, Gaskell wrote an acclaimed *Life of Charlotte Brontë* (1857), which in large part cemented Brontë's reputation and established for at least a generation how she was to be seen.

W.S. Williams became a regular and trusted correspondent. In the second letter, shown opposite, of 26 October 1852, she addresses him as 'My dear Sir' and ends, 'Believe me Yours sincerely, CBrontë'. Smith, Elder had by now published Charlotte's editions of her sisters' novels – Emily's *Wuthering Heights* and Anne's *Agnes Grey* – as well as her own *Shirley*. Her personal situation, however, was even more isolated: Charlotte's mother and two further sisters had died two decades earlier, but in 1848–9 Anne, Emily and Branwell all died in the space of barely a year, leaving Charlotte and her father alone at Haworth. Her literary friends and correspondence became even more important as a lifeline, although her publishers were keen to have another novel. Here she tells Williams she has returned a box of books to Cornhill (65 Cornhill was the firm's address in London – and later provided the name of their literary *Cornhill Magazine*) and has also included two volumes of a manuscript ('M.S.'):

> the third vol. is now so near completion that I trust, if all be well, I may calculate on its being ready in the course of two or three weeks. My wish is that the book should be published without Author's name.

This was to be *Villette* (1853), which like *Jane Eyre* drew on Brontë's own life experience, this time as a teacher in a girls' school in Brussels – the eponymous 'Villette'.

Charlotte Brontë, letter to W.S. Williams, 1852

Octbr 26th 1852

My dear Sir

I am sending a return-box of books to Cornhill – I take the opportunity of enclosing 2 vols. of M. S. The third vol. is now so near completion that I trust, if all be well, I may calculate on its being ready in the course of two or three weeks. My wish is that the book should be published without Author's name.

I shall feel obliged if you will intimate the safe arrival of the Manuscript –

Believe me
Yours sincerely
C Brontë

W. S. Williams Esqre

The moving Finger writes, & having writ,
Moves on: nor all thy Piety & Wit
Shall lure it back to cancel half a line
Nor all thy tears wash out a word of it.

=

"Domine, quo vadis?" – Legend of St Peter.

=

The Roman eagles were placed in a chapel in the camp, & worshipped by the soldiers. Gibbon I. 147.

Contest between the <u>Retiarius</u> & the <u>Secutor</u>, described by Juvenal VIII. 200.

=

The Christ of art became severe after the year 1000. Didron.

=

Panselinos – Ερμηνεια της ζωγραφικης – a book of rules for painters in their rendering of sacred subjects.

George Eliot 1819–1880

Reckoning that his daughter Mary Anne's plain looks would mean she had to earn her own money rather than marry into it, Robert Evans paid particular attention to her education. Her subsequent career as a writer more than vindicated his decision. Mary Anne (or Mary Ann or Marion: she used various spellings) became the de facto editor of the influential *Westminster Review*, writing articles and reviews on literature, art and theology, as well as on the social and political reform for which the *Review* was known. Widely read, she was at home in many languages – her translations of the latest German theology were made for her own interest as well as for income, although she had lost her conventional Anglican faith in her early twenties.

Alongside this, Evans was garnering increasing success as a novelist. She adopted her male nom de plume in 1857 to avoid being associated with a particular sort of fiction – what she called 'Silly Novels by Lady Novelists' – but also to distance her writing from the scandal that surrounded her private life. Her lack of conventional beauty did not, as it turned out, leave her devoid of romantic and sexual adventure, and from 1854 she lived with George Henry Lewes (and adopted his name), a married man unable to be divorced from his wife. This left her, if not quite a social outcast, nevertheless not accepted by much of society; indeed, she was pointedly snubbed by her own brother.

Eliot was known for the meticulous care for accuracy with which she approached her novels, and none more so than *Romola*. Written as an historical fiction set in fifteenth-century Florence, *Romola* was published in serial form in *The Cornhill Magazine* during 1862–3. Although she was already an experienced author, the novel's birth pangs were harder than anything she had felt before, not least because, as she realized, she had prepared too conscientiously for her task: her striving for historical accuracy kept the literary text from taking flight.

Working notebook of George Eliot (Mary Anne Evans)

Many of Eliot's notebooks survive, but this is the Bodleian's sole example, acquired by donation in 1971. Begun in 1862, the small book is full of material for the novel, in Greek, Latin, French, German, Spanish and Italian. On this page, Eliot ranges between notes on Rome from Gibbon's *Decline and Fall of the Roman Empire*, to questions of Byzantine and Western Christian art, probably drawn from A.N. Didron's *Iconographie chrétienne*, to a stanza from Edward Fitzgerald's version of the *Rubáiyát of Omar Khayyám*, the eleventh/twelfth-century Persian astronomer and poet:

> The moving Finger writes, & having writ,
> Moves on: nor all thy Piety & Wit
> Shall lure it back to cancel half a line
> Nor all thy tears wash out a word of it.

Fitzgerald's translation had become popular only in 1861, so Eliot's (slightly inaccurate) quotation from it here is very up to the minute.

The notebook itself is also of a particular type. A 'Patent Metallic Book', it featured a metal-point pencil (now missing) and specially prepared paper that gave the pencil the permanent properties of ink, relieving the writer of carrying round a possibly leaky fountain pen. The book has been written in from both ends, in Evans's stylish and clear hand. Small (70 × 110 mm) and smartly bound in dark blue leather with gold-stamped decoration, it has an internal pocket for receipts and stamps, the remains of a pinkish-red place marker, and a metal clasp to hold it closed.

George Eliot (Mary Anne Evans): 'Improved Patent Metallic Book'

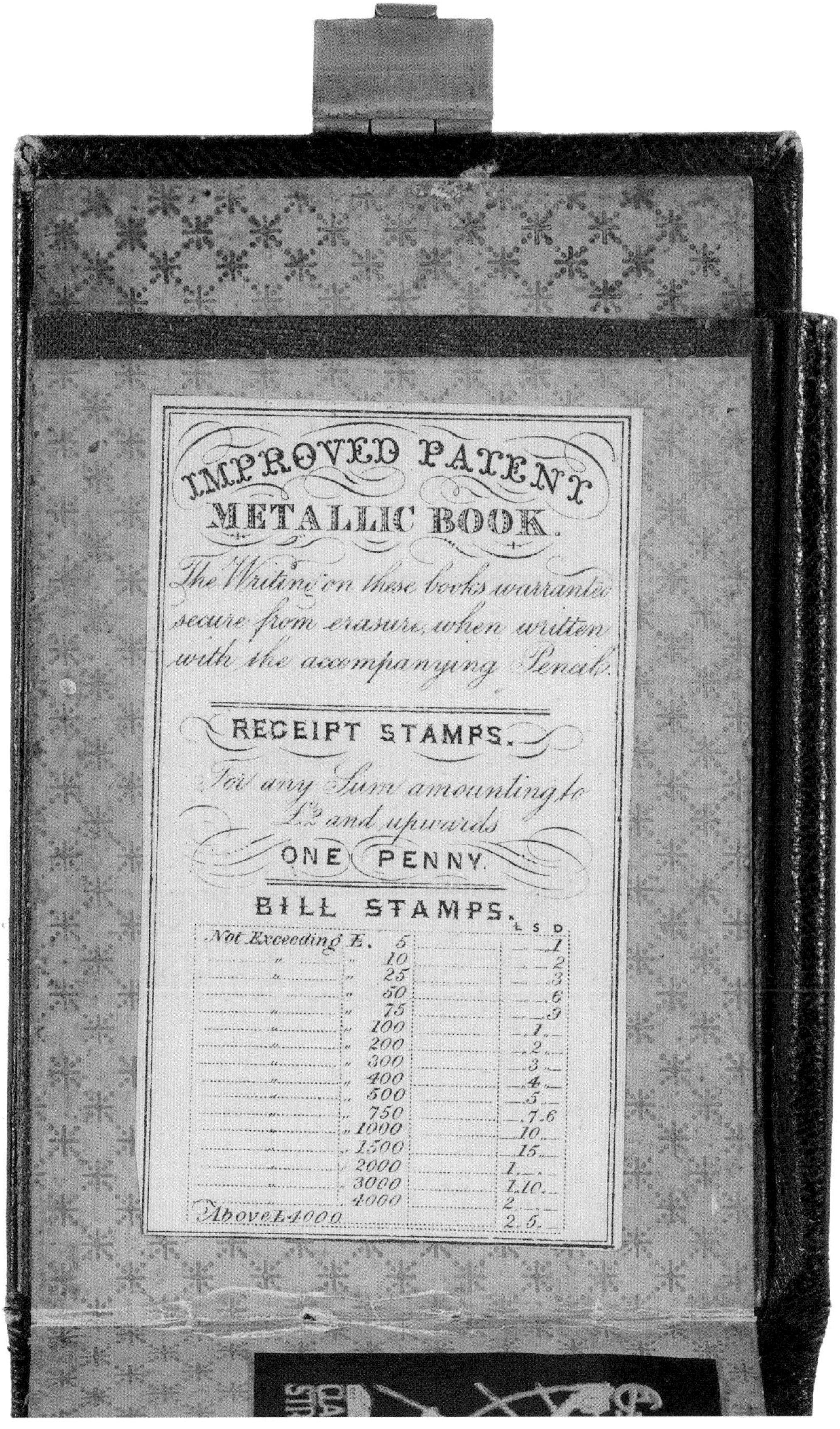
IMPROVED PATENT
METALLIC BOOK.
The Writing on these books warranted secure from erasure, when written with the accompanying Pencil.
RECEIPT STAMPS.
For any Sum amounting to £2 and upwards
ONE PENNY.
BILL STAMPS.
L S D
Not Exceeding £. 5 ... 1
" 10 ... 2
" 25 ... 3
" 50 ... 6
" 75 ... 9
" 100 ... 1
" 200 ... 2
" 300 ... 3
" 400 ... 4
" 500 ... 5
" 750 ... 7.6
" 1000 ... 10
" 1500 ... 15
" 2000 ... 1
" 3000 ... 1.10
" 4000 ... 2
Above £4000 ... 2.5

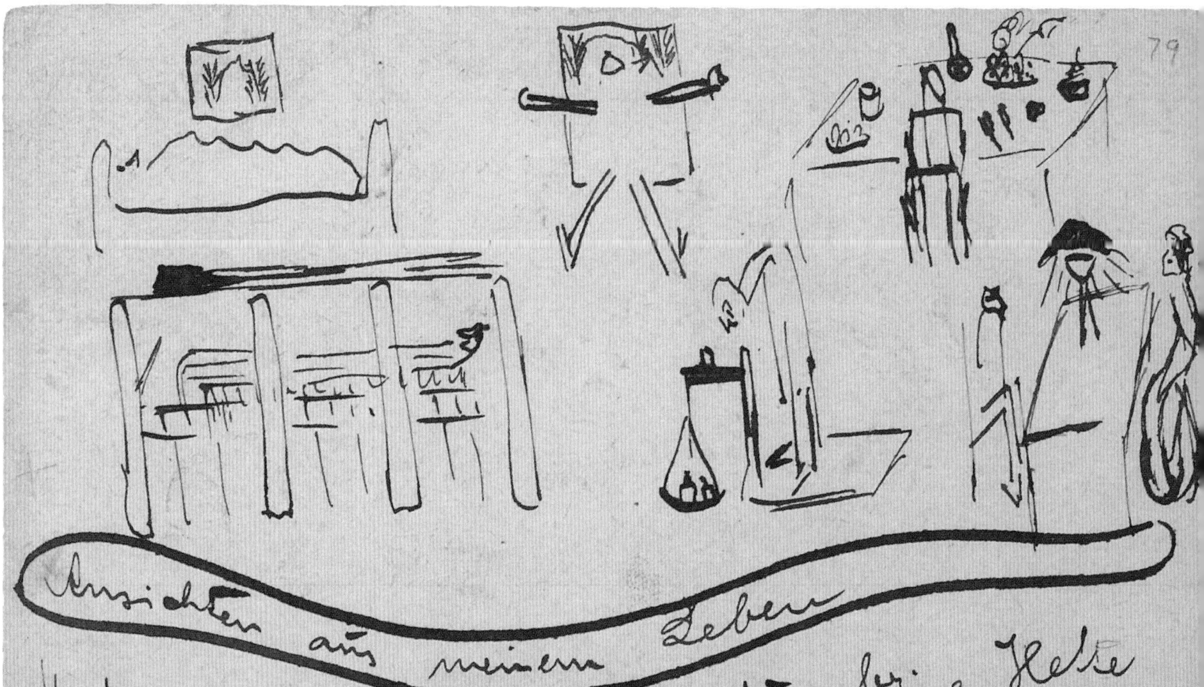

Und wie geht es Dir? Weihnachten bring Hefte
und Bücher, ich werde Dich prüfen. Soll ich übrigens

Franz Kafka 1883–1924

This postcard is a greeting from the enigmatic Czech novelist to his youngest and favourite sister Ottla. Writing from Austria in December 1918, Kafka punningly alludes to the German word for picture postcard (*Ansichtskarte*), with his hand-drawn 'pictures of my life' ('Ansichten aus meinem Leben'); but the life he portrays here is far from a holiday. Kafka had contracted tuberculosis, an incurable and wasting disease, in 1917 and he had been pensioned off from his job at an insurance company. He spent most of the rest of his life in sanatoria, which the sketch here of his being weighed reflects.

Kafka's manuscripts and papers came to his friend Max Brod, along with the request that he burn them. Brod, however, did not comply, and at the outbreak of war in 1939 took them with him from Prague to Tel Aviv, later sending them to Switzerland for safekeeping. Kafka's two brothers had died in infancy and all three sisters, Elli, Valli and Ottla, were murdered in concentration camps; Ottla died in Auschwitz in 1943. The ownership of the Kafka papers passed to his sisters' four daughters.

In 1961 Kafka's nieces agreed to deposit the material at the Bodleian Library to make it accessible to scholars and to facilitate a critical edition of his writings by a team led by Malcolm Pasley, who was instrumental in bringing the manuscripts to Oxford. With great generosity, Elli's and Valli's daughters, Gertrude Kaufmann and Marianna Steiner, bequeathed their share of the papers to the Bodleian. A further tranche of material was gifted by the Schocken family, with the help of Bodley's American Friends, and the Library joined together with the Deutsches Literaturarchiv in Marbach to purchase Kafka's letters to Ottla. In addition, part of the material saved by Brod remains in Jerusalem. By this winding path, directed as was so much of twentieth-century history by the results of the Holocaust, the Bodleian, the Literaturarchiv, the National Library of Israel and Ottla's descendants have all shared in preserving his memory.

Franz Kafka, postcard to his sister Ottla, 1918

5

Sir Geoffrey Faber, President

Richard de la Mare, Chairman. P. F. du Sautoy, Vice-Chairman

T. S. Eliot, W. J. Crawley, Morley Kennerley (U.S.A.), Alan Pringle, David Bland, Charles Monteith

FABER AND FABER LTD

PUBLISHERS

24 Russell Square London WC1

Fabbaf Westcent London Museum 9543

TSE/AM 8th December 1960

Miss Helen Gardner,
St. Hilda's College,
O X F O R D.

Dear Miss Gardner,

It is courteous of you to write to me about the brief which Mr. Rubinstein gave you. I only knew that copies had been given to a few other witnesses before the trial when Professor Pinto wrote to me and asked whether he could present his copy to the Library of Nottingham University. I accordingly asked him to send me his copy and I made alterations and deletions. Mr. Rubinstein only took some notes in longhand, and a great deal of the document is in his idiom rather than mine. Furthermore, there were some personal details which I was merely explaining to him and did not wish to be elicited in the witness box. I have written to Mr. Rubinstein, who has promised me to ask those persons to whom he had given my brief to return it to me.

In retrospect I am glad not to have been called upon, although at the time I felt rather let down. But my feelings toward Lawrence remain ambiguous and my desire to give witness in his favour was really rather as a protest against other books, such as LOLITA, which struck me as really evil, which much more deserve censoring. The great pity is that the Crown chose Lawrence's book for prosecution. One knows what will happen: once a book has been under the charge of obscenity not even a jury can give absolution, and the book will be bought by thousands out of curiosity who are quite incapable of understanding what Lawrence was after. And I feel pretty sure that I should have disliked Lawrence personally if I had known him!

Yours sincerely,

T. S. Eliot

T.S. Eliot 1888–1965

The trial of a novel whose author has been dead for thirty years hardly seems like news; but the prosecution in 1960 of Penguin Books for their publication of D.H. Lawrence's last novel, *Lady Chatterley's Lover*, was the talk of the town. *Lady Chatterley* had been published in Italy in 1928, but its volatile combination of sex and class, starkly portrayed, had caused it to be excluded from import to Britain. Penguin had not only published the unexpurgated version; they intended to produce a cheap 3/6d edition, putting the book within the means of almost anyone who wanted to read it.

Penguin's success at the trial rested on the shoulders of their solicitor, Michael Rubinstein, who appears at the beginning of this letter of T.S. (Thomas Stearns) Eliot to Miss (later Professor Dame) Helen Gardner, then fellow in English at St Hilda's College, Oxford. Rubinstein had prepared a constellation of expert witnesses who would come to court and swear that *Lady Chatterley* could not be found guilty under the Obscene Publications Act of 1959. Miss Gardner and Mr Eliot had corresponded for some years. He admired her academic work on his poetry, and when *The Sunday Times* had requested an interview with him for his seventieth birthday in 1958, he had agreed as long as Miss Gardner should conduct it.

In the end, as Eliot notes, he was not called to the witness box, but Gardner did give evidence in person, having been shown the brief that Eliot had prepared for Rubinstein. Despite his support for the defence, Eliot records here his ambivalence towards Lawrence and his concern that the publicity of the trial will only swell *Lady Chatterley*'s sales among those who would not understand it. In this he was correct: when Penguin published their second edition a month later, it sold its 200,000 print run on the first day.

Eliot was born in St Louis, Missouri, to a family with distinguished Unitarian roots, but his own religious journey took another direction.

Letter from T.S. Eliot to Helen Gardner about the *Lady Chatterley* trial

After settling in England, in 1927 he became a High Church Anglican, and from then on his faith underpinned his life and work. In 1935, commissioned by the Bishop of Chichester, he wrote *Murder in the Cathedral* about the martyrdom of Thomas Becket. Originally performed at Canterbury Cathedral, the play was such a success that it transferred to the Old Vic theatre in London. The year before, however, Eliot had been asked to write part of a pageant in support of the Forty-Five Churches Fund, which had been set up to raise money for the construction of new churches in London suburbs. *The Rock* was a sort of practice run for *Murder in the Cathedral*, though both Eliot himself and subsequent critics considered it much less successful, despite its raising £1,500 for the fund. With characters that include St Peter, Anglo-Saxon builders with cockney accents and modern Londoners, as well as a verse-speaking chorus, the drama centres on the building of a church by the creation of a community across time and space.

Eliot was dissatisfied with *The Rock*, but he printed some of the choruses he wrote for it in his *Collected Poems, 1909–1935*. That opposite, from the autograph manuscript preserved in the Bodleian, reads:

> Dwellings for all men
> Churches for all.
> Should the fruit fall, then,
> By the waste wall?
> Shall the fruit fall then
> The harvest be waste,
> When the Saviour of all men
> Our sowing has graced.

Eliot had become internationally famous as a poet and dramatist long before the trial. But even poets need to eat and, after a spell working in a bank, he was recruited in 1925 by Geoffrey Faber to work as literary editor and a director of his new publishing firm. Faber and Faber became Eliot's literary home, and his acumen established its run of 'Faber poets', which included W.H. Auden and Ted Hughes, for the next forty years.

T.S. Eliot, draft of *The Rock*, 1934

Under & over
Belfries so high
Seagulls will hover
Drowning their cry;
The new bells all ringing
With solemn accord
And the choristers singing
In the House of Our Lord.

~~Dwelling for~~
Dwellings for all men
Churches for all –
Shall the fruit fall, then,
By the waste wall?
Shall the fruit fall then
The harvest be waste,
When the Saviour of all men
Our sowing has graced.

SCIENTISTS

Cinnaber see vermilion

Cittrine

Coagulate or congeale or bring a liquid
☿ by long heate is coagulated into ☿ [illegible]
when they are almost cold after fusion. Severall
gested in fit proportion wth fixt bodys. & severall
lations at dry heat as of sand or ashes is best, & a moist hea
Cobalum a minerall by vitrification of wch th
Cochineel one graine of it dissolved in spirit of [illegible]
of water wth a discernable blew colour.
Cohobation ~~[illegible]~~ or repeated distillation
wth its caput mortuum & againe distilled. Ma
tions or congelations) becoms more flegmatick

Colcothar

Commixtion is when bodys are well mixed

Cones made of Iron or brasse to pour melted
Cones made of Paper called manica Hypocra

Copperas is vitrioll (i e of Copper) See Brim

Copper is somtims found perfect in the mine

Corall is a succulent soft & tender plant growi
soon as it comes into ye open aire is thereby turned i

Isaac Newton 1642–1727

Alchemy has come to have a bad name. Chemistry is science, but 'alchemy' implies hocus pocus, and its concern with turning base metal into gold an embarrassing mixture of greed and credulity. Yet in the seventeenth century the line between the two was not so clear. Since plants and animals grow and mutate and interact with one another to reproduce, the notion that the same might be true of metals and other inanimate matter was not (indeed, is not) so strange. In the book of Genesis, the Bible recorded God turning the inchoate matter of primal chaos into the finished world. So alchemists, too, tried to break parts of that creation down into its primal state, and reconstitute it in new and better forms. Nuclear physics is not so different.

Newton's concern with alchemy or chemistry, then, can be seen as related both to his serious interest in theology and to his work on the physics and mechanics of the motion of the universe, which his mathematics captured with such brilliant simplicity. The page shown here is part of a fragmentary alphabetical dictionary of (al)chemical terms, materials and apparatus, with entries starting with 'Abstraction' and ending with 'Urinous Salt'. It probably dates from the late 1660s or early 1670s, when Newton was seriously engaged in chemical questions, and might perhaps be considered a forerunner of his great *Index chemicus* of the 1680s.

Although he amassed a very large collection of alchemical texts, and made copious notes from them, this little work appears to be his own composition. This page runs from 'Cinnaber see Vermillion' to 'Deliquium'. Newton has left gaps where he has yet to supply a definition, for instance with 'Colcothar', an oxide of iron. The entry for 'Crucible' includes two small drawings of possible shapes for such vessels.

This little work came from the great auction of Newton's papers held at Sotheby's on 13–14 July 1936. It was acquired for the Library by the Friends of the Bodleian in 1967.

detail left and overleaf Isaac Newton, alphabetical dictionary of (al)chemical terms

Cinnabar see vermilion

Citrine

Coagulate or congeale or bring a liquid or soft body into a firme or solid Masse
☿ by long heate is coagulated into ☿ precip per se: Also it will coagulate being put upon Lea
when they are almost cold after fusion. Severall volatile spirits will coagulate being joyne
gested in fit proportion with fixt bodys. & severall liquors will coagulate spirit of urine. Ffi
lations at dry heat as of sand or ashes first, & a moist heat as Balne Mariæ Venter Equinus &c for further dissolut
Cobaltum a minerall by vitrification of wch they make Powder blew. (unifaction by
Cochineel one graine of it dissolved in spirit of Urin & then by degrees in faire water, tinged 125000
of water wth a discernable blew colour.
Cohobation ~~[illegible]~~ or repeated distillation is when ye liquor distilld off is againe
wth its caput mortuum & againe distilled. Many liquors by often cohobations (or better by
tions of congelations) become more flegmatick & yr caput mortuum more rich.

Colcothar

Commixtion when bodys are well mixed wth some powders in order to Calcination

Cones made of Iron or brasse to pour melted metalline substances into, a Mortar may usually
Cones made of Paper called manica Hypocratis for filtrations or solutions per deliquium.

Copperas is vitrioll (i.e. of Copper) See Brimstone

Copper is somtimes found perfect in the mine

Corall is a succulent soft & tender plant growing in ye bottom of the sea & propagating its sp
as soon as it comes into ye open aire is thereby turned into a Lapideous forme & may be corroded w
vinegar or by its spirit as Lapis stellaris & many ~~other~~ minerall stones may bee.
Crocus Metallorum is made of Antimony & Saltpeter ana: well dryed, mixed, fired in a
wth a coale & dulcified. Infused in white wine tis good for vomits.
Red Crocus Martis is filings of Iron calcined by flame in a Reverberatory furnace. Als
is turned to a red powder or Crocus by the fumes of Aqua fortis.

Crucible or earthen pots made in Holland &c to melt metalls &c in. 6 or 7 of them one within another are
a nest
Cuppel or Test. Gold being cuppelled wth much lead growes paler & heavier by ye volatile silver it se
Cucurbits from their shape, in relation to their heads they are usually called bodys. 
Sal Terræ Damnatæ is a fixt salt got by pouring hot water on ~~the salt~~ terra to imbibe its salt, yn filtrating

Decant yt is, when ye precipitate or fæces &c is settled to ye bottom pour of the liquor.

~~Decoct yt is boyle (or digest wth warmness) some substance put some substance in a warme~~
~~boyling liquor to extract its subtiler pts, see extraction.~~
Decoction is a liquor impregnated but not coloured wth ye subtile pts wch being hot
warme it hath extracted from some body immersed in it. Tis much used by Apothecarys.
extraction.

Decrepitate or calcine any body (as salt or Niter) till it leave cracking

deliquium. Liquors are made per deliquium when saline substances exposed to cold dew in
the moisture of the aire & soe run down (resolve) in a liquor. Somtimes they are layd on an in

-tion or keeping a liquor &c in a warme heat as in Balneo or Sand to make a further mixtion [illegible]
-, or maturation &c. If ye liquors bee penetrant or digestion long, tis best to seale them up hermetically

-illation when ye volatile pts of bodys are driven up by fire into Vapors wch condense into a liquor B
-ify or Edulcorate yt is take away all ye tast & savour of ye solvent from ye precipitate by
-ll affusions & abstractions of fresh water. Rectified spirit of wine is often used instead of water
-th away wth it all ye corrosive spirits that lodged in ye powder wch are sometimes hard to
-erated. Also distilled water of hard boyled white eggs is an excellent dulcifier.

Glasses have an Ovall bole wth a long stem .

-mells are severall mixtures of Minerall & Metalline glasses (as Calx of Tin by fire
-opake glasse &c). They are used also for annealing colours upon glasse, the art of colouring glas
through being lost. The colours (blew red &c) layd upon ye glasse are fluxed in ye furnace
-t is annealing & so fasten themselves to it. only the yellow wch is done wth Calx of Silver sinks
-ns Veneris is flowers of Sal Armoniack sublimed from dulcifyed Colcothar

-ear

-pireumatick or wch hath a fire fang or strong offensive tast of ye fire, wch is got by distilling wth too vehement fires.
-raction is when ye purest & best pts of any substance are taken from ye feculent by dig-
-us propper liquor wch dissolves & imbibes ym into it selfe & being soe impregnated it is
decanted from ye faeces after they are settled. Which liquor [illegible]
-r is called a Tincture, otherwise decoction &c. And if you further evaporate or distill it [illegible]
matter in the bottom come to a Mellago tis then called an Extract [illegible]
both wch, if made wthout heat, are usually called Infusions. [illegible] called fluxes
flux of Metalls is made more easy by Borax or Sandiver, or an equall mixture of Nitre & Tartar &c [illegible]
-ltration is when the purer pts of a liquor passe through some strainer (i.e. porous body)
-h wch ye grosser cannot. Tis best done in a funnell over or in wch is put single
-ble browne paper a little hollowed to hold the liquor wch will quickly run through & leave
-sser pt behind in the paper. You may fold ye paper conically to hold the
liquor without a funnell. Sometimes tis done per Lingulam that is long shreds of Cotton or woll
ye broade end being put into ye liquor wch will ascend (though not above 5 or
-ces & run downe into ye vessell into wch ye narrow end descends wch end must hang lower then ye liquor
-ores Veneris are darke greene christalls made by evaporating a solution of Verdigreas in Distilled Vinegar
-ores Sulphuris wch are yellow are made by mixing well powdered Sulphur wth Colcothar or Salt
-k dust or (wch is best) wthout any addition, in Sand.
-res Antimonij &c in naked fire: ye highest are white ye rest tending to red.
-ores Salis Armoniaci are sublimed from Salt or scales of Iron in Sand.
-ores Benzoin are white & may bee made by setting Benzoin in any Gally pot on a few coales
-ing them in a sheet of paper folded conically.
-ores Antimonij from a mixture of Antimony & Sal Armoniack, in Sand, are red.
-e simple flowers of Lead, Tin, Copper, Regulus of Antimony & of Antimony are made in naked fire wth
& heads. But they will not rise (like many other flowers) wthout a vent in ye top of the head [illegible]
-mination F (for calcination, fusion, cementation &c
-urnace. As 1 ye Wind furnace wch blows it selfe by attracting ye aire through a narrow passage
distilling furnace by naked fire, for things yt require a strong fire for distillation. & it differs not much
ye Wind furnace only ye glasse rests on a crosse barr of iron under wch bar is a hole to put in the
wch in ye wind furnace is put in at ye top. 3 The Reverberatory furnace where ye flame only
-ting under an arched roof acts upon ye body. 4 ye Sand furnace when ye vessel is set in
-sks heated by a fire made underneath. 5 Balneum or Balneum Mariæ when ye body is set to distill or digest in
water. Balneum Roris or Vaporosum ye glasse hanging in the steame of boyling water
Instead of this may bee used ye heat of horse dung (calld venter Equinus) &: brewsters grains
bran, saw dust, chopt hay or straw, a little moistned close pressed & covered. Or it may in
-s shell bee set under a hen. 7 Athanor, Piger Henricus, or furnus Acediæ for long digestions
being set in sand heated wth a Turret full of Charcoale wch is contrived to burne only at the
the upper coales continually sinking downe for a supply. Or the sand may bee heated
-mp & it is called the Lamp furnace. These are made of fire stones, or bricks

Edward Jenner 1749–1823

In 1980 the World Health Organization formally declared smallpox to have been eradicated from the human population. A disease that was once common – and fatal to about a fifth of those who contracted it – had been eliminated by the power of vaccination. Edward Jenner, a country doctor from Gloucestershire, was the driving force behind that success.

The idea that deliberately inducing a mild dose of a disease might give future protection from it was not new. In Britain, Lady Mary Wortley Montagu had introduced the practice from Constantinople, in 1721. Variolation, as it was called, took infected material from smallpox pustules and used it to infect the subject, who would then be protected from further illness. But the technique was not without risk, since no amount of smallpox could be guaranteed to be safe.

Jenner's breakthrough – famously associated with his observation of milkmaids – was to show that infection with a much milder disease, cowpox, would nevertheless provide protection against smallpox. In 1798 he published his findings for the first time, and from then on he was engaged in promoting the benefits of vaccination, a term derived from the Latin *vacca*, 'cow'.

Then, as now, there were vaccination sceptics. In 1800 John Ring, a London doctor, organized a testimonial to be signed by eminent physicians in support of the practice, and this was repeated in other parts of the country. In this letter, dated 12 December 1800, Jenner writes to William Fermor of Northamptonshire, about a Dr Vyvian, who would not sign the Oxford endorsement. He is scathing about vaccination denial:

> How sedulously we guard ourselves from the introduction of foreign Plagues, while a far greater than could be imported is sufferd unmolested to destroy annually its tens of thousands!

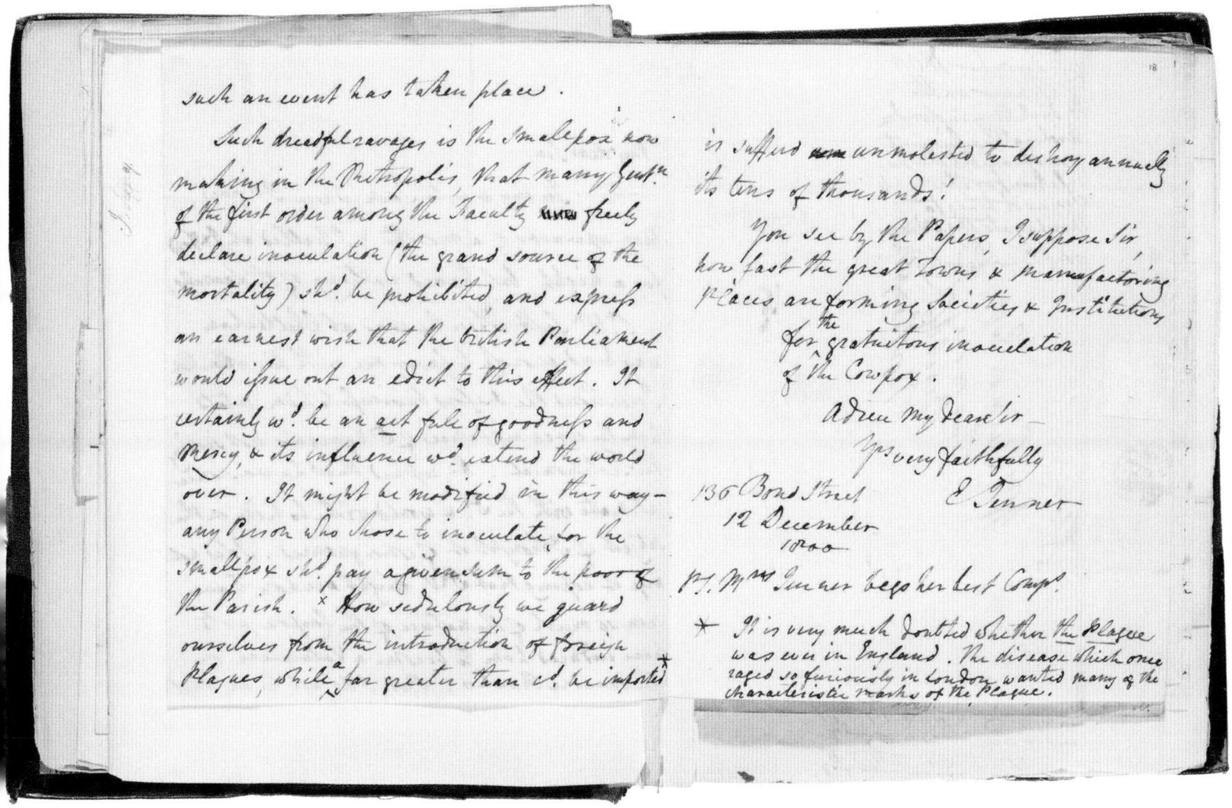

such an event has taken place.

Such dreadful ravages is the Smallpox now making in the Metropolis, that many Gentn of the first order among the Faculty freely declare inoculation (the grand source of the mortality) shd be prohibited, and express an earnest wish that the British Parliament would issue out an edict to this effect. It certainly wd be an act full of goodness and mercy, & its influence wd extend the world over. It might be modified in this way – any Person who chose to inoculate for the smallpox shd pay a given sum to the poor of the Parish. * How sedulously we guard ourselves from the introduction of Foreign Plagues, while a far greater than cd be imported is suffer'd unmolested to destroy annually its tens of thousands!

You see by the Papers, I suppose Sir, how fast the great Towns & manufacturing Places are forming Societies & Institutions for the gratuitous inoculation of the Cowpox.

Adieu my dear Sir

Yrs very faithfully

E Jenner

136 Bond Street
12 December
1800

P.S. Mrs Jenner begs her best Comps.

* It is very much doubted whether the Plague was ever in England. The disease which once raged so furiously in London wanted many of the characteristic marks of the Plague.

Edward Jenner, letter to William Fermor about vaccination, 1800

Luckily,

> the great Towns and manufactoring Places are forming Societies and Institutions for the gratuitous inoculation of the Cowpox.

Wealthy citizens from the burgeoning industrial towns were providing free vaccination for everyone.

It has been estimated that the eradication of smallpox has saved more lives than any other single medical initiative.

… ~~that are only~~ … to distinguish them from such as are optically ~~only appear to be~~ double … being in the same line of vision.

Captn Smyth R N & Sir James South in this Country & by Messrs Struve, Encke, & Bessel on the Continent. — The work before us contains the results of Mr Struve's observations at the Imperial Observatory at Dorpat of double Stars during a period of 20 years. When first established at Dorpat he had but very imperfect means of observation, but notwithstanding these disadvantages he formed a Catalogue of 795 double Stars with their approximate places. Some of them had already been determined by Sir Wm Herschel, others by Laland and the rest were his own. In 1824 he was furnished by the liberality of the Emperor of Russia with an instrument of unparalleled excellence and construction by … Struve. The … of glass made by the celebrated Fraunhoffer 9.43 inches in diameter and its focal length is 14 feet. That is the image formed in the tube is 14 feet from the lens. This telescope is mounted to move by Clock work parallel to the Equator so as exactly to counteract the effects of the earth's rotation by which means observations are made as if the earth were at rest.

…, 12 Lyncis. … good … also to … B … is a … Consists … Stars … Single … ordinary … ope the

unequal magnitudes in close approximation. The places of 500 of these double Stars were determined by him with great accuracy & perseverance. Since his time the search ~~has been~~ for double Stars has been prosecuted with infinite zeal and success by his son Sir John Herschel, by ~~Mr Struve, Bessel, Encke, Smyth and South, and by Mr Dunlop in New South~~ These eminent astronomers have increased Sir Wm Herschel's original Catalogue to more than 6000, exclusively of those in the Southern hemisphere. These 6000 result from the examination of about 120,000 Stars so that one star in 20 is double, but that ratio varies … the size of the Stars … less the smaller they … double Stars were …ed by Mr Dunlop in … Southern hemisphere, the … of those determined … John Herschel in that … the heavens has not … made public.

… double Stars were classed … Wm Herschel according … closeness of the Components and they have been … a test of the excellence … opes. For example in … 36 Andromedae, η Cor … Herculis & τ Serpentarii … stars are so near to … other that it is extremely … to separate them, … separately, and … impossible without a … te telescope

Mary Somerville 1780–1872

Together with Caroline Herschel, Mary Somerville was one of the first two women honorary members of the Royal Astronomical Society, elected in 1835. Indeed, she amassed honours thick and fast: a whole box in the Bodleian is required to house the accolades she was given by the Royal Society, the Royal Irish Academy and the Royal Geographical Society, to mention only a few of the British and foreign awards she accumulated in her lifetime. Just seven years after her death, a newly founded college for women in Oxford chose her name as its own. For a small-town Scottish girl with no formal schooling in maths or science, it was an extraordinary achievement.

Against the wishes of her father, Mary Fairfax, as she was born, seems always to have been attracted to mathematics, which she studied in secret. When she married and moved to London, she was able to expand her education; widowed with two children, she returned to Scotland, where she further advanced her mathematical abilities by arranging tuition by correspondence from William Wallace.

Mary's mathematical talent began to gain recognition. A second marriage (which produced two more children) in 1812 took her once again to London, where her husband, William Somerville, was physician to the Royal Hospital, Chelsea. Somerville encouraged her studies, and the couple became part of scientific London society.

In 1827 she was asked to translate and explain the latest five-volume work by the French mathematician Pierre-Simon Laplace on applied mathematical analysis, the *Mécanique céleste*. Consulting with the astronomer Sir John Herschel and the mathematicians Charles Babbage and Augustus De Morgan, she took three years to complete the task, and in 1837 *The Mechanism of the Heavens* was adopted as an advanced textbook in Cambridge University. Another book, *On the Connexion of the Physical Sciences*, in which she expounded the latest in Anglo-

Mary Somerville, working notes for *The Mechanism of the Heavens*

French scientific research, appeared in 1834 and was an immediate international success.

The pages illustrated give an idea of Mary's working method. Her talents lay particularly in what we would now call the public understanding of science. She could take complex mathematical and astrophysical questions and make them accessible to a less expert audience without sacrificing the science. Her working papers in the Bodleian radiate competence, organization and professionalism. Shown here are two parts of the writing process – an earlier, drafting stage for *Mechanism*, and the fair copy of *Connexion*, ready to be sent to the printer. Mary made her drafts using large loose pages divided into two columns. Her running text inhabits the right-hand column, with the left side free for additions and alterations. Sometimes whole sections were crossed out and substitute text inserted on extra pieces of paper. Her knowledge of the scientific literature is evident in her references, which here include both William Herschel and his son, Sir John.

By contrast, the final draft of *On the Connexion of the Physical Sciences* is copied into a book, at the front of which Somerville has noted which pages have already been sent to the printer. This section – 'Demonstration of the formula for calculating the time by an observation of the sun's Altitude' – displays her technical capabilities, with a precise diagram illustrating sextant measurements, and the worked-through example for her readers to follow. Her drafts contain a number of such worked examples on individual pieces of paper, ready to be inserted as needed.

Somerville could not escape the conventions of her day. A letter from the Royal Society announcing a bust to be placed in her honour was sent to her husband, not to herself. It will be

> a proud tribute to the powers of the female mind – and at the same time establish an imperishable record of the perfect compatibility of the most exemplary discharge of the softer duties of domestic life with the deepest researches in Mathematical Philosophy.

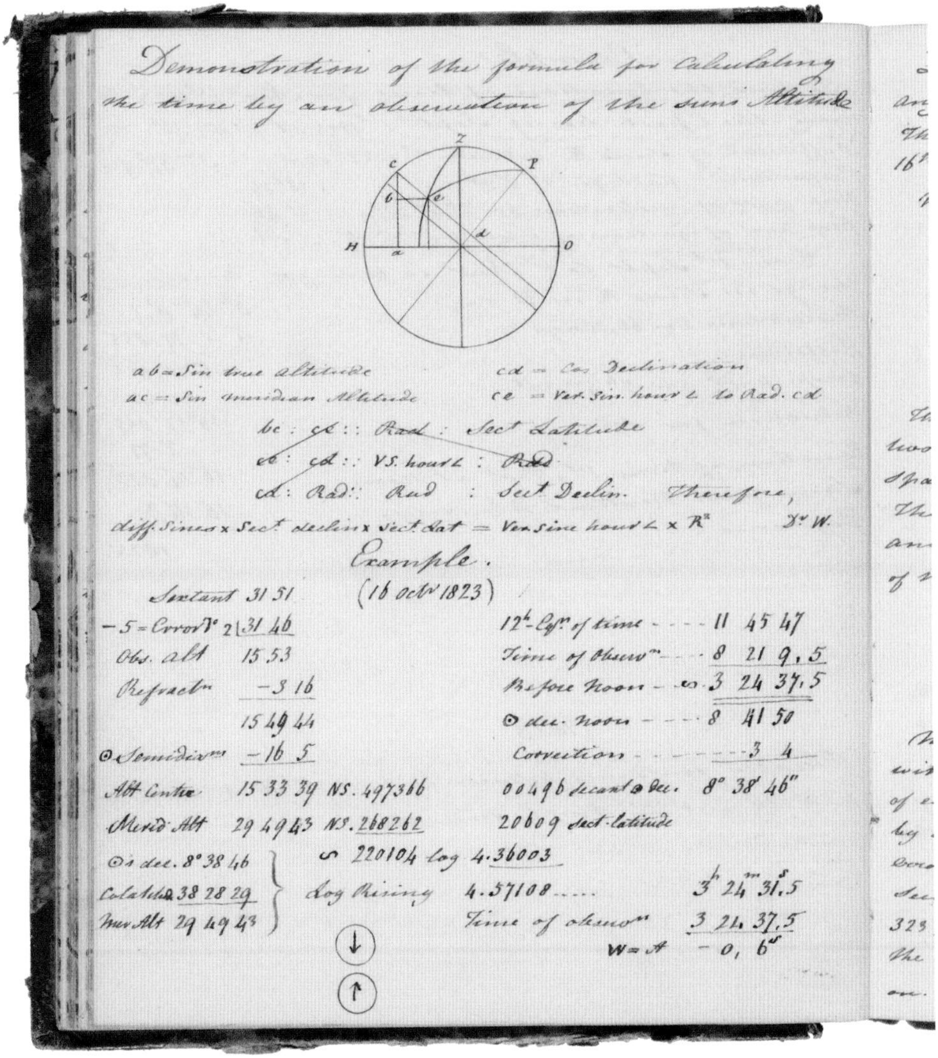

Mary Somerville, fair copy of *On the Connexion of the Physical Sciences*

Although she was not allowed to read her work to the Royal Society (her husband had to do it in her place), some of her contemporaries, including the great French scientist Laplace, saw her as an equal. On her death, *The Morning Post* declared her 'one of the most distinguished astronomers and philosophers'.

Library House, Hastings,
11th June,
Thursday,
1826.

My dearest Mammy

No letter from Lady Tam yet. Louisa is better to day, she was very much pleased yesterday with a box of the most beautiful things imaginable from Miss Noel; there were beautiful little wee wee baskets, one larger basket, and some pincushions in the form of little guitars, another carriage and Louisa is to have a dozen more carriages of different sorts. To day I have been doing some Italian, and I have written about Arronart, and made out a little alphabetical list of all the things I am going to write about from Bingley's Useful Knowledge, there are two dozen different things I wish to write about, and I have been puzzling hard at a sum in the rule of three which I could not do, the question is "If 750 men are allowed 22500 rations of bread per month how many rations will a garrison of 1200 men require"? I think by the time you come back I may

good deal of medicine before it would act, I am rather better to day as I have had no occasion to take any medicine, it was your going away that made me unwell yesterday. The whole party are as usual. My little lamb came here quite safe. I have got your mattress to sleep

upon, I find it is a very nice one. Will you talk to Mrs Clermont about Puff. Pray don't let Miss Briggs or any body else know about my determinations that I told you of. I lie down every day about a quarter of an hour after I have finished my dinner, for the time Mrs Montgomery thinks best, she allows me to wash in her dressing room morning and

evening, and to have her shawl to put over my feet when I lie down in the day, am I not a spoilt child. How are all your friends? From my room I have a full view of the Duke's house, and the house Lady Frances Morgan used to have. I have written you a long letter in revenge for it write me a much longer one I must now conclude, If you have too much to do, pray don't write to me at all, I am dying to ride over on horseback to Battle to meet you on Wednesday, I wish above every thing that such an arrangement would be made. Good bye, Yours affectionately A. Ada Byron.

Intended more communication but I have been busy till too late carriage at the door tomorrow more Bless thee. —

Lady Noel Byron
Reid's Hotel
Lower Grosvenor St
London

2 JU 2 1826

HASTINGS

Ada Byron
June 1826.

Ada Lovelace 1815–1852
Charles Babbage 1791–1871

The intelligence and vivacity of Ada Lovelace are evident throughout the many folders of her letters held on deposit at the Bodleian Library. It is hard to imagine that she was never strong and died from cancer aged only thirty-six. The correspondence encompasses her whole life, from signing a childish 'A D A', to her 'Mammy' (betraying her County Durham roots), aged perhaps three or four, to letters to 'Dearest Mama' in her final months, in which, despite the reassurances of Dr Lacock, she says she cannot see her future.

As a child, she was mostly tutored by a series of governesses and her mother, Anne Isabella Milbanke, Lady Byron, who had a long-standing interest in mathematics and geometry, and in education more generally: Lady Byron herself had been well taught and was later recognized as an educational reformer. In one letter, Ada says her mother's explanations of maths problems are so much better than those given by the textbook. Ada never knew her father, the poet Byron, since her parents separated soon after her birth and he died when she was eight; but her mother arranged a broad education for her daughter, including, in Ada's handwritten timetable, Arithmetic, Music, French and 'Out of doors'.

In spite of ill health, for much of Ada's life mathematics occupied her mind and gave her a sense of purpose. In the letter opposite, written when she was ten, she tells her mother:

> I have been puzzling hard at a sum in the rule of three which I could not do, the question is 'If 750 men are allowed 22500 rations of bread per month, how many rations will a garrison of 1200 men require?'

The layout of the letter, with the first written lines horizontally as usual, but afterwards continuing vertically up the page, was not uncommon at the time, presumably to save paper. Ada regularly writes this way, giving

Ada Lovelace (aged ten), letter to her mother about mathematics her letters a definite sense of puzzle, although with her even hand they are surprisingly easy to read. Writing vertically at the top of the page, she finishes, 'Good bye, Yours affectionately, A. Ada Byron'.

In another letter, from November 1840, after her marriage to William King (later Lord Lovelace) and the birth of her three children, Ada assures her mother that her status as wife and mother has not lessened the attraction of mathematics:

> Oh No! There is I think little danger of mathematics being 'eclipsed'. I have quite survived the simultaneous departure of my Sisters and the Sun, partly I imagine by aid of the Mathematics, which is an excellent resource on such occasions. I work on very slowly. This Mr De Morgan does not wish otherwise. On the contrary he cautioned me against a wish I had at one time to proceed rather too rapidly. (Dep. c. 368, fol. 187r)

Augustus De Morgan, professor of mathematics at University College, London, became Ada's tutor, mostly by correspondence, in 1840, through the intervention of his wife Sophia, a long-standing family friend. De Morgan was a specialist in calculus, and Ada's course seems to have been mostly working through his substantial textbook, *Differential and Integral Calculus* (published between 1836 and 1842). From virtually a standing start, in eighteen months she had become very proficient.

However, it's not for her skill in pure mathematics that Ada is remembered, but for her work with Charles Babbage and his attempts to produce a calculating machine. Mary Somerville introduced Ada and Lady Byron to Babbage in 1833. Babbage hosted regular gatherings of interesting people – regulars included Charles Dickens and Charles Darwin – and in the letter to 'My dear Mrs Somerville' shown here, the eighteen- or nineteen-year-old Ada asks the older woman for help:

> If you are going to Babbage's tonight, will you do me so great a favour as to call for me at 10, Wimpole St., and take me there. I am in a loss for a chaperon.

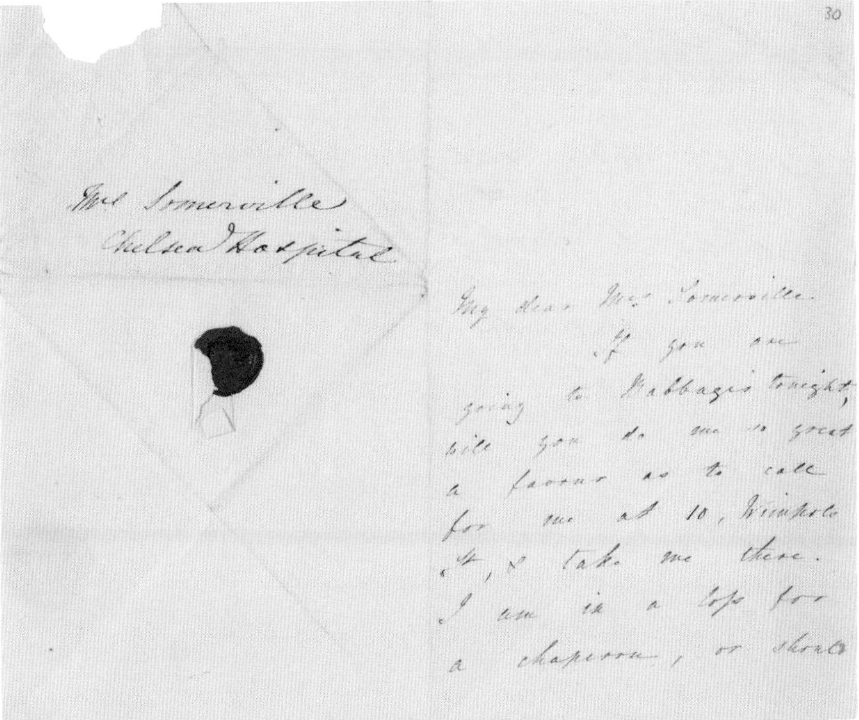

Mrs Somerville
Chelsea Hospital

My dear Mrs Somerville.
If you are going to Babbage's tonight, will you do me so great a favour as to call for me at 10, Wimpole St, & take me there. I am in a loss for a chaperon, or should

Ada Lovelace, letter to Mary Somerville, 1833

Babbage was already working on automata, including a 'silver lady', as well as his 'thinking machine', which he demonstrated at some of the soirées. He moved on from his first Difference Engine to a more sophisticated Analytical Engine, which he hoped would be able to give itself orders, depending on the results of its own earlier calculations – what Babbage called 'eating its own tail'. The machine, had it ever been built, was to be programmed by means of punched cards, like those invented by Joseph Jacquard to run his mechanical weaving looms in Lyon.

Ada's fascination with the possibilities of mechanical calculation was part of her desire to improve her mathematics. Babbage writes in 1839 that he is still working to find her a tutor, and it may have been he who suggested De Morgan. When Babbage was invited to Turin by Luigi Menabrea, who was working along similar lines, Ada was asked to

also the rest of Note D — There is still one trifling misapprehension about the Variable cards — A Variable card may order any number of Variables to receive the same number upon them at the same instant of time — But a Variable card ~~cannot ord~~ never can be directed to order more than one Variable to be given off at once because the mill could not receive it and the mechanism would not permit it. All this it was impossible for you to know by intuition and the more I read your notes the more surprised I am at them and regret not having earlier explored so rich a vein of the noblest metal.

The account of them stands thus

A	Sent to Lady L.	F	Returned by Lady L
B	With C.B	G	Where is it gone??
C	Ditto	H	With C B
D	Sent to Lady L		
E	With C B		

I have not seen
am ashamed to a
tiously just the whol
I will atte
tomorrow and

1 Dorset St Manch
2 July 1843

46
till I can possi-
in his hands
commands
truly Yours
Babbage

translate the Italian's article on Babbage's machines. This translation and her extensive commentary (twice as long as the original text), published in 1843, are the basis of her reputation in computational science. She added eight illustrative appendices, A to H, of which the most important was Appendix G, her explanation of how a machine could calculate the so-called Bernoulli series of numbers – work that has been called the first computer program. The letter opposite, from Babbage, sets out the stages the various appendices had reached, and on the previous page he records his admiration for her work:

> I like much the improved form of the Bernouilli [*sic*] Note … I am very reluctant to return the admirable and philosophic view of the Anal. Engine contained in Note A. Pray do not alter it and do let me have it returned on Monday.

The Analytical Engine was Babbage's idea, but Ada's description of what it might achieve with minimal human intervention, creating its own processes as it worked, was a mathematical and imaginative step far in advance of mere mechanical calculation.

Charles Babbage, letter to Ada Lovelace, 1843

in the Geology of S. America, in which I am much interested. it is the recent elevation of the land. — That such has taken place & to a considerable amount on this coast I have abundant proofs. Have you ever noticed on land elevated from 30 to 200 ft above the sea, any <u>large</u> beds of marine shells, of which did not appear carried there by man? I think it probable that such might occur at Ri: Grande or South Brazil; if you have any information on this head, I should be most grateful for such a communication. — My direction in England is Shrewsbury or indeed to the C. of Good Hope on my road there. I am g you will think me a very troublesome correspondent; I only wish I could send you instead of Geological questions & details, some specimens which would be worthy of your acceptance. — The Beagle now proceeds direct to the Galapagos, from thence across the Pacifick to Sydney, C. of Good Hope to England. — I confess I am so little accustomed to these long expeditions, that I look forward to this last stage, with more interest, than the whole of the voyage. I have the pleasure to remain. Your obliged & obedient servant

Chas. Darwin

Charles Darwin 1809–1882

Charles Darwin's early life was full of false starts. He did poorly at school; he followed his father's wishes and went to Edinburgh University to become a physician, but left without a degree; he followed his elder brother, Erasmus, to Cambridge to become a clergyman, but found it not to his taste. From childhood, however, he had been drawn to natural history, and at Cambridge he met a young professor of botany, J.S. Henslow, whose tutelage and friendship were to change his life.

With Henslow's teaching, Darwin not only passed his degree, but passed it well; and it was Henslow who put him in the way of a berth on a two-year round-the-world voyage, via South America, on a scientific survey ship, HMS *Beagle*. In the event, the trip was to last five years, from 1831 to 1836, and, in Darwin's own words, it 'determined my whole career'.

HMS *Beagle* reached Buenos Aires late in 1832, and it was probably there that Darwin met Henry Stephen Fox, a British diplomat and distant cousin with similar interests in botany and natural history. Fox wrote to Darwin in 1833 and Darwin here replies from Lima, Peru, the last stop in South America before what was to become the *Beagle*'s most celebrated landfall, the Galapagos Islands. In Lima, Darwin observed a political revolution, but his letter to Fox is all about the extraordinary geology of the continent, whose formation was still debated. The letter ends:

> The Beagle now proceeds direct to the Galapagos, from thence across the Pacifick to Sydney, C. of Good Hope to England. – I confess, I am so little accustomed to these long expeditions, that I look forward to this last stage, with more interest, than the whole of the voyage.

The seasick Darwin was clearly finding shipboard life wearisome; but we must remember that he had no idea of the wonders of the islands he was about to encounter.

Charles Darwin, letter to Henry Fox, 1833

Indess weilt im heil'gen Osten
Seine Bude könnt' verrosten
Während er nach Hohem strebt
Und in weiter Ferne lebt.

—

Dass die Mauern nicht erkalten
Nimmt er hier herein den Alten
Der da predigt unentwegt
Und die Rechenkünste pflegt.

—

Die Folianten ernste Reih
Denket sich gar mancherlei
Wundern sich, dass so ein Mann
Ohne sie hier hausen kann.

—

Grollen: Was will dieser hier?
Raucht Tabak und spielt Klavier
Der Barbar geht ein und aus
Weshalb blieb er nicht zuhaus?

—

Dieser aber oft und gerne
Denkt des Hausherrn in der Ferne
Freut sich, bis er diesen Mann
In der Nähe sehen kann.

—

Mit herzlichem Dank und Gruss

Albert Einstein

Mai 1931.

Albert Einstein 1879–1955

By the time he came to spend a few weeks in Oxford, in May 1931, Albert Einstein was a Nobel laureate in physics and an internationally known figure. Enticing him away from his academic life in Berlin had not been easy. He and his wife, Elsa, had spent a few hours in Oxford in 1921, but invitations to make longer visits had not so far met with success. Physics was not one of the university's strengths, and there were few colleagues in the city whom Einstein might have regarded as interesting. Nonetheless, Frederick Lindemann, Professor of Experimental Philosophy, as the chair in physics was known, who had engineered the earlier visit, made repeated attempts to lure him back, hoping that Einstein's presence would bolster his campaign to breathe new life into his subject and counter the prevailing prejudice against the sciences. Although well disposed to Lindemann, Einstein managed to avoid saying yes, citing ill health, prior commitments and his poor English as reasons for not coming. Finally, however, persistence paid off, and in 1927 Einstein agreed to come and give three public lectures funded by the Rhodes Trust, which offered the considerable sum of £500: 'It is very important to me that in England, where my work has received greater recognition than anywhere else in the world, I should not like to give the impression of ingratitude.' Even so, it was not until 1 May 1931 that Einstein finally arrived in Lindemann's college, Christ Church.

Einstein found his first college dinner 'a bizarre and boring affair' ('eine ebenso bizarre wie langweilige Angelegenheit'), describing the all-male fellowship as 'the holy brotherhood in tails' ('der heiligen Brüdershaar im Frack'). Slowly, however, he came to appreciate Oxford life, in particular the musical evenings he enjoyed with the German-speaking Deneke sisters of Lady Margaret Hall, who borrowed a violin and invited him to take part in string quartets at their home. These occasions were some of Einstein's favourite memories of this and subsequent visits, and Margaret Deneke recalled the skill with which he played.

Albert Einstein, poem for R.H. Dundas, 1931

The lectures themselves could not really have been called a success, since few of his hearers could follow his German, and even fewer his mathematics. His initial audience of 500 was vastly reduced on the two subsequent occasions; he did not blame them. It was for the second lecture that he prepared the blackboard of equations that is now preserved in the Oxford Museum of the History of Science. Einstein himself was opposed to its being retained as a kind of secular relic, and claimed later that he no longer believed what he had written.

If few could converse with him in German, nevertheless his Oxford hosts were drawn to Einstein's modest good humour and charm. Christ Church had put him up in the rooms of the college's ancient historian, R.H. Dundas, who was travelling in India, and as an expression of his thanks to his unseen host, Einstein left a gently comic poem in Dundas's well-used visitors' book, in which his host's books, grumbling, ask themselves what this 'barbarian' is doing in their room. He 'smokes tobacco and plays the piano' but ignores them completely: 'why didn't he stay at home?':

> Grollen: Was will dieser hier?
> Raucht Tabak und spielt Klavier
> Der Barbar geht ein und aus
> Weshalb blieb er nicht zuhaus?

The visitor signs off, 'With heartfelt thanks and greetings, Albert Einstein, May 1931':

> Mit herzlichen Dank und Gruss
> Albert Einstein
> Mai 1931.

In March 1933, the election of the National Socialists in Germany caused Einstein to give up his German citizenship and resign his membership of the Prussian Academy; his home in Berlin was looted and his property confiscated. In effect, he was an unemployed refugee. Lindemann tried to find a way to bring him permanently to Oxford, but it was at the Institute of Advanced Studies in Princeton that Albert and Elsa finally found a home.

Albert Einstein, portrait photograph

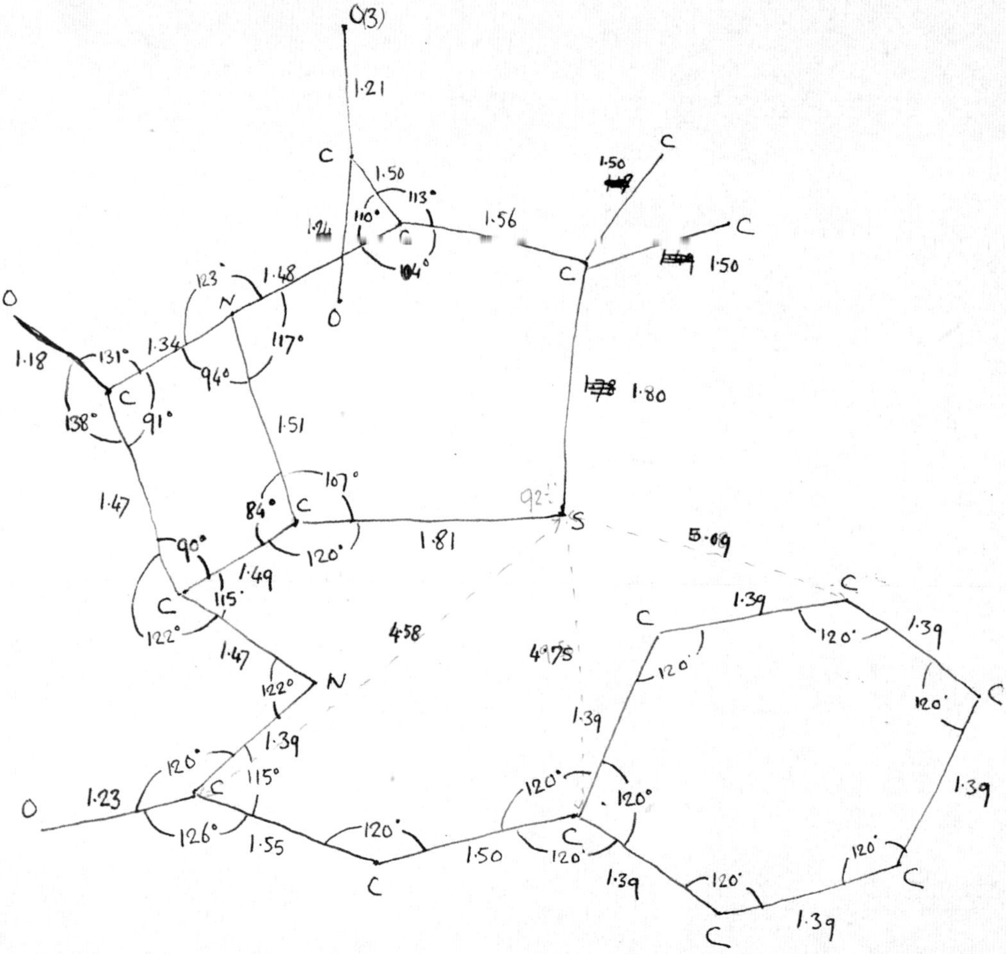

O(3)
1.21
C
1.50
113°
110°
1.24
C
1.56
104°
1.50
C
C
1.50
C
123°
1.48
N
O
O
117°
1.18
131°
1.34
94°
C
1.80
138°
91°
1.51
107°
1.47
84°
C
S
92°
90°
1.81
5.09
120°
1.49
C
C
115°
C
1.39
122°
1.39
4.58
4.75
120°
1.47
N
122°
120°
C
1.39
1.39
120°
120°
O
1.23
C
115°
120°
120°
1.39
126°
C
1.55
120°
1.50
120°
120°
1.39
120°
C
C
1.39
C

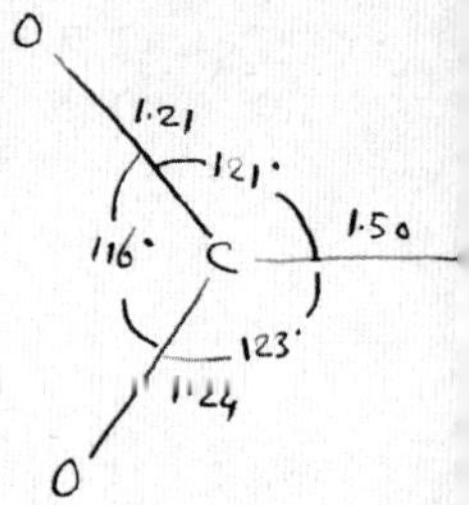

O
1.21
121°
1.50
116°
C
123°
1.24
O

Dorothy Crowfoot Hodgkin 1910–1994

Only two girls, Dorothy Crowfoot (as she then was) and her friend Norah Pusey, were allowed to join the boys for chemistry lessons at their school in Norfolk in the 1920s. Dorothy's interest had begun early, encouraged by a family friend who was a chemist from the Wellcome Laboratories in Khartoum in the Sudan, where her father was director of education and antiquities, and by her mother, an expert in ancient textiles. In her first year at Somerville College, Oxford, Dorothy combined her interests in archaeology and chemistry, analysing glass mosaic pieces from Jerash in Trans-Jordan; but her focus finally settled on X-ray crystallography. After a PhD in Cambridge, she pursued a lifetime of studies of the molecular structure of insulin, cholesterol, vitamin B12 and penicillin. She was one of the earliest women to be elected to the Royal Society, in 1947; she won the Nobel Prize for Chemistry in 1964; and she was awarded the Order of Merit in 1965, the first woman to be so honoured since Florence Nightingale in 1907.

Dorothy Crowfoot Hodgkin worked with the Oxford team attempting to isolate and understand the properties of penicillin. Their aim was to take Alexander Fleming's 1929 discovery from the laboratory bench through to successful clinical applications. The work of Howard Florey, Norman Heatley and Ernst Chain, which made the breakthrough, was underpinned by Dorothy's painstaking deduction of penicillin's molecular structure. The many boxes of her papers at the Bodleian illustrate the methodical discipline that lies behind eureka moments. They preserve multiple, handwritten tables of measurements from her photographic trials, her graphical plotting of the results, and her increasingly complete drawings of the final structure – shown in her diagram here. Most of this work was done in wartime conditions: one note mentions the inaccessibility of the lab after dark because it wasn't fitted with blackout curtains, to prevent it being visible to enemy bombers.

Dorothy Crowfoot Hodgkin, draft for molecular structure of penicillin

And, like Ginger Rogers keeping pace with Fred Astaire, but 'backwards and in high heels', Hodgkin combined her pioneering chemistry with her undergraduate teaching, her position as a fellow of Somerville and bringing up three children while her husband, Thomas, a historian of Africa and the Arab world, worked in Staffordshire. Thomas could visit only at weekends, so the couple wrote to one another every day, with Dorothy mixing the chemical and the familial side by side. In the letter opposite she shifts from the excitement of a step forward with penicillin, to news of a Rockefeller foundation grant, to the 'frightful cold' of Joyce, the children's nurse.

Her delight in her work was matched by a self-effacing manner, warmth and generosity, an openness to ideas and genuine pleasure in the achievements of others. Visitors to her lab noted the unusual informality – together with an expectation of scientific rigour. Yet, for all her dedication to her chemistry, Hodgkin had a wide view of the world. Her upbringing in the Middle East, her marriage to a historian of Africa and her friendship with Somerville's Quaker principal, Margery Fry, all contributed to her strong socialist political awareness. She supported nuclear disarmament and believed in the power of communication and open discussion to find ways to further peace, travelling widely, including visits to the Soviet Union and Vietnam, to make personal links with scientists there. From 1975 to 1988 she was president of Pugwash, the series of international Conferences on Science and World Affairs that aimed to prevent any further use of atomic weapons.

At her memorial service in Oxford in 1995, Max Perutz said:

> There was magic about her person. She had no enemies, not even amongst those whose scientific theories she demolished ... Just as her X-ray cameras bared the intrinsic beauty beneath the rough surface of things, so the warmth and gentleness of her approach to people uncovered in everyone, even the most hardened scientific crook, some hidden kernel of goodness. It was marvellous to have her drop in on you in your lab, like the Spring.

Dorothy Crowfoot Hodgkin, letter to her husband, Thomas, 1943

Sept. 29' 1943.

My darling,

This is a very exciting day.

1/ the first half of penicillin — the stuff we began to look at last year — has been synthesised and proved identical with the natural product. Grand.

2/ a telegram has come from Rockefeller making the grant. So that bit of worry is past. I can't help wondering if they've kindly sent the cable before getting the report.

Apart from that things are going all right but Joyce has got a frightful cold & it's a bit doubtful whether she can get out this afternoon. I took Luke to school this morning & successfully passed him on to Mrs. Hicks.

Somehow or other nothing much but work is happening just now.

REFORMERS

Martin Luther 1483–1546

The Library's founder, Sir Thomas Bodley (1545–1613), was born into a staunchly Protestant Exeter family. Indeed, Bodley's father was so dedicated to his religion that, when the Catholic Queen Mary came to the English throne (1553–8), he led his family into exile rather than trim his beliefs. The Bodleys made their way down through the Rhineland, ending up in Geneva, stronghold of the Protestant theologian John Calvin. The young Thomas was taught by Calvin himself, as part of a curriculum that was particularly strong in the ancient and learned languages of Hebrew, Greek and Latin.

The family returned to England in 1559, when Mary had been succeeded by her sister Elizabeth. Thomas enrolled at Magdalen College, Oxford, took his degree and embarked on a successful career as a scholar and diplomat. It was only in the latter part of his life, after his marriage in 1586 to Ann Ball, widow of a prosperous Totnes pilchard merchant, that financial security allowed him to embark on the project for which he is now best remembered: the foundation of a library. Strictly speaking, this was a refoundation of the library established with the books of Duke Humfrey of Gloucester in 1488. Bodley was a hands-on benefactor, writing the Library's statutes, collecting books and appointing the first Librarian, Thomas James.

Given his strong roots in the Reformation, we might imagine that Bodley would have preferred to collect only particular sorts of book. Instead, from the first he was determined to include every learned work he and his agents could lay their hands on: this Protestant had a catholic taste in collecting. Medieval Catholic texts in Latin shared shelf space with material in Hebrew, Arabic, Syriac, Persian and Chinese, even while others regarded such works as mere curiosities. Bodley's library was to be a resource for 'the republic of the learned'.

Nevertheless, Sir Thomas would surely have been particularly pleased with the Library's acquisition in 1865 of the little book shown here – a group of proverbs (*Sprichwörte*) in German, handwritten by Martin Luther, architect of the Reformation in Europe. The little paper pocket book is incomplete, but the preservation of the surviving thirty-four pages attests to their status as a kind of relic of the man who changed the face of European religion.

Luther defied family expectations that he become a lawyer, and entered an Augustinian monastery in Erfurt. It was not a happy choice: despite academic success and a series of administrative posts in the order, his dissatisfaction with the Catholic Church and the authority of the pope grew increasingly strong. As the story goes, Luther made his position clear when in 1517 he nailed his Ninety-five Theses to the door of Wittenberg Castle church. Timing was everything: had he lived a little earlier, Luther's objections would have been a local quarrel; but the invention of the printing press made it easy for his Theses to spread.

His contention with the church led to Luther's excommunication, with the status of an outlaw, at the Diet of Worms in 1521. He was rescued from an uncertain future by the emperor Frederick III. Enclosed for his own safety at the Wartburg Castle in Eisenach, Luther translated the New Testament into German. His was not the first vernacular translation, but his inspired use of language and understanding of the potential of printing made it an unprecedented success. This and his prolific production of vernacular hymns shaped the German language as well as the Protestant religion.

The vernacular proverbs shown here illustrate Luther's belief that religion had to speak to people where they were. The pointing finger especially notes the comforting claim, 'God is the fool's guardian' ('Gott ist der narren furmunde'). Almost as interesting as the text, however, is the striking red ink in which it is written. Unlike most medieval and early modern inks, which were brown or black, made from soot or oak galls, bound together with gum, this was probably made from brazil wood. Although brazil-wood ink later became relatively common, Luther's use here marks him out as an early adopter.

overleaf Martin Luther, book of German proverbs

22\.

Du wolst mich lieb haben
Wolst mich schlagen
Hast mir zum ars geschissen. Aber nicht
Gegen dem baum sol ~~mich~~ man sich neigen
davon man schatten hat
Auff dem kopchen sitzen lausen
Schimpfschelten lige doch
Schimpff wil sich machen
. Der schimpffest von N. mit seiner
Reit yhr schais zum ars.
Schier gest wie ein keer
Junge hunde muessen lernen
Hat das gemein gebet verloren
Ich wil yhm bass brieffe mach schon
Hat das gemein geschrey verloren
Becher mit allen schwencken
Er darff der mühe nicht

Larven verbeyssen Frumheit

Ein liebe sucht das ander. D. hoff drunke

Viel ist ehrlich

Wenig ist Gottlich

Kopff und zagel

Schopff und schwantz

Jnn einen sawrapffel beyssen

Beyssen ehir mancht essen

Verbeyssen

Gott ist der narren furmund

Durch den korb fallen

Ein schlechten daher setzen

Ein riegel dafur schieben

Wischt das maul und geht davon

Wer [illegible] das er narr ist

Er kans nicht zu marckt bringen

Es ist nicht eines schuld sondern der

[illegible] wunder [illegible] [illegible] [illegible] [illegible]

[illegible] felschen [illegible] [illegible]

Right Honble

I am fully Senceible of the great Fatigue you must unavoidebley Suffer from the Weighty affairs of your high Office And the Multiplycity of applications Continually rolling in upon you, for which reason I refrain as much as possible from giving any interuption by approaching you Yet cannot Conceal my Concern for that if the affair of Not settling Catt Island be wholly neglected and no Measures Concerted relating thereto until the Parliament shall meet and be moved to buy out the Lords Proprietors, there will then be so much other business on foot as will postpone this; I should therefore be glad of opertunety to say something to you upon it in Order to take Time by the foretop, and also perticulerly to acquaint you, and you only, that I know of a good Sum of Money wch has laid Many years unapply'd, it is a Considerable Larger Sum than what the Parliament have Lately Granted for Settling Foreign & other Protestants in Georgia, and wch I am perswaded you may with ease (but I cannot) get for making an Ellegant & Deffenceible Settlement on Catt Island

I had no Knowledge of this Money until within a few Months, and I also Know of a Close designe to apply to the Parliament for the Same at the begining of Next Sessions, But I conceive you can lay an Anchor to Windward of them and get that Money appropriated for the effectually Settling Catt Island, if you shall think fit to take it in hand, before others can endeavour for it.

My Resolution of acquainting none but your honr wth this matter is

D 1/39. P. S. from

Thomas Coram 1668–1751

The Foundling Hospital in Coram's Fields is the best-known legacy of the life of Thomas Coram, but it was by no means the only philanthropic venture of a man who believed that 'every one ought, in duty to do any good they can'. What motivated his interest in needy and abandoned children is not known, although his own mother died when he was very young and he was sent to sea at the age of ten or eleven. Apprenticed to a Thames shipwright, he spent his twenties and thirties travelling between Boston, Massachusetts, and Taunton in Devon, building ships for the merchant trade. He returned to England permanently in 1704, with an American wife, Eunice, and a thorough knowledge of commercial seafaring.

Thomas and Eunice had no family, but his route from home to work in London took him past destitute children living on the streets. Having seen foundling hospitals in Paris, Thomas began a campaign to establish one in London, but it was seventeen years before he was successful; conventional wisdom held that caring for illegitimate children would only encourage the poor to produce more of them. He himself was too much of the rough and ready businessman, with a sailor's use of language, to win over the aristocrats at the heart of government. His brisk style and nautical frame of reference is evident in this letter about money for settlements in Georgia, where he speaks of 'tak[ing] Time by the foretop' (seizing an opportunity) and 'lay[ing] an Anchor to Windward' (slipping in ahead of rivals).

Eventually, he hit on the idea of persuading 'ladies of quality and distinction' to support the cause, and when twenty-one such ladies at Court added their names to his petition, success was guaranteed. The Foundling Hospital opened its doors to the first forty children in 1740. William Hogarth and G.F. Handel both supported Coram's cause: Hogarth organized a paying show of his own and others' pictures and Handel gave benefit concerts of *Messiah*. The entrance fees from both supported the foundation, which continues its work today.

Thomas Coram, letter concerning settlements in Georgia

Servt. Rea : dings &c	Scripture – with aspira : tion – Practice Book &c slowly –	Conduct	Make thots & Conduct = Humility, with Shame = Love of God & solacing with thots of heaven holy & happy
Relaxn. Thots & Conver : sation walking out &c = Ask on coming out of compy.	Recapit: Readings – or per : notables – or get perlord: when Eyes &c = Topics for Talks of all minds ready always – = Set down per notables	NB	
			Set down main faults &c
			Set down: Day particulars once pr. Day, & examine them
mind to be im : press'd	Love of Xt. constraining &c = Satan, but God &c = God's Eye &c	Sensuality mor : tify	Frequent approxima : tions = resolves = you can give Plea : sure to God, or grieve him
	Golden Rule: Do good to all around you & daily ask, what Good &c &c	NB	
		Recreaty.	Cowper = Shakespeare's works = Biography = Memoir
Faults to be chiefly watched	Sensuality: (by substitu : tion) mens thots &c Peevishness — Heat in argument &c	Ser.	occasionally think of own faults & cultivate Love of God (honour)

William Wilberforce 1759–1833
John Newton 1725–1807

William Wilberforce was elected to Parliament aged twenty-one and spent the next forty-five years fighting for others. Born in Hull, Wilberforce had not yet graduated from Cambridge when he became the town's member of parliament in 1780. For most of his career he represented the county of Yorkshire, only switching late in life to a constituency in Sussex, when the journey north became too arduous for his failing health. With family money behind him, and a strong Christian faith, Wilberforce was able to maintain a political independence that allowed him to work for the causes closest to his heart.

Outwardly at least, the even tenor of Wilberforce's life could not have been further from the extraordinary journey of John Newton, who lost his mother at the age of six and made his first sea voyage with his shipmaster father at eleven. He made a career in the merchant marine, with a brief but traumatic spell pressed into service in the Royal Navy, which was ended by his transfer to a slave ship, *Pegasus*, bound for West Africa. He left *Pegasus* to try his luck in the slave trade on the Guinea coast, but instead spent two years in conditions of slavery himself. This was the place, he later recalled, where he hit rock bottom. In 1748, finally returning home on a ship captained by a friend of his father's who had been asked to look for him, Newton was caught in a ferocious storm. He began to pray and, as the ship limped to port, read the Bible. Ever after, he remembered that night, 21 March, as the date of his conversion.

Initially, however, his life was little different. Slaving was still viewed as a respectable occupation, and Newton continued to command slave ships. It was only when he discovered evangelical Christianity, and absorbed the ideas of John and Charles Wesley, among others, that his mind was changed. In his spare time, he studied for ordination, although he was not sure into which denomination; his face and beliefs were not an easy fit. Eventually, in 1764, he was appointed to the Anglican parish of Olney in

William Wilberforce, spiritual diary, 1790

Buckinghamshire. His sailor's pea jacket and rough and ready style were unconventional, but his assiduous pastoral care and passionate preaching, alongside a natural ecumenism, gained him many friends. It was here, with his parishioner, the poet William Cowper, that he published his *Olney Hymns* (1779), of which the best known today is probably 'Amazing Grace':

> Amazing grace! How sweet the sound!
> That saved a wretch like me.
> I once was lost, but now am found;
> Was blind but now I see.
>
> Through many dangers, toils, and snares,
> I have already come,
> 'Tis grace hath brought me safe thus far,
> And grace will lead me home.

In 1780 Newton moved to the church of St Mary Woolnoth in the City of London, which provided him with an influential setting for his preaching and helped make his home a centre for evangelical thinking. It was here that Wilberforce came for advice and spiritual direction. Although he had flirted briefly with evangelical beliefs in his teens, Wilberforce had reverted to mainstream Anglicanism, but a conversion experience in 1785 sent him to Newton, whom he had met as a boy. Should he give up politics and devote himself solely to God? Newton convinced him to carry on in Parliament, and Wilberforce resolved to work with even greater diligence for others. For the remainder of his life, supported by Newton, Wilberforce worked for the abolition of the slave trade and slavery as an institution.

Wilberforce was never someone to do things by halves. The document on the previous page is part of a spiritual diary or timetable written on 10 October 1790 at Yoxall Lodge in Staffordshire, home of fellow abolitionist Henry Thornton. His large, fast handwriting gives a sense of his busy life – and also, perhaps, of his weak eyesight. The page begins with Scripture, and includes time for prayer, the recollection of faults and recreation, which here includes reading the poems of Cowper. The lower pointing hand note on the right-hand page highlights his thought that 'you can give Pleasure to God, or grieve him'.

William Wilberforce, notes for speech on 'Slaves Chief Grievances'

Slaves Chief grievances

Conceded by Collins, Mathison Scanty food, clothg Lodging

Koster seem to be inferred for Medical Care.

from their own documents

III Sold for Masters debts & apart from Land (never form as the Base [illegible] down hill & [illegible] inclined plane

III Mere Personalty family Separation

no Song like Swan

II No Personal protection — from Lord & [illegible]

[illegible]

II Not giving evidence [illegible] Friend

[illegible] white but what Legislature

II No legal protection Burkes Preamble

Laws a Mockery

III Colour

I Degradation & Low Estimation

as many proofs as Babel's [illegible] & others in [illegible]

evidenced by Work under Whip

12 [illegible] as not know [illegible]

14 Marriage not allowed [illegible] make them

no [illegible]

13 Indecent flogging of Females

[illegible] 13

15 Fornication & Seduction Grievance at [illegible] who for

want of knowing Language of Babel

Religion wanted & cant complain

V Education Ditto

VI Manumission Hindrance

Laws of King [illegible] neglected

Sunday Market & other [illegible] works

V Burial African

baptism, marriage, burial [illegible] grave

IV Popular feeling all agst them which commonly

which a Different animal [illegible]

mere Colour Degradation

My dear Sir,

I know not where you are, but I suppose a letter sent to Palace Yard, will soon find you.

I deferr'd thanking you for your very kind, & very acceptable Present, till I could say I had read it. Indeed I have not properly read it yet, but I have devoured it. My first perusal, tho' without missing a word, has been hasty. I hope to peruse it more leisurely But from this cursory survey, I trust I am warranted to tell you that I have already found it profitable, for Instruction, for Correction & for Reproof. And therefore I must wait upon you with an Intercalary letter.

I think, you know by this time, that I do not much deal in Ceremonials & Compliments. But I should stifle the feelings of ~~the~~ my heart, were I wholly to suppress mentioning, the satisfaction, the pleasure, the joy, your publication has given me. To God be all the glory. The best Men are but Instruments of his pleasure, & have no sufficiency as of themselves even to think aright. We can remember the time, when you could not have written this book, & when I would not have read it, if it had been put into my hands. The difference between what we ~~w~~ are, & what we once were, & what many still are, is all of Grace. According to his Mercy he has saved us.

I had written thus far, when the Post-man brought your letter. I am glad I made a beginning befor it came. It is true, My dear Sir I am pretty much engaged in my way; but could you think it possible, that I should be content with dipping in a book of Yours? Had you written upon any other subject, my love & respect for you, would have made me impatient to read. On the other hand had your book, come without a Name, without any Circumstance that could lead me to guess at the Author, it would have engross'd my attention. You compel me, Sir to say, that I deem it the most valuable & important

publi

Despite the intensity on display here, Wilberforce's religion, as John Wolffe has commented, was never austere. He was a warm and generous character who drew others to him; and he was a compelling speaker, especially in parliamentary debate, his technique relying on thorough preparation rather than rhetorical tricks. This was still the age when it was frowned upon to write out a speech in advance and simply read it aloud. The Wilberforce boxes in the Bodleian are full of notes he made for speeches, often creased from having been folded into a pocket, and consisting of a series of numbered points that he could expand *ex tempore*. The second document here is the first of two pages enumerating the 'Slaves Chief Grievances'. He notes that even those who opposed abolition concede that they have 'Scanty food, clothing, Lodging, Medical Care', as well as:

> I Degradation and Low Estimation
> I^{4} Marriage not allowed
> I^{3} Indecent floggings & undress
> I^{5} Fornication and Seduction Grievances
> V Religion Want of & Education Ditto.

In 1797 Wilberforce published his *A Practical View of the Prevailing Religious System of Professed Christians, in the Higher and Middle Classes of this Country, Contrasted with Real Christianity*, about the gap he perceived between the way of life of most of those who called themselves Christians and how he believed a Christian life should truly be lived. He sent a copy to Newton, who replied, in the letter opposite, dated 2 April 1797:

> We can remember the time, when you could not have written this book, and when I would not have read it, if it had been put into my hands. The difference between what we are, and what we once were, and what many still are, is all of Grace. According to his Mercy he has saved us.

Newton died in 1807, having seen Wilberforce's efforts come to fruition, and the Bill for Abolition succeed in Parliament.

John Newton, letter to Wilberforce, 1797

1. It is generally admitted now that Examinations on Clinical subjects cannot be made from books.
The pupil must be at the bed side & his acquirements must be judged of by bed-side Physicians or Surgeons.
Now of all things nursing is the most clinical of all Arts.
The 'Doctor' is a judge no doubt of the results
But he is no judge, indeed he has no knowledge of the processes by which the result is arrived at.
[Ask any really eminent Clinical Physician like yourself. You all say this, & most justly.]
Only the long practised, trained & training Matron (Superintendent) can do this: And even she cannot certify with confidence, except after farther long years of experience of each individual Nurse, whether the Nurse can so compose herself as to meet the many emergencies incident to her calling — or whether she has the patience,

Florence Nightingale 1820–1910

The pages opposite and overleaf are part of a letter of 1872 from Florence Nightingale to Henry Acland, Regius Professor of Medicine at Oxford and member (later president) of the General Medical Council (GMC). Nightingale was a prolific correspondent, even by Victorian standards when post might be delivered several times a day. Her life was one of campaigning but, since she was for many years an invalid, a really good, forceful letter was often her weapon of choice.

Nightingale and Acland maintained a correspondence over many years, particularly on the subject of nurse training and registration, topics very close to her heart. The issue was how the competence of nurses could be assessed. Should this be by examination, as was the case with physicians, or were the skills required by nurses not such as could be assessed on paper? As might be expected, the GMC – established in 1858 to survey and regulate the landscape of professional medicine – tended towards the former. Nightingale was very firmly in the opposing camp.

In the letter, she makes two main points:

> 1. It is generally admitted now that Examinations on Clinical subjects cannot be made from books.
> The pupil must be at the bed side.

Her argument is that, although 'Physicians or Surgeons' can attest to whether the patient is improving, they cannot know how that result was achieved: 'Only the long-practised, <u>trained</u> and <u>training</u> Matron (Superintendent) can do this.' It takes an experienced nurse to judge an aspiring colleague; paper qualifications will not do.

Secondly she points to a quality even harder to assess:

> Nursing is not only an Art <u>but a character.</u> And how can this be arrived at by Examination? It cannot.

27

2. I come now to my second reason, which I must pray to be allowed to give very shortly:—

Nursing is not only an art but a character.

And how can this be arrived at by Examination? It cannot.

Nursing depends more than any other occupation, (except the charge of teaching children — perhaps even more than that —) on the woman as a character — not merely on her learning the technical details of her trade.

This is so obvious that, to one like yourself, I feel it would be presumptuous to insist on it further.

Rather, I would ask you to insist upon it with Poor-Law authorities, with whom the question is now becoming one of such importance.

These reasons appear to be final, do not they?, as against any Examination & Registration by the Medical Council.

[There might possibly arise the question:— suppose any Nurse-training Committee, after sufficient experience should decide

> Nursing depends more than any other occupation, (except the charge of teaching children – perhaps even more than that –) on the woman as a character – not merely on her learning the technical details of her trade. This is so obvious that, to one like yourself, I feel it would be presumptuous to insist on it further.

Nightingale ends the page decisively:

> These reasons appear to be final, do not they?, as against any Examination and Registration by the Medical Council.

Before the creation of the GMC, medical qualifications in the United Kingdom were something of a Wild West. The 1841 Census suggests that around a third of all doctors were unqualified, and there were nineteen separate medical regulatory bodies. The GMC was to provide centralized standards, backed by consistency in examination and registration. Florence Nightingale was not opposed to nurse registration per se, but she was strongly opposed to treating nurses and physicians (not to mention the special case of midwives) as the same sort of animal. It was reasonable to require doctors to pass written examinations, for example, but the qualities essential in a nurse should be recognized as very different: 'A really good but diffident nurse might fail in being on the Register at all, while a forward glib bad nurse might stand high in the Examination.'

Nightingale made her name nursing at Scutari in the Crimean War. She became an icon of the times – 'The Lady with the Lamp' and a 'Ministering Angel'. But her real success came from her strength in statistics (she was elected a fellow of the Statistical Society of London in 1858) and organization, which allowed her to look with objectivity at what we would now call 'health outcomes'. She forged an alliance with George Godwin, editor of the journal *The Builder*, to plan ideal hospitals, which would be orientated to sunlight, with ventilation, quiet and good sight-lines so nurses could see their patients. Warmth, cleanliness and good diet made up the rest of her prescription for convalescence.

Nightingale lived to be ninety and never stopped working, despite frequent ill health. She ends her letter to Acland, characteristically: 'in great press of business and illness, ever believe me your faithful servant, Florence Nightingale'.

Florence Nightingale, letter to Henry Acland, 1872

Emmeline Pankhurst 1858–1928

In photographs of the time, 'Mrs Pankhurst' – her married status was an important mark of respectability – with her conventional dress and striking hats, seems an unlikely protester. But the self-described 'hooligan' was the leader of the militant wing of the women's suffrage movement in Britain, the Women's Social and Political Union (WSPU). She and her daughter Christabel were among the group of women activists regularly imprisoned and force-fed in Holloway Gaol. Pankhurst was a charismatic speaker and personality, while Christabel oversaw organization.

She writes here to Miss Evelyn Sharp, and the date of the letter, 31 October 1910, is instructive. In July of that year, the first attempt at a Conciliation Bill, allowing women the vote on the same terms as men, had failed in Parliament. Only men who owned or rented property worth £10 per annum could be electors. Extending these terms to women would enfranchise comparatively few and, so the Liberal and Labour parties feared, those it did would be likely to vote Conservative. When the Bill was defeated, Pankhurst planned a deputation of women to Parliament Square on 18 November, where she would speak to the prime minister.

Sharp was a children's author and feature writer for *The Manchester Guardian*, who had been converted to militancy in 1906, when the newspaper sent her to cover a speech by another WSPU supporter, Elizabeth Robins. She became a key member of the movement. She had promised her mother, however, that she would do nothing that might get her gaoled, and it is this promise that must have occasioned a letter to Pankhurst explaining that she could not join the demonstration. Pankhurst writes back sympathetically:

> Don't worry! After all it would never do for our best speakers to get shut up for they will be needed to keep up popular indignation while the rest of us are in prison.

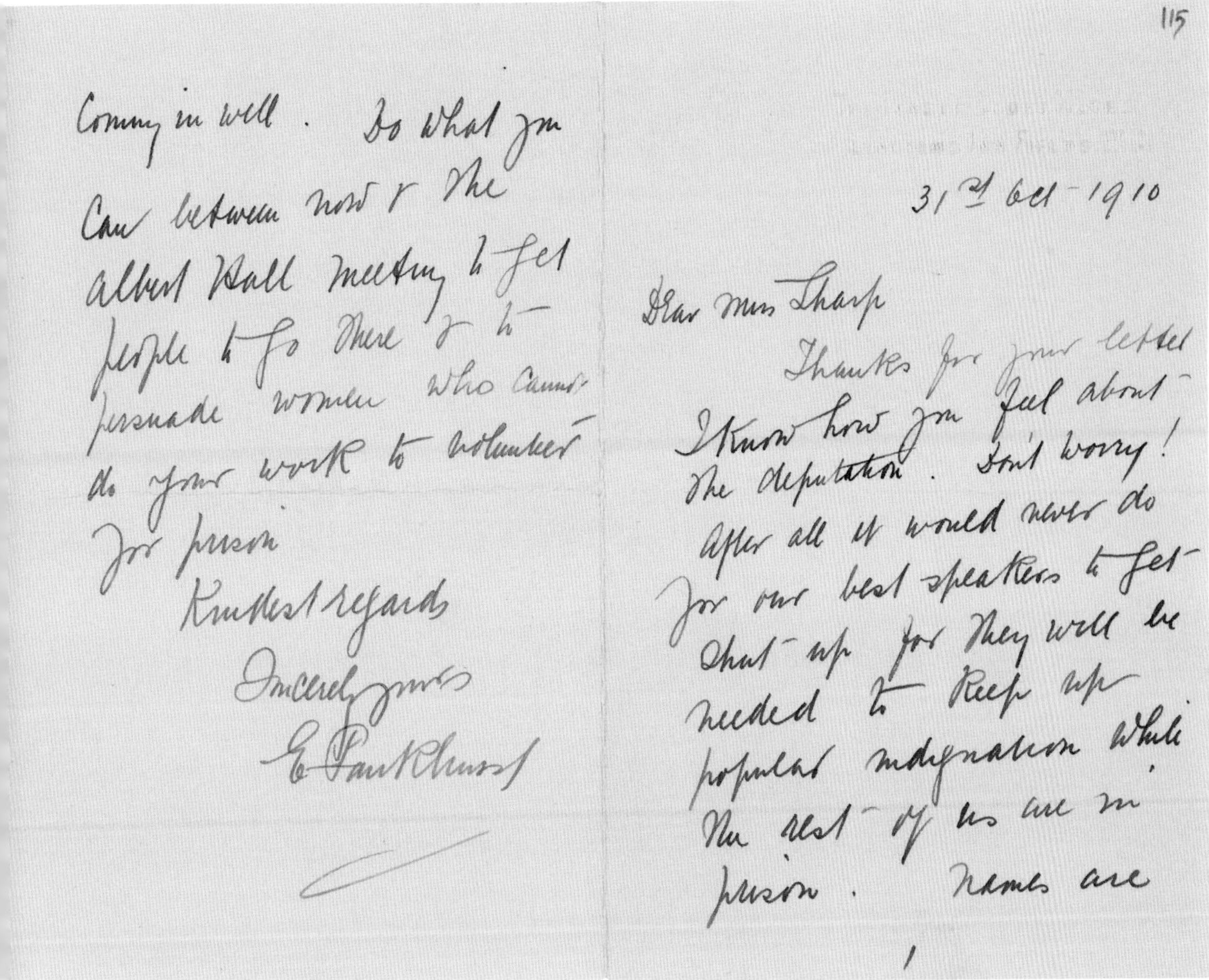

115

31st Oct 1910

Dear Miss Sharp

Thanks for your letter. I know how you feel about the deputation. Don't worry! After all it would never do for our best speakers to get shut up for they will be needed to keep up popular indignation while the rest of us are in prison. Names are

coming in well. Do what you can between now & the Albert Hall meeting to get people to go there & to persuade women who cannot do your work to volunteer for prison

Kindest regards

Sincerely yours

E Pankhurst

Emmeline Pankhurst, letter to Evelyn Sharp, 1910

Sharp was right to worry. 'Black Friday', as 18 November is known, was to become infamous for the brutal response of the police to the women's deputation.

Eleanor Rathbone 1872–1946

'I do not believe that I belong to that small class of persons who justify public portraits.' The modesty was genuine on the part of Eleanor Rathbone, and yet her remarkable life gives the lie to her assessment of herself. Generations of Rathbones had used their wealth for the benefit of others, particularly in Liverpool, their home city. The money came from timber and shipping, but never from slaves: their Quaker heritage made that unthinkable. Eleanor was brought up to understand that public service was an obligation, as a repayment for the comfort of her own upbringing. With almost no formal schooling, she nevertheless persuaded her parents to allow her to go to Somerville Hall, Oxford (before it had become a college of the university) to study 'Greats' – Latin, Greek and ancient history and philosophy – and there she flourished, both academically and in the further development of her socially reformist ideas.

Rathbone arrived at Oxford as a feminist, and her time at Somerville only confirmed her views on how women's potential was squandered, and their lives, and those of their children, made precarious by their legal position and government policy. Returning to Liverpool, she threw herself into the cause of women's suffrage and into efforts for the relief of family poverty, including a groundbreaking *Report of an Inquiry into the Conditions of Dock Labour at the Liverpool Docks* (1904), which highlighted the hardships brought about by the casualization of labour and what we would now call 'zero-hours contracts'. In 1906 women were allowed to stand for election to the city council, and from 1909 till 1935 Rathbone sat as an Independent, to the annoyance of her historically Liberal family, promoting public housing schemes and provision for widows and orphaned children.

Although she remained active in Liverpool politics, Rathbone began to make a mark on the national stage. She played a large part in the

National Union of Women's Suffrage Societies – the 'constitutional' wing of the movement – eventually becoming its leader. During the First World War, she crafted a policy for support payments to be paid directly to women rather than to their husbands, a plan which many years later was accepted by government in the system of family allowances. William Beveridge, architect of the post-war British welfare state, described her argument as 'one of the most important modern treatises on distributive economics'. Throughout her career, she researched her causes and presented her conclusions with rigour and force.

Somewhat to her surprise, Rathbone was elected to Parliament in 1929 as an Independent, and she held the anomalous Combined Universities seat, which represented graduates of universities other than Oxford and Cambridge, until her death. Now she began to operate internationally as well as nationally. She spoke on female genital mutilation in Africa, child marriage in India, the republican movement in Spain and the position of refugees around the world. With the National Socialists in power in Germany, she was determinedly anti-appeasement; she highlighted the Nazi treatment of the Jews, and denounced the policy of internment for German and Jewish refugees who had fled to Britain.

In this letter of 29 August 1940, she replies to Gilbert Murray, retired Regius Professor of Greek at Oxford and a fellow campaigner and internationalist, who had written about the case of Emil Müller-Sturmheim, one of the organizers of the Free Austrian Movement in London. Müller-Sturmheim had fled Vienna in July 1938, but was interned under the British government's policy towards 'enemy aliens'. Rathbone replies here in characteristic no-nonsense style. She had already been working to extend exemptions, and she thinks 'The new category for anti-Nazis seems to be the best chance for this man (See White P[aper] enclosed)'; she suggests waiting until the tribunal to deal with this group has been appointed. Was he, though, interned at 'Lingfield' [Racecourse – one of the government camps]? If so, 'that must mean that he is going to U.S.A.'

At her death, *The Manchester Guardian* (3 January 1946) wrote of Eleanor Rathbone, 'No parliamentary career has been more useful and fruitful.' She would have wanted no other memorial.

overleaf Eleanor Rathbone, letter to Gilbert Murray, 1940

[1940?] 169

50, ROMNEY STREET,
WESTMINSTER, S.W.1.

Aug. 29th [1940]

Dear Professor Murray,

Many apologies for neglecting your letter of August 8. Am still rather buried beneath the refugee avalanche but emerging & the new jobs are certainly lessening.

<u>Dr E.M. Sternheim</u>. The new category for anti-Nazis seems to be the last chance for this man (see White P. enclosure). But as you have already reported in terms to Jenkin Williams, no use for me to butt in. I suggest your waiting till the Tribunal to deal with this category is appointed & then send it your own & other people's evidence, if possible all together. — But if Sternheim is at

Lengfield, saying that must mean that he is going to U.S.A. – That's the Camp where for the last month or so has been used solely for assembling the emigrés

Yours sincerely

Eleanor F. Rathbone

~~See~~ ~~end~~

9

Superintendent,
Yeravda Central Prison,
(Poona).

My dearest Charlie,

I have your letter.

God's grace has been wonderful. Those days were days of basking in the sunshine of His presence. There was not one step taken out of self will. Never have I experienced such an immediate, definite response to prayer.

Yes, it was well you stayed there. I knew what it would mean for you to remain there. And yet I did not take a moment to decide in reply to your

you speak of is far subtler & wears the cloak of respectability. Ours in India looks as bad as it is & therefore in a way less difficult perhaps to fight.

I have almost regained my lost strength.

Our love to you and all the members of the ever growing family,

Yours

7/10/32

Mohan

Mohandas Gandhi 1869–1948

Sent from prison in Pune and marked with the censor's red imprimatur, the pages opposite are the first and last of a letter from Mohandas Gandhi to his English friend Charlie – Charles Freer Andrews. The date, 20 October 1932, is about a month after Gandhi had called off the hunger strike he had staged over the question of electoral representation for the Indian Dalit, or 'untouchable', community. The British had arranged separate seats for each caste group, but Gandhi wished to abolish the idea of untouchability, while also ensuring that the Dalit were not ignored. After six days of fasting, he agreed a deal with the Dalit leader, B.R. Ambedkar, establishing a single Hindu electorate, regardless of caste, with a guaranteed number of Dalit representatives.

Gandhi and Andrews, an Anglican priest and campaigner for Indian independence, had been friends since a meeting in Durban in 1914. A teacher at St Stephen's College, Delhi, Andrews was nicknamed from his initials, 'Christ's Faithful Apostle'. The confidence in which Gandhi holds him is shown both in his greeting – 'My dearest Charlie' – and by the signature – 'Mohan'; to his fellow Indians, Gandhi signed himself 'Bapu' – 'father'. Andrews was in England when Gandhi announced his hunger strike. He was ready to travel immediately to India in support, but Gandhi persuaded him that he could be of more use to the cause in England.

Here, having 'almost regained my lost strength', the Hindu Gandhi writes of his fast in strikingly religious language, of a sort that would resonate with Andrews:

> God's grace has been wonderful. Those days were days of basking in the sunshine of His presence. There was not one step taken out of self will. Never have I experienced such an immediate, definite response to prayer.

Later in his imprisonment, the British allowed Gandhi a typewriter and secretary, so that only the earliest of his prison letters, like this one, were written by hand.

Mohandas Gandhi, letter to Charles Freer Andrews, 1932

FRIENDS AND RIVALS

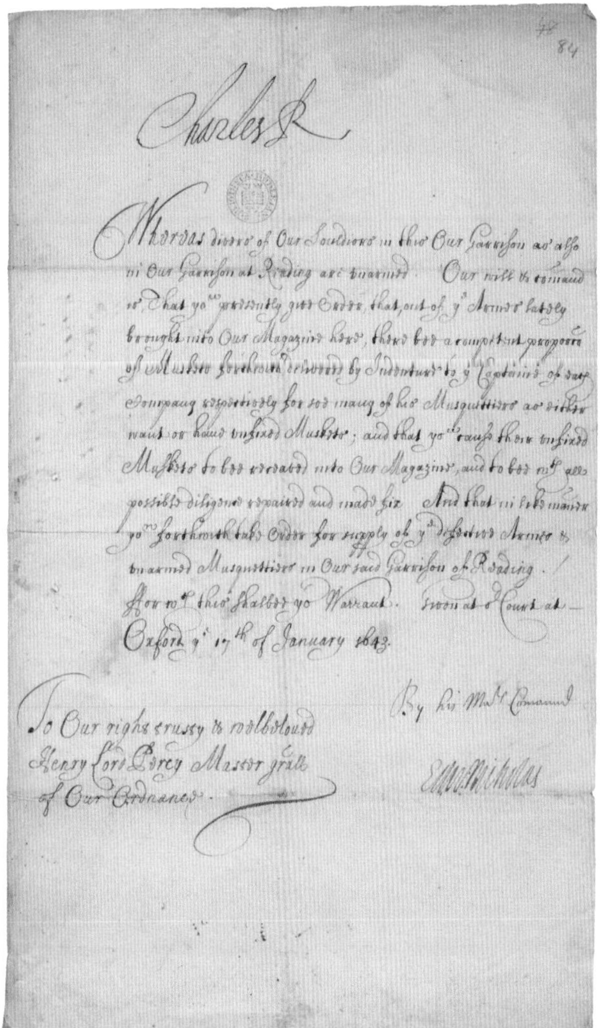

84

Charles R

Whereas divers of Our Souldiers in this Our Garrison as also in Our Garrison at Reading are unarmed. Our will & comand is, That yo^u presently give Order, that, out of y^e Armes lately brought into Our Magazine here, there bee a competent proporc̃on of Muskets forthwith delivered by Indenture to ye Captaine of each Company respectively for soe many of his Musquettiers as either want or have unfixed Muskets; and that yo^u cause their unfixed Muskets to bee received into Our Magazine, and to bee wth all possible diligence repaired and made fit. And that in like manner yo^u forthwith take Order for supply of ye defective Armes & unarmed Musquettiers in Our said Garrison of Reading. ffor wch this shalbee yor Warrant. Given at o^r Court at Oxford y^e 17th of January 1643.

By his Ma^ts Comand

Edw. Nicholas

To Our right trusty & welbeloved Henry Lord Percy Master g^rall of Our Ordnance.

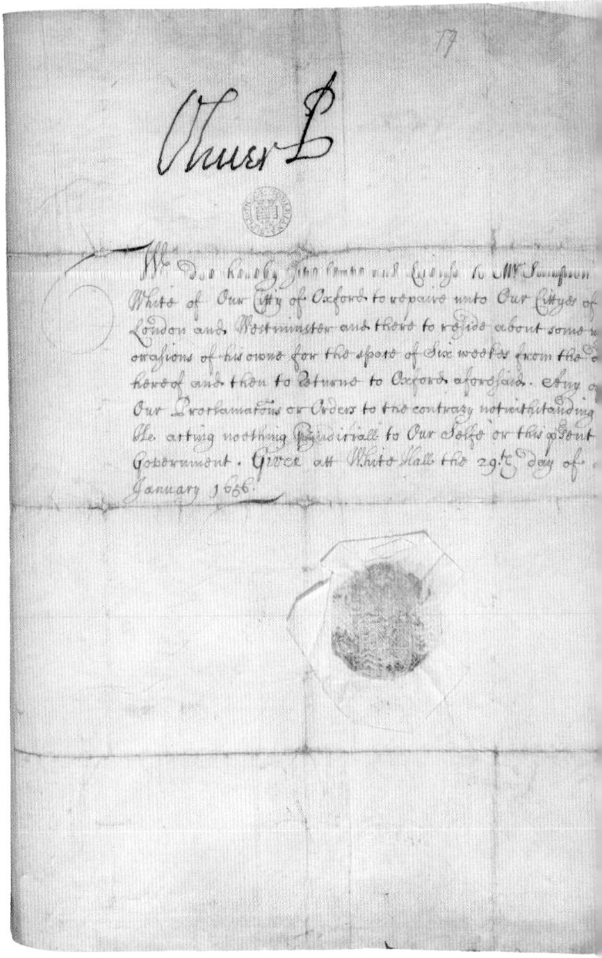

17

Oliver P

Wee doe hereby give leave and Licence to Mr Sampson White of Our Citty of Oxford to repaire unto Our Cittyes of London and Westminster and there to reside about some [illegible] occasions of his owne for the space of Six weekes from the [illegible] hereof and then to returne to Oxford aforesaid. Any [illegible] Our Proclamations or Orders to the contrary notwithstanding [illegible] he acting nothing prejudiciall to Our Selfe or this p^sent Government. Given att White Hall the 29th day of [illegible] January 1656.

Charles I 1600–1649
Oliver Cromwell 1599–1658

Almost exact contemporaries, Charles I and Oliver Cromwell found themselves on opposite sides in the English Civil War (1642–51). The Puritan, middle-class Cromwell, member of parliament for Huntingdon, seemed the reverse of Charles, a high Anglican married to a Roman Catholic, who believed in the divine right of kings. Charles's increasingly absolutist behaviour crystallized resistance to the monarchy, and Cromwell became a commander in the Parliamentarians' New Model Army pitted against the king's forces. When, after a series of battles, the 'right but repulsive' Roundhead army was victorious over the 'wrong but romantic' Cavaliers, Cromwell was one of the signatories of the king's death warrant after his conviction for high treason, before being himself installed as Lord Protector – head of state and head of the government – in the new republican Commonwealth.

The war was not just to be a military coup. In a remarkable series of discussions about political sovereignty held in St Mary's Church, Putney, in 1647, the military commanders debated what form of government was best. There were radical opinions: in the famous words of Colonel Thomas Rainsborough, 'the poorest he that is in England has a life to live as the greatest he'.

Yet, as their signatures here show, Cromwell and Charles were perhaps not so different. The king signed this order of 1643 approving the arming of the garrisons at Reading and Oxford with his regnal name Charles R(ex) and the text refers to him in the plural – the royal 'we'. Cromwell signed the second document, a letter of 1656 allowing travel from Oxford to London, using his own official signature, Oliver P(rotector). He too is referred to in the plural ('Our Citty of Oxford'), and was also styled 'His Hinesse ye Lord Protector'. At Cromwell's death in 1658, his son, Richard, took over as Protector; but his weakness was a factor in the reinstatement of the monarchy two years later.

Charles and Cromwell are both commemorated on the Bodleian Benefactors' Board, as donors to the Library.

left Signature of Charles I, 1643
right Signature of Oliver Cromwell, 1656

134

158

Mount Vernon 22d Feby 1788

Dear Sir,

If this letter should get to your hand in time, I beg you would send me five bushels of clean and fresh Red clover seed, and the like quantity of Timothy by the Vessel which you say would sail for Alexandria soon after the Delaware should be freed from Ice.

By a letter which I have just received from Mr Smith of Carlisle dated the 5th Inst. I am informed that he had at that time £200 of my money in his possession which he would send to you by the first safe conveyance—out of this please to pay yourself.—

I will write more fully to you in a few days.—In the meanwhile

I am Dear Sir

Yr most Obed Servt

G: Washington

George Washington 1732–1799
Thomas Jefferson 1743–1826

These two letters catch two friends from Virginia, the first and third presidents of the newly created United States of America, in quieter moments of their lives.

Washington had achieved hero status as commander of the American forces in the War of Independence from the British, which had begun in 1775. In 1787 he led the delegation of his home state of Virginia at the Constitutional Convention, which met in Philadelphia to draw up Articles of Confederation – deciding the future relationship of the thirteen states that had contested the war. Washington was unanimously elected as the convention's presiding officer, and it was confidently expected that he would be elected as the new nation's first president – which in the spring of 1789 he duly was. But in the meantime Washington had returned to his family home at Mount Vernon, and on 22 February 1788, when this letter was written (his fifty-sixth birthday), was busy considering the sowing of new crops. He writes here to Clement Biddle, owner of a shipping firm (and a wartime general), to ask him to send 'five bushels of clean and fresh red-clover seed, and the like quantity of Timothy [hay seed]' – both fodder crops that were also good for the soil. Washington took a careful interest in the agriculture of his land and was particular about its cultivation.

Washington asks for the seed to be shipped as soon as the Delaware river is free from ice. Biddle replied at the beginning of March: he had put the order, and a volume of newspapers, on board the sloop *Charming Polly*, bound for Alexandria, Virginia, but a sudden severe frost looked to prevent her from sailing for some days to come. As soon as the weather permitted, the ship would sail.

Washington arranges payment via his attorney (and another former army commander), Thomas Smith of Carlisle, Pennsylvania. Smith has £200 of his money, and will send it to Biddle 'by the first safe conveyance'. In his reply, Biddle says that Smith had sent the money in gold, which in

George Washington, letter to Clement Biddle, 1788

fact had a value of only £192 13*s.* 4*d.*, and which he had credited as $400 to Washington's account. The new nation had adopted the dollar as currency in 1785, but a dual system is clearly still in operation.

Thomas Jefferson, the primary author of the Declaration of Independence in 1776, served as president from 1801 to 1809. He retired to his family plantation at Monticello, just outside Charlottesville, Virginia, and set about the foundation of a university. Jefferson was something of a Renaissance man, and was minutely involved in every aspect of the university's development. He designed the classical buildings, drew up the curriculum and appointed the staff, including himself as the first rector.

The University of Virginia opened in 1825, and in December of that year Jefferson wrote the letter shown here to John McLean, United States Postmaster General since 1817, 'to ask a favor'. Jefferson is concerned that the students are walking every day the mile to the post office in Charlottesville to pick up their post. Not only is this a waste of good studying time, but it provides the young men with opportunities 'to get into irregularities inconsistent with the college regulations and injurious to themselves'. In some detail, Jefferson explains how McLean could establish a sort of branch office at the university, so the students would have no need to go into town. He recommends Mr Arthur Brockenbrough, the university proctor (and a Jefferson appointee) as its postmaster.

McLean replied on 5 January 1826. He is sorry that he cannot do exactly as Jefferson requests. Such a plan had been tried at academic institutions elsewhere and proved unsatisfactory. He cannot, he feels, make an exception for Jefferson, in spite of his high regard for the former president. However, he has instructed the Charlottesville postmaster to arrange to send mail via Arthur Brockenbrough, and he hopes that the effect will turn out much the same. Five days later, Jefferson replied, assuring McLean that he would never expect special treatment and thanking him for his help.

Thomas Jefferson, letter to John McLean, 1825

Sir Monticello Dec. 30. 25.

I have to ask a favor of you in behalf of the University of Virginia, the motives to which I am in hopes you will approve, while it would seem scarcely to disturb at all the arrangements of your office. this Institution is exactly one mile from Charlottesville, the nearest post-office. it's order requires that as little occasion as possible for going to the town should be given to the Students. one or more mails arrive or depart every day in the week, and thus gives to every Student an excuse for going there every day. besides the time wasted in the walk, they are liable, when there, to get into irregularities inconsistent with the college regulations and injurious to themselves. all this would be avoided by establishing a deposit there for the letters of the inhabitants of the place. these during the year now ended have amounted to between 2. and 300. grown persons, will be between 3. and 400. the year now beginning, and will probably increase 1. or 200. every year for some time to come. that deposit, it is believed would recieve at present more letters than Charlottesville; and nearly all the future additions will be to that. if this accomodation can be admitted (without discontinuing the office at Charlottesville, which is not proposed) it will much promote the order it is so desirable should prevail among the youths of the University. the present mail road at that place is a bow of about 400. yards length, of which the cord passes thro' two private gates along the front of the University buildings, in one of which the office shall be kept, so as to save, by the direct line, the time which the rider might lose in exchanging his mails. if this measure should meet your approbation, I would recommend as Postmaster for the University Arthur S. Brockenbrough Esqr., Proctor of the University, a gentleman worthy of every confidence which may be reposed in him. and to the service you would render the institution, it would add a gratification to myself, it's Rector, and a motive the more for acknoleging to you my great esteem and respect.

Th: Jefferson

P.S. for further particulars I must refer you to mr Rives our representative, intimately acquainted with all the localities worthy of enquiry.

Royal Institution of Great Britain,

ALBEMARLE STREET.

23*d* *April*, 1836.

SYLLABUS
OF A COURSE OF LECTURES
ON THE
HISTORY OF LANDSCAPE PAINTING,
BY
JOHN CONSTABLE, Esq. R. A.

To be delivered on the following Thursdays at Three o'Clock.

Lecture I. May 26.—The real Origin of Landscape—Coeval in Italy and Germany in its rise and Early progress—Further Advanced in Germany in the Fifteenth Century—Albert Durer—Influence of his Works in Italy—Titian—impressed by them and in *his* hands Landscape assumed its real dignity and grandeur—and entitled him to the appellation of the "*Father of Landscape*"—the "St. Peter Martyr."

Lecture II. June 2.—Establishment of Landscape—the Bolognese School—by this School Landscape first made a distinct and separate Class of Art—the Sixteenth and Seventeenth Centuries—the Caracci—Domenichino—Albano—Mola—Landscape soon after perfected in Rome—the Poussins—Claude Lorraine—Bourdon—Salvator Rosa—The "Bambocciate"—Peter de Laar—Both—Berghem—the deterioration of Landscape—its Decline in the Eighteenth Century.

Lecture III. June 9.—Landscape of the Dutch and Flemish Schools—emanates from the School of Albert Durer—forming separate and distinct branches—Rubens—Rembrandt—Ruysdaal—Cuyp—the marks which characterize the two schools—their decline also in the Eighteenth Century.

Lecture IV. June 16.—The decline and revival of Art—imitation of preceding excellence the main cause of the decline—opposed to original Study—the Restoration of Painting takes place in England—Reynolds—Hogarth—West—Wilson—Gainsborough—when Landscape at length resumes its birthright—and appears with new powers.

London: William Nicol, Printer to the Royal Institution.

Admit

William Wordsworth Esq

and friends

to the Course

John Constable

35 Charlotte Street July 3rd

John Constable 1776–1837
J.M.W. Turner 1775–1851

At the end of the eighteenth century, English landscape painting was transformed by two extraordinary artists. With technical as well as visionary brilliance, they overturned the perfect flat surface of the canvas, while using apparently simple images to express a deeper meaning about the nature of belonging.

Constable's vision of England is now so ubiquitous it is difficult to imagine his struggle for recognition. Deeply rooted in the countryside around the river Stour, his art was founded on long observation. Responsibilities to the family business meant that his desire to become an artist was almost derailed, but he was grateful for the financial support that allowed him to carry on through the long years of misunderstanding and little success. Unlike the precocious Turner, who was making money from his art by the age of eleven, Constable's road was hard and slow. Whereas Turner was elected an associate of the Royal Academy at twenty-four, Constable repeatedly failed in the members' ballot, succeeding only in 1819, at the age of forty-three.

Nevertheless, when fame arrived it did not leave him; indeed, the landscape of his childhood was known as 'Constable country' even before his death. Where he had once been blackballed from the artistic elite, between 1833 and 1836 he gave a series of lectures on the history of landscape painting, at the Literary and Scientific Society of Hampstead, the Worcester Literary and Scientific Institution and, as shown here, at the Royal Institution in London.

This ticket details the content of the four lectures, beginning with late medieval European painting, through the classical landscapes of Poussin and Claude, to the glorious Dutch and Flemish schools of the seventeenth century. Lecture IV turns closer to home, with 'Restoration of Painting' in England, 'when Landscape at length resumes its birthright – and appears with new powers'. The Royal Institution lectures were attended

John Constable, endorsed ticket to a lecture

by a variety of eminent figures in science and literature. Here, from his home address in Charlotte Street, Constable has personalized the ticket for the admittance of the poet 'William Wordsworth Esq[uire] and friends'. Unsurprisingly, the great poet of the English landscape was interested in hearing its great visual interpreter speak.

Turner was equally a student of European painting. With immense energy and stamina – as he approached everything – he travelled the continent, recording in hundreds of sketchbooks what he had seen and translating it into his own visual language. The Bodleian preserves Turner's fast and careless handwriting in a few scrappy letters; but it also holds three small watercolours 'attributed to' him, among a large collection of topographical painting and drawing collected by the antiquarian S.A. Warner and bequeathed to the Library in 1948.

We cannot be sure that the attractive little view of Newark Castle shown opposite is really by Turner (although it bears his initials), but he is certainly known to have visited Newark and painted there. Although perhaps best loved now for his large, late impressionistic works, such as *The Fighting Temeraire*, much of Turner's bread and butter work was in the illustration of topographical almanacs, where his watercolours were turned into steel-plate engravings and published in series of 'picturesque views of England and Wales'. Turner made thousands of watercolour sketches for such projects, so it is not unreasonable to think that this attractive little picture is the genuine article.

J.M.W. Turner, view of Newark Castle

To
Edmond Malone Esqr

Mr Bentham presents his Compliments to Mr Malone, and would take it as a particular favour, if he could inform him, whether the Charter of Queen Eli-zabeth granted for the foundation of Westminster School is extant any where in print, and, whether in print or manuscript, if he could put him in a way to see it, without any such formality as that of an application to the Dean and Chapter, in whose custody the original must be of course.

Queen's Square Place Westmr   Oct. 7/97.

Jeremy Bentham 1748–1832
John Stuart Mill 1806–1873

Quite why the philosopher and reformer Jeremy Bentham is writing in October 1797 to the lawyer and Shakespeare scholar Edmund Malone to ask him about the whereabouts of a published copy of the Elizabethan foundation charter for Westminster School is unclear. Whatever the reason, his request was unsuccessful, for Malone replied on 26 October to say that he knew of no such printed version. Westminster was Bentham's alma mater, and it is fair to say that he hated it. Having learned Greek at home since the age of three, at the age of seven he went to Westminster, where the headmaster was a friend of his father, and was a fish out of water. Small, musical, not particularly sporty and interested in serious learning, he was lonely and isolated; later in life he described the school as 'a wretched place for instruction'.

Nevertheless, he went up to Oxford aged fourteen and graduated at sixteen. His father's ambition was that his clever son become Lord Chancellor; but, although he qualified as a lawyer, Bentham's interest was not in practice but in reform. Appalled by the situation of the worst-off in society, for much of his long and busy life he pressed for renewal and change, whether it be in education, prisons and the penitential system, the Poor Law, the legal system or Parliament, to name but a few of his radical causes. His decades-long campaign for the abolition of the offshore prison hulk ships, where convicts were kept in appalling conditions, was joined to a plan for a new sort of penitentiary, the Panopticon. Although it never came to pass, he was prepared even into his sixties to take on the post of governor, as soon as his new model prison might be built.

Bentham was a close friend of the writer James Mill, who rented a house from Bentham close to his own in Queen Square Place, Westminster. In his *Autobiography*, James's eldest son, the radical philosopher and advocate of women's suffrage John Stuart Mill recalled frequent visits by Bentham, and time spent together at Bentham's

Jeremy Bentham, letter to Edmund Malone, 1797

various country residences. There, away from London, Mill acquired an appreciation of landscape: 'This sojourn was, I think, an important circumstance of my education. Nothing contributes more to nourish elevation of sentiments in a people, than the large and free character of their habitations.'

Mill also read Bentham's writings, especially those on utilitarianism – the proposition that the aim of government should be the greatest happiness of the greatest number – with enormous excitement. His own reworking of the ideas resulted in a classic text, *Utilitarianism*, which along with his work *On Liberty* made him the foremost political philosopher of his day.

Mill's own home schooling was as intense as Bentham's had been, and he later believed it had contributed to a sort of nervous breakdown in his twenties. His recovery was at least in part effected by his reading of poetry, and especially Wordsworth: 'What made Wordsworth's poems a medicine for my state of mind was that they expressed, not mere outward beauty, but states of feeling, and of thought coloured by feeling, under the excitement of beauty.'

It's not surprising, then, that when Mill and two friends, Henry Cole (later director of the South Kensington Museum, now the V&A) and Horace Grant, made a walking tour of the Lake District in July and August 1831, they should call on Wordsworth. At first, as his diary of the tour (shown opposite) recalls, they kept finding the poet out, although they were impressed by his sister, Dorothy. Finally, however, the great man was at home at Rydal Mount:

> We remained four whole days at Ambleside chiefly for the purpose of seeing Wordsworth, with whom we passed as much of that time as we could, and were amply repaid both in pleasure, intellectual excitement, and instruction. Our walks were chiefly short ones. Wordsworth conducted us to several beautiful spots, and his own grounds contain in a very limited extent, so great a variety of prospects that they are almost a compendium of the whole Westmoreland mountains.

John Stuart Mill, diary entry of a visit to William Wordsworth, 1831

neighbourhood, and walked up Patterdale to the pass at its head, in the mountain Kirkstone, 56 ~~already~~ noticed in a former part of this journal & a carriage road, though a difficult one, ascends this pass, from the higher parts of which, on looking back, nothing is visible but the sky, the wild sides of the pass, and a glimpse of Brother's Water at ~~the~~ its foot. The descent to Ambleside by the side of Stock Ghyll is less striking, but still very fine: the scenery of Ambleside, considered as grand mountain-scenery, will scarcely bear examination after the more striking scenes which I had witnessed since I left it, but the beauty of the home-scenes and of the more rich and graceful Windermere is even more delightful from the contrast.

We remained four whole days at Ambleside, chiefly for the purpose of seeing Wordsworth, with whom we passed as much of that time as we could, and were amply repaid both in pleasure, ~~moral~~ intellectual excitement, and instruction. Our walks were chiefly short ones; ~~by Wordsw-~~ Wordsworth conducted us to several beautiful spots, & his own grounds contain ~~on~~ in a very limited extent, so great a variety of prospects that they are almost a compendium of the whole Westmoreland mountains. We walked again to Troutbeck, Kempbyrd, a considerable part of one day in going down

by his perfect knowledge of his thought. The room was quite unchanged. It was in every respect as if he had resided in it yesterday – the writing materials, the books, all the indications of habitual occupation – Only one change I observed: a plate on ~~the~~ his accustomed chair – ~~The~~ with ~~an~~ a inscription "This was the Prince Consort's chair from 18– to 1861."

In ~~less than~~ less than five minutes from my entry, ~~the~~ an opposite door opened, & the Queen appeared.

She was still in Widow's mourning, & seemed stouter than when I last saw her, but this was perhaps only from her dress. I bowed deeply when she entered, & raised my head with unusual slowness, that I might have a moment for recovery. Her countenance was grave, but serene & kind – & she said, in a most musical voice, "It is some time since we met".

William Ewart Gladstone 1809–1898
Benjamin Disraeli 1804–1881

The history of nineteenth-century politics is full of remarkable careers, but none more so than the duelling fortunes of Mr Gladstone and Mr Disraeli. For many years, in and out of office, the two men battled it out at the dispatch box of the House of Commons, alternating as members of successive cabinets and even as prime minister. They were different in party – Gladstone was a Liberal, Disraeli a Tory; background – Gladstone the son of an evangelical baronet, Disraeli from a mercantile, literary Jewish family; education – Gladstone Eton and Oxford, Disraeli an articled clerk with a law firm in Old Jewry; and appearance – Gladstone sternly traditional, Disraeli with his oiled ringlets and rings worn over white gloves. 'Dizzy', a successful novelist, was a great favourite of Queen Victoria; as he said to Matthew Arnold, 'Everyone likes flattery, and when you come to Royalty you should lay it on with a trowel.' In contrast, the queen complained that Mr Gladstone 'speaks to me as if I was a public meeting.'

In his recollections of his career (opposite), Disraeli recalls his first meeting with Victoria after the death of Prince Albert in 1861. He had been invited to the wedding of the Prince of Wales in March 1863, and shortly afterwards was given a private audience with the queen, which took place in Prince Albert's favourite sitting room, left exactly as it had been when he was alive:

> Only one change I observed: a plate on his accustomed chair, with an inscription 'This was the Prince Consorts chair from 18– to 1861'. In less than five minutes from my entry, an opposite door opened, and the Queen appeared.
>
> She was still in Widows mourning, and seemed stouter than when I last saw her … I bowed deeply when she entered, and raised my head with unusual slowness, that I might have a moment for recovery. Her countenance was grave, but serene and kind – & she said, in a most musical voice, 'It is some time since we met'.

Benjamin Disraeli, diary entry concerning a meeting with Queen Victoria, 1863

The letters between Disraeli and Gladstone in the Bodleian, which holds the Hughenden Deposit of Disraeli's papers (named after his country estate), are not always temperate. On occasion, each forgoes a courteous 'Dear Sir' to complain of the language one has used of the other. Nevertheless, there were times when politics was to be put aside. Disraeli's wife, Mary Anne, died in December 1872, and after a decent interval, on 19 January 1873, Gladstone wrote to express his and his family's sympathy. The letter, part of which is shown here, is worth quoting in full, for its style as well as its sentiments:

> Dear Mr Disraeli
>
> My reluctance to intrude on the sacredness and freshness of your sorrow may now I think properly give way to a yet stronger reluctance to forego adding our small but very sincere tribute of sympathy to those abundant manifestations of it which have been yielded in so many forms.
>
> You and I were, as I believe, married in the same year. It has been permitted to both of us to enjoy a priceless boon through a third of a century. Spared myself the blow which has fallen on you, I can form some conception of what it must have been and be. I do not presume to offer you the consolation, which you will seek from another and higher quarter. I offer only the assurance which all who know you, all who knew Lady Beaconsfield, and especially those among them who like myself enjoyed for a length of time her marked though unmerited regard, may perhaps tender without impropriety: the assurance that in this trying hour they feel deeply for you, and with you.
>
> Believe me
> Sincerely yours
> W.E. Gladstone

W.E. Gladstone, letter of condolence to Disraeli, 1873

abundant manifestations
of it which have been yielded
in so many forms.

You and I were, as I believe,
married in the same year.
It has been permitted to both
of us to enjoy a priceless
boon through a third of a
century. Spared myself
the blow which has fallen on
you, I can form some concep-
tion of what it must have
been and be. I do not presume
to offer you the consolation,
which you will seek from
another and higher quarter.
I offer only the assurance
which all who know you,
all who knew Lady Beaconsfield, and especially those
among them who like my-
self enjoyed for a length
of time her marked though
unmerited regard, may
perhaps tender without im-
propriety; the assurance

and there were scattered bird-songs, jolly, broken warbles, – ('just one more warble before I turn in', sort of idea) – all in the proper setting of umbrageous dusk & midsummer – and only those d—d sausage balloons hanging a few miles away – (& high time they came down too) – I don't often take an evening stroll; usually bolt back to my room to my candle & book – But we'd had an easy day owing ~~to~~ the wet weather, which cleared at sunset.

What a humbug you'll think me! For we are still dallying on the brink. What a cutting-up we'll get some fine day. I see Wilfred Owen's verse in the Nation. The sonnet is not up to his form. But I have faith in him. He will do well if you & R.G. look after him, & stop him writing preciosities. Dear little Wilfred... have you seen him yet? Craiglockhart gave me two friends – he, & Rivers, whom I adore. I am weakly amiable tonight... Of late I've been moody & nerve-ridden. Reading Whitman put me right. He is a glorious old lad... Did you ever hear F. Delius's music to his Sea-Drift?... O music! I am starving for it, Robert – Here's my only poem for ages – Is it any good?

I stood with the Dead.

I stood with the Dead, so forsaken & ~~[illegible]~~ still.
When dawn was grey I stood with the dead:
And my slow heart said, 'You must kill; you must kill:
'Soldier, soldier; morning is red.'
On the shapes of the slain in their crumpled disgrace
I stared for a while through the thin, cold rain...
'O lad that I loved, there is rain on your face;
'And your eyes are blurred ~~late~~ & sick like the plain.'

I stood with the Dead; they were dead; they were dead;
My heart & my head beat to a march of dismay:
And the gusts of the wind came dulled by the guns...
'Fall in!' I shouted; 'Fall in for your pay!'...

love – S

Wilfred Owen 1893–1918
Siegfried Sassoon 1886–1967

'Dottyville' was the name given by Siegfried Sassoon in 1917 to Craiglockhart War Hospital, near Edinburgh. Housed in a disused hydropathic hotel ('hydro') in the village of Slateford, it was open only from October 1916 to March 1919, its patients officers (other ranks were treated elsewhere) shell-shocked by their experiences on the front line. Craiglockhart has an important place in the diagnosis and treatment of traumatic shock, especially at a time when the reality of the symptoms of neurasthenia was disputed – the men were surely malingering – and would have earned its corner of history, even without its association with two of the greatest First World War poets, Wilfred Owen and Siegfried Sassoon. But Sassoon's memories of the hospital's regime, and especially the therapeutic relationships formed by the percipient psychologist W.H. Rivers, alongside *The Hydra*, the hospital magazine edited by Owen, have ensured that its pioneering work has continued to be known and valued.

Owen and Sassoon met at Craiglockhart in the summer of 1917. Both had seen the worst of the trenches, and Sassoon had been awarded the Military Cross for an individual act of bravery – he was known as 'Mad Jack' by his men. He was already a published poet, and his use of direct speech to bring his everyday experience to life gave Owen a transformed sense of how poetry might express the reality of this new sort of war. They were divided by class, wealth and confidence, but the need to write brought them together, and Sassoon's encouragement enabled Owen to find his poetic voice.

Discharged from Craiglockhart, after a short spell in Palestine Sassoon had rejoined his old battalion in France in May 1918, and it is from here that he writes, on 19 June, to another poet, Robert Nichols. Nichols's poor health had curtailed his own active service, and he saw himself as stuck behind a desk. 'But what a pity it is that we can't change places for a fortnight,' Sassoon begins; 'Here am I, aching for a quiet house to hide in and get

Siegfried Sassoon, letter to Robert Nichols, 1918

poems off my chest, while you need just what I've had my fill of since March!'

The focus is solidly on poetry:

> I see Wilfred Owen's verse in the Nation. The sonnet is not up to his form. But I have faith in him. He will do well if you and R[obert] G[raves] look after him, and stop him writing preciosities. Dear little Wilfred … have you seen him yet? Craiglockhart gave me two friends – he, and Rivers, whom I adore.

Owen certainly had stopped writing 'preciosities', and for that he had to thank not only Sassoon and his fellow poets, but also Arthur Brock, his Craiglockhart doctor. Brock believed shell shock arose out of a broken connection with normal life – a connection that should be re-established by involving the patient in work, or 'ergotherapy', cure by functioning. For Owen, this consisted in editing *The Hydra*, the site of his first published poems. His convalescence at Craiglockhart enabled his development into perhaps the finest of the extraordinary poets of the war to end all wars.

Owen had been excited to meet the older, published writer at Craiglockhart. On 22 August 1917, he wrote to his cousin Leslie Gunston:

> At last I have an event worth a letter. I have beknownst myself to Siegfried Sassoon. Went in to him last night (my second call). The first visit was one morning last week. The sun blazed into his room, making his purple dressing suit of a brilliance almost matching my sonnet!

At least seven drafts of the poem shown here (dating from September–October 1917) are known; Owen's eventual title was 'Anthem for Doomed Youth'. It was included in the first published collection of Owen's *Poems* edited by Sassoon in 1920. The first draft, with amendments written in Sassoon's hand, is now in the British Library.

'Mad Jack' Sassoon lived into his eighties. Wilfred Owen returned to the front and was killed on 4 November 1918, a week before the Armistice.

Wilfred Owen, draft of 'Anthem for Doomed Youth', 1917

Anthem to Dead Youth.

What passing bells for you who die in herds?
– Only the monstrous anger of more guns.
Only the stuttering rifles' rattled words
Can patter out your hasty orisons.
No chants for you, nor balms, nor wreaths, nor bells,
Nor any voice of mourning, save the choirs,
The shrill demented choirs of wailing shells;
And bugles calling for you ~~fo~~ from sad shires.

What candles may we hold to speed you all?
Not in the hands of boys, but in their eyes
Shall shine the holy lights of long goodbyes.
The pallor of girls' brows shall be your pall;
Your flowers the tenderness of mortal minds;
And each slow dusk, a drawing-down of blinds.

MUCH HADHAM 66

HOGLANDS,
PERRY GREEN,
MUCH HADHAM,
HERTS.

30th January 1959.

Dear David Astor,

I have now cleaned up the sculpture and it looks very much better, - in fact you may think it is too bright, but London will soon tone it down. I have given it a coat of varnish which makes it look a little shiny to begin with, but this also will wear off.

I think if the gardener washes it down with a sponge and warm water every now and then, (oftener in winter than in summer) say about once a month. Also I will send my assistant at intervals to see when it next needs our attention again.

I am glad I have been able to do this because I like to think the sculpture looks well.

The Arts Council will be delivering it next Tuesday afternoon 3rd February, about 2-30. I hope this is alright.

With warm regards to you both.

Yrs sincerely
Henry Moore

Barbara Hepworth 1903–1975
Henry Moore 1898–1986

Fiction would judge it too much of a coincidence that two of the greatest sculptors of the twentieth century should be born within five years and ten miles of one another, and in Yorkshire at that; and that the two, Barbara Hepworth from Wakefield and Henry Moore from Castleford, should be fellow students at the Leeds School of Art in 1920 and at the Royal College of Art in London in 1921. Both worked by carving directly into stone, as well as casting monumental figures in bronze.

Moore was commissioned as a war artist in 1939, making a remarkable series of drawings of Londoners sheltering from the Blitz in the tunnels of the Underground. When their own London flat was bombed, he and his wife moved to a farmhouse, Hoglands, in the Hertfordshire hamlet of Perry Green. Similarly, in 1939 Hepworth and her husband, the artist Ben Nicholson, moved to St Ives in Cornwall, where the sea-struck light attracted a growing artistic community. For both, these were moves to places where the landscape inspired their creativity for the rest of their lives.

It's a long way to Yorkshire from Cliveden, the family mansion in Berkshire where the Hon. David Astor, son of Waldorf and Nancy Astor, and editor of *The Observer* newspaper, grew up. David Astor and his wife had homes in St John's Wood, London (overlooking Lord's cricket ground) and Oxfordshire, which they filled with art. He was an admirer of Moore, and in 1954 had bought, for £3,000, his over-life-size bronze *King and Queen*. Meaning it originally for his country house, Astor liked the piece so much he kept it in his London garden so he could see it every day.

Astor lent *King and Queen* to an Arts Council exhibition at King's Lynn in 1958. Moore was concerned that the city air had dirtied and degraded its surface, but Astor was unwilling to 'banish' the sculpture to Oxfordshire. Was there not some way, he asked, that Moore's assistant

Henry Moore, letter to David Astor, 1959

could come and clean it every six months or so, and the Astors' gardener would 'wash it down at frequent intervals'? The letter overleaf records the arrangement they came to. Moore has given the piece a polish and varnish, and will send his assistant when it next needs attention. In addition, the gardener should go over it with 'a sponge and warm water every now and then … say about once a month'.

Astor continued to collect. At the 1963 Battersea Park sculpture exhibition he saw Barbara Hepworth's *Single Form (Memorial)* and wrote to her to ask if it was for sale: he and his wife had 'fallen under [its] spell'. They wanted it 'for our place in the country where we already have one of your works'. Hepworth had made the original *Single Form* for the memorial to the United Nations Secretary General, Dag Hammarskjöld, and a twenty-one-foot version was to be sited in the pool outside the United Nations building in New York. She told Astor she had known Hammarskjöld, 'and my whole heart went into the work'.

Only two casts of the figure as shown at Battersea existed, and Hepworth quoted a price of 6,500 guineas (£6,825). Even for a wealthy Astor, it seems, this was a bit steep, and in the letter opposite, on her elegant, 'tracing paper' stationery, Hepworth does a little judicious bargaining:

> I write this note not to worry you – but merely to say that the siting of this sculpture matters more to me than money. So that providing my costs and commissions are covered my 'reward' for the work is more of a spiritual satisfaction than material one.

Astor, however, was too slow. One cast was bought by the Blaustein Foundation, which had supported the original commission for the United Nations, and was taken to the United States, while the other was bought by London County Council for permanent display in the park, where it can still be seen.

Barbara Hepworth, letter to David Astor, 1963

Personal

BARA HEPWORTH

13th. August, 1963.

The Hon. F.D.L. Astor,
12, Elm Tree Road,
London, N.W.8.

Dear David Astor,

Thank you for your kind letter of July,

I agree that the figure I quoted for "Single Form", which was the London Selling Price, sounded formidable; but you will appreciate that in the open market (with commission on top of very high casting fees) this price is inevitable.

As you are, however, my "private patron" I have ascertained that I could afford to make a reduction to you and your wife of 15% and because the Dag Memorial would have such a beautiful home with you, I would even go further than this if, by chance, it brought the sculpture within your reach? (Such as £5,500)

I write this note not to worry you - but merely to say that the siting of this sculpture matters more to me than money. So that providing my costs and commissions are covered my "reward" for the work is more of a spiritual satisfaction than material one.

With my kindest regards,

Yours very sincerely,

Barbara Hepworth

WYN STUDIO
IVES
RNWALL
IVES 905

TRAVELLERS AND ADVENTURERS

WR alig8

Ianuier ha xxxi iour
la lune xxx.

iii a La circuncision
. b N. Octaues saint estienne
xi c N. Octaues saint iehan.
. d N. Octaues des innocens.
xix e N. Saint simeon.
viii f Id. Lepyphanie
. g Id. Saint seurin.
xvi a Id. Saint felix
v b Id. Saint adrien
. c Id. Saint pol lhermite.
xiii d Id. Saint sauueur
ii e Id. Saint satir
. f Id. Saint hylaire
x g Kl. Saint felix
a Kl. Saint mor
xviii b Kl. Saint marcel.

Walter Ralegh 1554–1618

Ralegh was always searching for the next big thing. Tall and good-looking, well read, with a gift for writing, and possessing social contacts in Elizabeth I's court, he could have lived a quiet, literary life. Instead, his restless ambition took him soldiering in Ireland, colonizing in Virginia, and hunting for gold in South America. Fascinated by the legends of El Dorado – the empire of gold to be found in the lost cities of ancient peoples – he travelled up the Orinoco to Guiana. Although he returned empty-handed, his report of the journey, *The Discoverie of the Large, Rich and Bewtiful Empyre of Guiana* (1596), was widely read across Europe. Twenty years later, after a spell confined in the Tower, he tried again; but the second voyage was if anything less successful than the first. All his dreams had been tied up in the expedition and he could hardly believe it had failed.

Ralegh captivated many who knew him; but equally he had enemies at court. In particular, he was said to be an atheist, in an age when religion was a matter of great contention; the rumours of his lack of belief even occasioned an investigation in 1594. Nevertheless, outwardly he was a worshipping member of the Church of England. All the more interesting, then, that he owned the beautiful – but Catholic – Book of Hours, the first page of which is shown here. Books of Hours direct personal prayers throughout the year, and, this page shows the saints and religious feast days to be commemorated in the month of January. The text itself is in Latin, but the rubrics are in French: 'Janvier ha xxxi jour' ('January has 31 days'). Ralegh marks his ownership with a signature in the top margin.

The manuscript book was written in France in the fifteenth century. It had entered the Library by 1615, within Ralegh's lifetime, suggesting that he admired its fine quality rather than its devotional utility. Ralegh and Thomas Bodley, both Devon men, were old acquaintances.

Walter Ralegh, signature in a Book of Hours

The Mussule plum
Ripe August 24

John Tradescant the Elder d.1638

Some travellers are curious to meet other peoples, but the force behind John Tradescant's journeys was his love of plants. Gardener and plantsman to some of the greatest names in England, he plied his trade for Lord Salisbury, Lord Wotton and the duke of Buckingham, before setting up his own garden, nursery and museum of rarities in Lambeth, south of London and still at this time rural. So famous was his collection here that in 1630 Charles I made him 'Keeper of our gardens, Vines and Silke-wormes' at Oatlands Palace in Surrey, followed by an appointment as custodian of the Oxford Physic Garden in 1637. Tradescant had reached the pinnacle of his profession.

From at least his time as gardener to Lord Salisbury, Tradescant travelled to acquire plants. His first known journey, made for Salisbury in 1611, was through the Low Countries to Paris, buying for the gardens at Hatfield House. It may have been during his time at Hatfield that the manuscript shown opposite was made. Known as 'The Tradescants' Orchard', it contains sixty-six watercolour drawings of cultivated fruit, sometimes accompanied by birds and insects, organized by their time of ripening – here, 'The Mussule plum Ripe August 24'. Although the precise relation of the book to Tradescant has never been certain, it has been suggested as a twin to 'A Booke of Mr. Tradescant's choicest Flowers and Plants, exquisitely limned in vellum by Mr. Alex. Marshall', which Tradescant kept at Lambeth.

His link to our second illustrated page, however, is quite clear. It comes from his own account of a voyage undertaken with Sir Dudley Digges in 1618–19. Digges had been appointed as an ambassador to Muscovy, and Tradescant – with the agreement of his employer, Lord Wotton – accompanied him to Archangel on the coast of Russia via the northernmost tip of Norway, the North Cape. While Digges and his aides negotiated with the tsar, Tradescant was free to search out, collect and

'The Mussule plum', from 'The Tradescants' Orchard'

catalogue the native coastal flora and fauna, the first time anything of this sort had been attempted in Russia. Tradescant's twenty-four-page account of the voyage is written in a rather rustic hand and without any attempt at literary style, but its early date and the eyewitness account it preserves are full of interest.

The page opposite records the end of the voyage, which sailed via Gravesend in Kent to land on 'tewsday the 22 of of [sic] August … At Saynt Katharin's [dock] Neer London'. Although his narrative of the voyage is done, Tradescant goes on to list 'Things By Me observed'. These include the Russian times for sowing wheat, barley, oats and peas, as well as details about the construction of houses he saw en route – all interesting given the northerly latitudes of the trip:

> Now for ther warmthe they have stooves whearin they heate ther meat whiche is so well Don that it Givethe Great Content to All Strangers. for Beds I have Scene None of the Ruses But think for the most part they Sleepe upon Bedsteads & Most of ther Beding is Beare Skins & other Skins.

A year or so later (1620–21), another manuscript records Tradescant having signed as a gentleman volunteer on the pinnace *Mercurie*, as part of the expedition commanded by Sir Robert Mansell to put down the pirates who were harassing English shipping off the Barbary Coast of North Africa. The collecting bug was so strong, it seems, that he was prepared to risk naval action in order to make landfall when he could, to enhance his knowledge and his collections. Tradescant's ability to introduce and cultivate rare and exotic plants for his employers' gardens was an important element in his success.

Latterly, Tradescant's interests expanded to include rare and curious things of many sorts, and the museum he established at his house at Lambeth became as famous as the garden. He bequeathed his collections to his son, another John, from whom they were acquired by Elias Ashmole, and became the basis for the first public museum in England, opened in 1683 and still, as the Ashmolean, free to visitors to Oxford today.

John Tradescant the Elder, account of a voyage to Russia

Cam to Grabesend on tewsday the 22 of of August we landed At Seynt Katharins Neer London wheer God Be thanked we Ended our viage having No on man Sick God Be thanked

Things By Me obserbed
Inprimis for the sowing of Rie the seare In Ruly ther wheat In June theese two Graynes Growe some 13 monthes Before they Be Reaped By Reson of the snow falling In August or september & so Lithe tile the man After
ther harbest Is In August & the Begining of september ther Barly oats & Pease theye sowe In may the Last & Comonly Reaped the first of August or the Last of July
I habe Bin showed oats whiche wer Good whiche wer sowne & mowne & Reaped threshed In 6 weeks
for ther howses they Be made All of long peeces of fire Being half Cut Away on theinsyd they be Glased withe Glas Called slude ther Ruffes Be flat Almost & Cut Bordes of A handfull thick Layd longwayes Donne the Ruffe they habe the Rinds of Birche trees under the Bords whiche Be As Broad A yearing Calfe or Broader & 3 yards long whiche they Lay the Edges on one Another & Doo Defend the wet & Raine & snowe
Now for ther warmthe they habe stoobes wheerin they heat ther meat whiche Is so well Don that It Gibethe Great Content to All strangers
for Beds I habe seene None of the Rusys But think for the most part they sleepe vpon Bedsteads & most of ther Beding Is Beare skins & other skins

3

100 Addison Road

Kensington London W

Liverpool

(2)

Dear Mr Christy -

Thank you for your letter about Bath & Bournemouth. I have entered them on my list. I am afraid I was not clear about South Shields as you say "you are sorry". I only meant I would not go to sea side pleasure places for £5.5; I will always go to the Newcastle Geographical for nothing because I like places like Newcastle & South Shields - that is all.
Hull made itself very charming & the local paper said I was of "quaint but modest appearance" which was grateful & comforting. I have just finished here there were 200 people who could not get in so the L G S is going to catch it from the outcasts.

Yours very truly

M H Kingsley

11 - 12 97

Mary Kingsley 1862–1900

Mary Kingsley died in Africa, having volunteered to nurse prisoners in the Boer War. Working with typhoid patients, she contracted the disease herself. By her own wish, she was left alone to die, and was buried at sea; she was thirty-seven years old. Her life as a traveller had begun scarcely eight years earlier, with the death of her invalid mother in 1892. This left Mary with a small income and freedom to do as she pleased. Although her formal schooling had been sparse, her doctor father had written about his own extensive travels, and she had used his library to teach herself Arabic and Syriac.

She began with a short trip to the Canary Islands to get her bearings, afterwards deciding to concentrate on the West African coast. In the introduction to her second book, *West African Studies* (1899), she claims that her goal is to complete 'a great book my father, George Kingsley, had left at his death unfinished'. Whatever her motive, Mary was immediately entranced by the African peoples. In her four months in Sierra Leone and the surrounding area, she travelled as a lone woman, living with local people and soaking up their culture. She had a generous spirit, along with a quick observational eye and an open mind – 'a mere photographic plate' is her characteristically self-deprecating description.

Determined to return to Africa, Mary spent her time at home in London writing up her journey. Her firm and funny style made *Travels in West Africa* (1897) an immediate success; it netted her £3,000 in its first year of sales. She worked hard to prepare properly for the second trip, making contacts at the British Museum and plans for the identification and collection of flora and fauna. She set off in 1895, landing again in Sierra Leone, but then making her way along the coast and on, by canoe, up the Ogowe (Ogooué) river in Gabon. She was particularly interested in African religion – then often called 'fetish' or 'juju' – and spent time with the Fang people, who were known for their cannibalism:

Mary Kingsley, letter to her lecture agent, 1897

> So I went out … to West Africa where all authorities agreed that Africans were at their wildest and worst. It was no desire to get killed and eaten that made me go. (Preface, *West African Studies*)

The journey only confirmed her love of Africa and Africans. Paddling by night along 'the great, black winding river', under 'star and moonlit heavens', was, for the woman from Islington, the time of her life.

She returned to England as something of a celebrity, and embarked on a series of speaking engagements – although on occasion Victorian mores dictated that her lecture be read out for her by a man as she sat alongside. In the document overleaf, she writes to her lecture agent, Mr Christy. She has put Bath and Bournemouth into her diary, but reassures him that, although

> I would not go to sea side pleasure places for [a fee of] £5 5s, I will always go to the Newcastle Geographical [Society] for that because I like places like Newcastle & South Shields.

Sierra Leone was one thing, but Margate was a step too far!

Kingsley was set on scholarship as well as adventure. She corresponded with Dr E.B. Tylor, a foundational figure in cultural anthropology and the first professor of anthropology at Oxford University. They held differing views on the definition of fetish, with Tylor confining it to those spirits linked to a material object, but Kingsley's experience suggesting something different. In the letter opposite, she writes to Tylor's wife:

> I should much like to ask Dr Tylor if he could give me help in the matter of a class of important spirits that possess the power of becoming incarnate without the link of previously existing matter – in contradiction to the common spirit who must appear in previously existant matter.

Kingsley always takes the indigenous beliefs seriously.

Personally intrepid, she was socially conservative, opposing women's suffrage and horrified by the rumour that she wore trousers on her travels. But she opposed missionaries and colonization, as disrespectful of African culture.

Mary Kingsley, letter concerning African spirits

I should much like to ask Dr Tylor if he could give me help in the matter of a class of important spirits that possess the power of becoming incarnate. without the assistance of previously existing matter – in contradistinction to the common spirit who must appear in previously existant matter – my first named friend I may remark is none of your filmy white man ghosts – but good solid stuff – when he goes he does not leave behind him an ash – like a witch does when by certain proper mediums you have kept him, or her, burning with – his, or her, own light too long. But I defer these questions until you think Dr Tylor is both well enough & willing to deal with them

Sincerely hoping you have both profited much by your Whitby holiday

I remain Yours very truly

M. Kingsley.

FRIDTJOF NANSEN

TELEGRAMADRESSE: NANSEN, LYSAKER

LYSAKER DEN

Dear Sir Aurel, p.t. Haukelid-seter Aug. 3rd 1928

Many thanks for your very kind letter of July 6th, which I just received here in the mountains where I spend my holiday. I am of course keenly interested in your discovery of definite evidence of "desication" in the "tame" deserts of Makran and Kalat, and look much forward to see your description of it. I had the impression that Johan Gunnar Andersson's discovery of a site from the stone-age not very high above present water-level at Koko Nor indicates that there cannot have been any appreciable "desication" since that period in that region, but I have not seen his final description of his discoveries, he only told me about them. There is of course the possibility that conditions may have differed much in different regions. I congratulate you upon your new great work, which again I am sure will mean new remarkable additions to our knowledge about these interesting regions.

Wishing you all possible success and health for your great work I am

Yours very sincerely

Fridtjof Nansen

Fridtjof Nansen 1861–1930

The brutal conditions of polar exploration quickly divided the amateur from the professional; and the difference between the two was often fatal. Of the professionals, few proved themselves as well equipped physically, temperamentally and intellectually for the challenges of the farthest north as Fridtjof Nansen. And yet, although the eight years he spent actively in Arctic exploration made him internationally famous and admired, they were a relatively small part of a remarkable life.

Nansen's fascination with the highest latitudes was born not from nationalism or the adventurer's desire to do the as yet undone, but from science. He set out on his pioneering crossing of Greenland on skis in 1888 only when he had submitted his doctoral dissertation on the neuroanatomy of lower-order marine creatures – an equally pioneering field. His planning for the journey was faultless. He himself was a champion skater and skier, and he recruited only similarly qualified men, including two Sámi from Finland, who were used to survival in extreme conditions. Much of the equipment they were to haul (without dogs) had been specially commissioned and designed. Equally important was his mindset: previous expeditions had travelled west to east, but Nansen thought that the opposite direction – towards habitation – was more likely to succeed. This meant the team could only go forwards; there was no backward route to safety. Crucially, though, he was light on his mental feet; and when adverse conditions suggested a complete change of route part-way through the journey, he didn't hesitate to make it. Forty-nine days after setting out, the six-strong party reached their goal at the Danish settlement of Godthaab (now Nuuk).

Now for the pole itself. From studying artefacts making landfall from a sunken ship, the meteorologist Henrik Mohn had theorized the existence of an ocean current from east to west in the polar sea, and possibly right over the top of the world. But the danger for an expedition ship wishing to

Fridtjof Nansen, letter to Aurel Stein, 1928

harness the current was being trapped and crushed in the winter ice. Once again, Nansen laid careful plans. He commissioned a purpose-built craft that would be pushed up and out of the ice as it formed, sitting almost on top of the frozen sea. *Fram* is still the ship that has travelled both farther north and – after Nansen gave it to Roald Amundsen for his Antarctic journey – farther south than any other.

Begun in 1893, the drifting journey was slow, but by January 1895 *Fram* had beaten the northerly record. Still, Nansen realized that they would only reach the pole on foot, so in March he and Hjalmar Johansen, the expedition's dog-driving expert, set off by sled. By early April they had beaten the previous record latitude, but Nansen also calculated that, if they did not retreat, they would be unable to reach safety. Pragmatism again took precedence over principle, and although the homeward leg took them till September, they made the last part of it on *Fram*, now free from the encircling ice.

Nansen wrote up his best-selling narrative of the journey, *Farthest North*, in only weeks, but publication of the scientific material the voyage had collected was a task of years, during which he established his academic and curatorial career as a leading oceanographer, while also taking a position as a firm advocate of Norwegian separation from Sweden. He was offered various positions in politics, which he declined, although on more than one occasion he acted as a high-level envoy, including travelling to persuade Prince Charles of Denmark to become king of the newly independent Norwegian state.

In the First World War Nansen was active in pursuit of peace, supporting the creation of the League of Nations; he represented Norway at the General Assembly of the League in 1920. He became particularly concerned with the plight of refugees and prisoners of war, of whatever nationality. He developed a 'Nansen passport' to allow stateless persons to cross borders, and his repatriation work for the League was judged to have returned more than 400,000 people to their homelands. In 1922 he was awarded the Nobel Peace Prize, donating his prize money to international relief work. For the rest of his life he worked for the refugee cause, acting on behalf of those displaced by the Russian Revolution, the Greco-Turkish War and the Turkish-Armenian conflict.

Despite his involvement in world affairs, Nansen never relinquished his academic interests. The letter shown here is his second to Sir Aurel Stein, an extraordinary Hungarian-British explorer and archaeologist of the Silk Road, whose travels had taken him along the entire route from China to Pakistan. Stein had sent Nansen a copy of his two most recent articles following in the steps of Alexander the Great on the Indian North-West Frontier. Nansen replies from his holiday in the mountains at Haukeliseter between Oslo and Bergen, although his printed notepaper bears the address of the house he designed for his family at Lysaker, Oslo. The letter discusses the deserts of north India and Pakistan, which Nansen links to studies in Chinese archaeology by Johan Gunnar Andersson, and especially to his finds at Koko Nor, now known as Qinghai Lake. Andersson, a geologist as well as archaeologist, had been part of the Swedish Antarctic Expedition of 1901–3, which may partly explain Nansen's knowledgeable response, 'although I have not seen his final description of his discoveries, he only told me about them'. But the polar regions are also deserts in their own way, and the process of desiccation – drying by wind – is pertinent to their landscape.

Nansen's response to Stein was more than formally generous. In the same year, Stein was nominated as an external member of the Royal Norwegian Academy, an honour he attributed to Nansen's support.

Baghdad Ap. 28 - 1920 Satanism and the world order 70

Dear Professor Gilbert Murray

Will you let me presume on a very long acquaintance to write to you on the subject of an article of yours in the Contemporary, of which certain paragraphs have been conveyed to us by telegram. They are those dealing with the bombing of an Arab village. And if you will still further forgive me I'm not going to mince matters.

The facts as you state them are incorrect & give a wholly wrong – very harmful impression. There is no such thing as bombing at night in this country – I do not think that we should do it if we could, but the choice is not forced upon us, because it would be impossible to do. You can bomb towns by night, but not a small collection of straw huts in a vast & uniform plain – it would be sheer waste of ammunition. Any punishment of the

Gertrude Bell 1868–1926

By 1920, when the letter shown here was written, Professor Gilbert Murray was an internationally known figure. His day job as professor of Greek at Oxford University was only one of his multiple interests. His massive daily correspondence, which is preserved in many dozens of boxes in the Bodleian Library, covers matters as diverse as British and Irish theatre, Liberal politics, the League of Nations and national education policy, as well as Latin translation and Greek drama. All sorts of people sought his knowledge and asked his advice, generally addressing him in the manner of supplicants to the Oracle at Delphi.

Gertrude Bell, the letter writer here, is rather less deferential. Though never less than polite, she has no intention of letting him get away with publishing as fact something on which he is ignorant:

> The facts as you state them are incorrect & give a wholly wrong & very harmful impression. There is no such thing as bombing at night in this country – I do not think that we should do it if we could, but the choice is not forced upon us, because it would be impossible to do. You can bomb London by night, but not a small collection of straw huts in a vast & uniform plain – it would be sheer waste of ammunition.

Bell knew whereof she spoke. Her letter is sent from Baghdad, where she had been made Oriental Secretary by Sir Percy Cox, chief political officer with the British government's Mesopotamian Expeditionary Force – the only woman to hold a formal rank. Her task was liaison with the incoming Arab government in what was to become Iraq, one of the new political structures in the Middle East after the First World War. Bell and another pro-Arab British military adviser, T.E. Lawrence, pressed the claim of a leader of the Arab uprising, Faisal, who was made the first king of the new country.

Gertrude Bell, letter to Gilbert Murray, 1920

Her knowledge of the Middle East was deeply rooted. A woman of restless energy from a wealthy north-eastern family, the athletic Bell was given a good education, which culminated in a first-class degree in history at Lady Margaret Hall, Oxford, which she achieved in only two years. Although women's exam papers at this time were classified, they could not formally be awarded degrees; for the next several years, Bell cast around, looking for an outlet as big as her talents. She travelled in many parts of the world and spent a period as a mountaineer, testing her strength and bravery against the physical challenge of the Alps.

Her knowledge of the East began partly through family connections – the British diplomat Sir Frank Lascelles was her brother-in-law; her love of history, her capacity for languages and her intrepid physical toughness drew her to the archaeology of the region, and for about ten years before the war she took part in and led a series of important excavations in Anatolia, Syria and Mesopotamia, the last of these covering territory unknown to western scholars. Her published accounts of the expeditions, illustrated by her own striking photographs, gained her scholarly attention. During and after the war archaeology remained at the heart of her interests, and after the creation of Iraq she worked for the establishment of a national museum and library in Baghdad.

Bell lived her life according to her own rules, and she had the money and connections to do this. She regularly returned to the family home near Northallerton – but never for very long: her life in the Middle East allowed her a freedom that British society made difficult. She approved of Mary Ward's campaign to get more women into local government, where they could promote the education and welfare of the less well-off; but she was firmly against the idea of women's suffrage and actively supported the Women's National Anti-Suffrage League.

Her altercation with Gilbert Murray ended in conciliation: she asked him to send her some of his books unavailable to her in Baghdad; he explained that his meaning had been misconstrued. They parted as friends.

Gertrude Bell and T.E. Lawrence, Cairo, 1921

Chapter XXII

On this day Feisal asked me if I would wear Arab clothes like his own while in the camp. I would find it better for my own part, since it was a comfortable dress in which to live Arab fashion as we must do. Besides the tribesmen would then understand how to take me. The only wearers of khaki in their experience had been Turkish officers before whom they took up an attitude of instinctive defence. If I wore Meccan clothes like him or like Sharraf they would behave to me as though I were really one of the leaders, and I would be able to slip in and out of his tent without making a sensation which he had to explain away each time to strangers.

para)

I agreed at once, very gladly, for army uniform was abominable for camel-riding or when sitting about on the ground, and the Arab things, which I had learned to manage before the war, were cleaner & more decent in the desert. Hejris was pleased too, and exercised his fancy in fitting me out in splendid white silk and gold-embroidered wedding garments which had been sent to Feisal lately (was it a hint?) by his great-aunt in Mecca. I took a stroll in the new looseness of them round the palm-gardens of Mubarak and Buka, to reaccustom myself to their feel.

These villages were pleasant little places, all built of mud brick on the high earth mounds encircling the palm-gardens. Nakhl Mubarak lay to the north, and Buka just south of it across a thorny valley. The houses were small, mud-washed inside, cool and very clean, furnished with a mat or two, a coffee mortar, and food pots and trays. The narrow streets were shaded by an occasional well-grown tree. In the two villages there might have been five hundred houses, though they were scattered and hidden away beyond my power to judge. The earth embankments round the villages were sometimes fifty feet in height, for the most part artificially formed from the surplus earth dug out between the trees, from house rubbish, and from stones out of the Wadi.

para)

The banks were to defend the cultivated area from the floods of Wadi Yenbo, which otherwise would quickly fill the gardens, since they, to be irrigable, had to be below the level of the valley floor. The narrow plots were divided by fences of palm-ribs or by mud walls, with narrow streams of sweet water flowing in high-level channels round them. Each garden gate was over water, with a bridge to it of three or four parallel palm-logs built up for the passage of donkeys or camels. Each plot had its mud sluice, scooped away when its turn for watering came. The palms, very regularly planted in ordered lines and well cared for, were the main crop, but between the boles were grown barley, radishes, marrows, cucumbers, tobacco and henna. Villages higher up Wadi Yenbo were cool enough to grow grapes.

The views from the little knolls behind our camp were very fine. Rudhwa lay to the north of us, looking about fifteen miles away, with one part or other of it continually wrapped in rain-clouds. It was the biggest feature in sight, and dominated Wadi Yenbo, which was a broad scrub covered plain, relieved by occasional trees and by odd-coloured and odd-shaped rocks projecting from its bed at intervals. All the villages in the main bed were on its northern side, and their water came out in strongly-running springs, a foot or so below the gravel surface of the valley. The sources had been enclosed in narrow stone-lined channels and led underground from place to place as far as they would carry. The Nakhl Mubarak springs the last running water in Wadi Yenbo before it reached the sea.

para)

Above Nakhl Mubarak the valley drew in a little, till it seemed less than two miles wide. It ran north east for some distance to a fork, where the Bugaa branch went off southward from the main stream. Bugaa was half Harb and half Juheina: the villages beyond it, Nijeil and Madsus, with Ain Ali and Shaatha were wholly Harb, like Bir Said. Beyond the fork the country appeared to rise rapidly, and to get mountainous. Buwat itself was said to be on the watershed between Wadi Hamdh and Wadi Yenbo, only twelve miles from the Railway.

After the landing ground was finished I felt that I had better get back to Yenbo, to think seriously about an amphibious defence of its port, for Feisal's stand in Nakhl Mubarak could in the nature of things only be a pause. The Navy had promised its every help at Yenbo, and we settled that I should consult Zeid, and act with him as we thought fit. Also by getting back at once I would meet the aeroplane due next day, and would be able to tell the pilot and observer what I knew of the lie of the country, and where the Turks probably were. In this country of

T.E. Lawrence (Lawrence of Arabia)

1888–1935

'Ned' Lawrence, as he was known to family, was many different men. Was he the illegitimate son of a well-off landowner who won a scholarship to Oxford, or the poor boy who ran away to join the army? Was he Colonel Lawrence, hero of the East, or Private Ross of the RAF Photographic Unit, or even T.E. Shaw of the Tank Corps? Five foot five, he saw himself as a giant among men. Lawrence was a myth-maker about himself as well as a participant in history.

A summer journey to Lebanon and Syria in 1909 led to an undergraduate dissertation on Crusader castles; on graduation, he joined an excavation in Syria, learning the language and culture, and becoming a supporter of Arab independence. After the outbreak of war in 1914, he joined military intelligence in Cairo. With British approval, he took an active part in the Arab uprising against the Ottoman Empire under the emir Faisal, leading the capture of the strategically important port of Aqabah. He blamed himself for what he saw as the subsequent Allied betrayal of the Arabs, who had overthrown the Turks only to be made subject to French control.

Nevertheless, as Colonel Lawrence he attended the 1919 Conference of Versailles as Faisal's adviser and translator, while as a fellow of All Souls College, Oxford, he wrote up his account of the uprising, *Seven Pillars of Wisdom*. The fearless desert traveller lost his first draft while changing trains at Reading station. Rewriting a second from memory, he finally worked up a third, polished version (the Bodleian copy), finished in February 1922.

The manuscript is in an unusual lockable binding, and Lawrence was careful about who might read it. The chapter shown here begins with Faisal's suggestion that Lawrence wear Arab clothing: 'I took a stroll in the new looseness of them round the palm-gardens of Mubarak and Bruka, to reaccustom myself to their feel.' Some of Lawrence's Arab dress is now in the Ashmolean Museum.

T.E. Lawrence, *Seven Pillars of Wisdom*, third draft, 1922

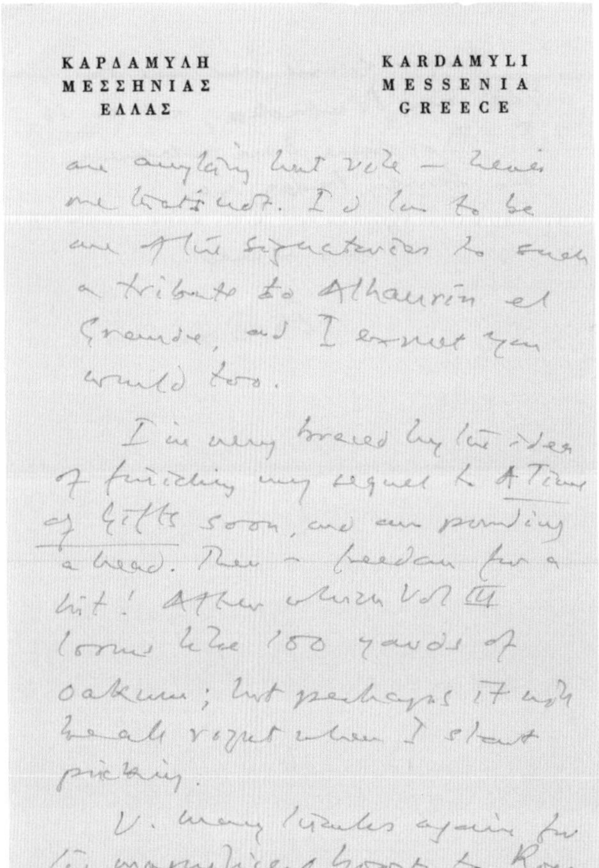
ΚΑΡΔΑΜΥΛΗ
ΜΕΣΣΗΝΙΑΣ
ΕΛΛΑΣ

KARDAMYLI
MESSENIA
GREECE

are anything but vile — believe me that's not. I'd love to be one of the signatories to such a tribute to Alhaurín el Grande, and I expect you would too.

I'm very braced by the idea of finishing my sequel to A Time of Gifts soon, and am pounding ahead. Then – freedom for a bit! After which Vol III looms like 100 yards of oakum; but perhaps it will be all right when I start picking.

V. many thanks again for the magnificent boost to Roger H's book.

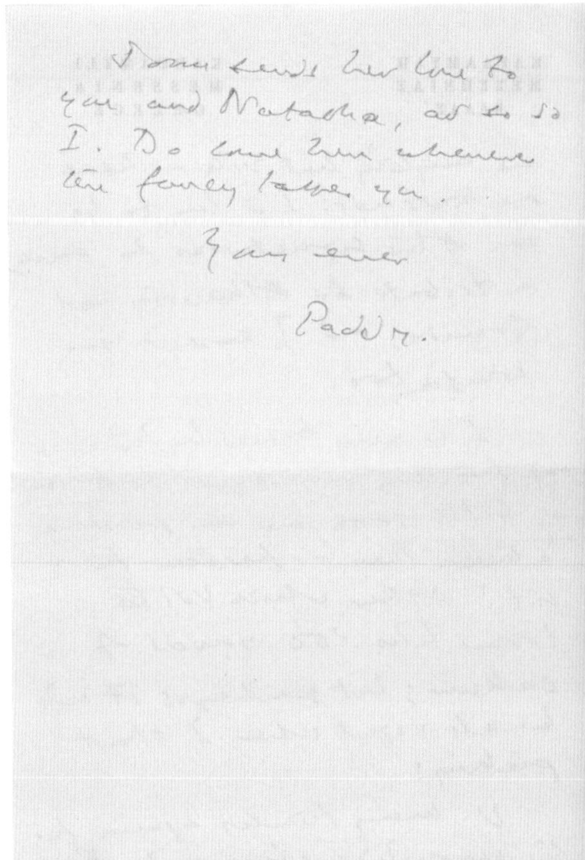
Joan sends her love to you and Natasha, as do I. Do come here whenever the fancy takes you.

Yours ever

Paddy.

Patrick Leigh Fermor 1915–2011

Like his close contemporary Laurie Lee, 'Paddy' Leigh Fermor, as he signs himself in this letter to the poet Stephen Spender, is best known for going for a walk. Lee, from the tiny Gloucestershire village of Slad, set off for Spain, but the more cosmopolitan Leigh Fermor aimed to cross the whole of Europe, ending in Istanbul – or, as he always called it, Constantinople.

Lee supported himself by busking with his violin, but Leigh Fermor – almost equally out of funds – made his way mostly on charm; he could get on with anyone. A lucky encounter transformed his early rough sleeping into a series of beds in castles and aristocratic houses, talking for his supper as he went. But he listened as well as talked, and since the date was 1933, there was plenty to listen to, as he passed through Germany, Austria and points east.

Lee only wrote up his journey, *As I Walked Out One Midsummer Morning*, in 1969, and it was even longer before Leigh Fermor published *A Time of Gifts* (1977), the first volume in a promised trilogy about the journey. It was an instant success, capturing his excitement, recognition of shared culture, and innocence. In the years between, Leigh Fermor's life had been one of wartime adventure and bravery in Greece and Crete, for which he was awarded the Distinguished Service Order (DSO).

Greece was the country of Leigh Fermor's heart. This letter, dated '16? vii 84', is addressed from the house he and his wife, Joan, built in the wild region in the southern Peloponnese, about which he also wrote. Here he claims:

> I'm very braced by the idea of finishing my sequel to A Time of Gifts soon, and am pounding ahead. Then – freedom for a bit! After which Vol III looms like 100 yards of oakum. (Mani 1958)

Oakum picking – pulling apart old rope to make caulking for ships – was a practice common in Victorian prisons and workhouses. Not surprising, then, that volume III was only published posthumously.

Patrick Leigh Fermor, letter to Stephen Spender, 1984

COMPOSERS

57
for Guadagni
Larghetto
Thou art gone upon high
Thou hast led captivity captive
and recei - ved gifts ved gifts for men, yea even for thine

George Frideric Handel 1685–1759

The first performance of *Messiah*, conducted by the composer from the harpsichord, was a benefit performance in aid of prisoners and other good causes, in the New Musick Room, Fishamble Street, Dublin, on 13 April 1742. Seven years later, on 27 May 1749, Handel staged another charity concert, this time in aid of the new chapel at Thomas Coram's Foundling Hospital in Lamb's Conduit Fields in London. A sell-out society event with royal patronage, this first concert featured a newly composed Foundling Hospital anthem and the Fireworks Music, finishing with a showstopper – the Hallelujah Chorus.

We don't know what drew Handel to supporting Coram's foundation, but this was the start of an association that remained important to him for the rest of his life. He presented the new chapel with an organ and marked its inauguration with a performance of *Messiah* in May 1750. This was such a success that he agreed to give a second performance a fortnight later. From then on, Handel gave one or two performances of *Messiah* in the hospital every Easter, and it has been calculated that the oratorio alone raised around £6,000 to support the foundation's work. In return, the hospital concerts established *Messiah* as an audience favourite.

The page opposite is from Handel's original *Messiah* conducting score, which he used for all his performances. Most of the score is written out in a beautifully clear version by his principal copyist, J.C. Smith, but there are some pages (including the one shown here) and numerous notes in the composer's own hand; alterations were necessary depending on the musical forces he had to hand for any one performance.

Handel rewrote the settings of some of the movements for the 1750 performances, including altering 'But who may abide the day of his coming' to the version generally performed today to suit Gaetano Guadagni whose name, along with those of Signora (Caterina) Galli and Miss (Cecilia) Young – all well-known singers – is added by Handel here.

G.F. Handel, *Messiah* conducting score

125
Thema v. J. B.

Clara Schumann 1819–1896

A child prodigy at the piano, who made her debut in Leipzig at the age of nine, Clara Wieck developed into an international virtuoso, teacher and composer, in demand until the end of her life. It was at one of her early concerts that she met her future husband, the composer Robert Schumann, who was so impressed by her playing that he came to take lessons from her piano-teacher father. They married the day before her twenty-first birthday and had eight children.

Nine years older than Clara, in his lifetime Robert was much less successful and appreciated than his wife. She championed his music in her concerts, but always with an eye on what would please the public; alongside her family responsibilities, she managed her career with skill. After Robert's attempted suicide and two-year confinement in an asylum, where she was not allowed to visit him until shortly before his death in 1856, she needed all her considerable talents to maintain both family and career together.

Clara's fame gave the couple a wide circle of friends and acquaintances, in particular the violinist Joseph Joachim, with whom she often played concerts, and the composer Johannes Brahms, whose career they assisted and encouraged. Clara gave many of his works their first public performance, and she chose his *Variations on a Theme by Haydn*, op. 56, arranged for two pianos, as the last piece she played in concert, in 1891.

The album leaf opposite is in the nature of a rather elaborate autograph by Clara – not an uncommon gift at the time. She has written out two lines of a theme from the last movement, Allegretto con variazioni, of Brahms's String Quartet No. 3 in B flat major, op. 67 ('*Thema v. J.B.*'), a piece she especially admired. It was played by a quartet led by Joachim at Clara's house in Berlin, before its first public performance in October 1876.

Clara Schumann, album leaf

Schilflied.
gedichtet von N. Lenau
Andante con moto
p
pp
Sempre piano
Cresc.
pp
Cresc.

Felix Mendelssohn Bartholdy 1809–1847

Felix Mendelssohn was the sort of friend it was a pleasure to have visit. Instead of bringing flowers or wine, he was more likely to write you a little music. When he and his wife, Cécile, stayed with her relatives, the Benecke family, in London in 1842, he left the family a gift that became his *Six Christmas Pieces*, op. 72. The page shown opposite is the beginning of his setting of the fifth of the *Schilflieder* – 'Reed Songs' – by Nikolaus Lenau, written out and illustrated by the composer as a gift for his friend Henrietta Keyl, sometime during the winter of 1844–5. Mendelssohn – talented in drawing and painting as well as music – has matched the words and the watercolour to perfection:

Auf dem Teich, dem regungslosen,	On the lake's unruffled surface
Weilt des Mondes holder Glanz,	The moonbeams linger,
Flechtend seine bleichen Rosen	Weaving their pale roses
In des Schilfes grünen Kranz.	In the green garland of reeds.

Although such gifts of album leaves, meant for inclusion in private collections of music, art and poetry, were common, only one other illustrated example by Mendelssohn survives. It is possible he made this one in return for a drawing that Keyl's son had given to Cécile Mendelssohn the summer before.

Mendelssohn himself was a great compiler of such albums. He began one as a Christmas gift for Cécile in 1836 and continued it after their marriage the next year. This 'Wedding Album', as it is now known, is a treasure trove, containing drawing, painting and music by Mendelssohn himself, pieces by others copied out by him, and poetry and prose in the hands of Goethe, Schiller and Lessing. He has also included a remarkable autograph collection of music by other composers. Mendelssohn himself had been considered something of a child prodigy, playing his first public

Felix Mendelssohn Bartholdy, *Schilflied*

concert around the age of nine, so it is interesting to discover an autograph leaf by that greatest of child musicians, Mozart (his *Allegro in G minor for piano*, K. 312), along with others by Beethoven and Haydn. His prize, however, must have been two leaves containing four choral preludes from the *Orgelbüchlein*, BMV 636, by J.S. Bach, of which the first, 'Vater unser im Himmelreich', is shown here.

Bach spent almost the last thirty years of his life providing music for four of the largest churches in Leipzig, where Mendelssohn was to become conductor of the city's Gewandhaus Orchestra. At a time when Bach's work had fallen out of fashion, Mendelssohn was deeply influenced by his music, having been introduced to it perhaps by an aunt who had been a pupil of Bach's son Wilhelm Friedemann Bach, and who had collected a number of original manuscripts of his works. In Berlin in 1829, he conducted the first performance of the *St Matthew Passion* since Bach's death in 1750 and championed a revival of interest in his music. It's unsurprising, then, that Mendelssohn wanted to include a Bach autograph in the 'Wedding Album' for Cécile. Unfortunately, recent research has decided that the little pieces he acquired are not, in fact, in Bach's own hand, as the album claims, but in that of his pupil and later copyist Christian Gottlob Meissner.

The album tradition continued after Felix and Cécile's wedding. They kept a joint diary recording their honeymoon journey from Frankfurt, travelling up the Rhine, with pen and ink illustrations that appear to be mostly by Felix, although Cécile herself could also draw. Here he illustrates her entry for Tuesday 11 April (1837), when they had reached Strasbourg. She describes their reading newspapers over breakfast, when they were visited by Herr Berg: 'Jeremiah and Jerusalem rolled into one. His Lamentations.' The witty sketch marvellously catches the couple's intimacy, their recognizable breakfast, and their clear unwillingness to put down their (different) newspapers, despite the appearance of Herr Berg and his outsize umbrella.

The extended Mendelssohn family were, like Felix himself, keen collectors, and so a great deal of material from the composer's lifetime has been preserved. Its donation to the Bodleian, however, is a different

Christian Gottlob Meissner, *Choral Prelude* by J.S. Bach

story – one that explains the shelfmark of the material in the Library: M. Deneke Mendelssohn. Felix and Cécile's daughter Marie married Carl Victor Benecke, son of the family for whom he had written *Six Christmas Pieces*. They in turn had a son, Paul, who, along with another Mendelssohn grandchild, Lily Wach, became the custodian of the family papers. Paul lived in Oxford near two musical neighbours, Helena Deneke, a fellow of Lady Margaret Hall, and her sister Margaret, who was an admirer and collector of Mendelssohn's music and memorabilia. The sisters held musical evenings at their home – welcoming Albert Einstein, among others, to play with other accomplished amateurs. Paul came to trust the two women, slowly handing over his own family heirlooms, for safekeeping. To complete the collection, Margaret travelled to Switzerland to meet Lily Wach's daughter Maria, and negotiated the purchase of Mendelssohn material by the Bodleian. At Margaret's death, Helena gave her sister's remarkable collection to the Library, asking that it be known specifically as the M. Deneke Mendelssohn collection, to make it clear that it was Margaret and not she herself who was ultimately responsible for such a generous gift.

Mendelssohn's florid handwriting is itself something of a work of art, and the formation of a number of the letters when he writes in German, although not uncommon for the time, makes it hard to decipher for modern readers used to English letter forms. For example, his *e* looks rather like a small English *n* and his *h* like a cursive *f*, while his final *s* resembles a *b*. In comparison, when he writes in Italian to add the expression marks above the stave, his script is immediately legible.

Felix and Cécile Mendelssohn Bartholdy, honeymoon diary entry, 1837

spielt. Ich gewann einen an
Spinnel Doktor

Elise Lutteroths Geburtstag, wir
schreiben ihr beide zu diesem
angelangt. Am Kaffeetische
stein ... wir ihre Gesundheit.
Mein Unwohlsein am Abend
veranlasst Felix des andern
Morgens

Mittwoch 12ten

zu Mme Passavant zu gehen
um sie nach ihrem Befinden zu
fragen. — Unser Spaziergang
auf den Berge. Felix fand ...

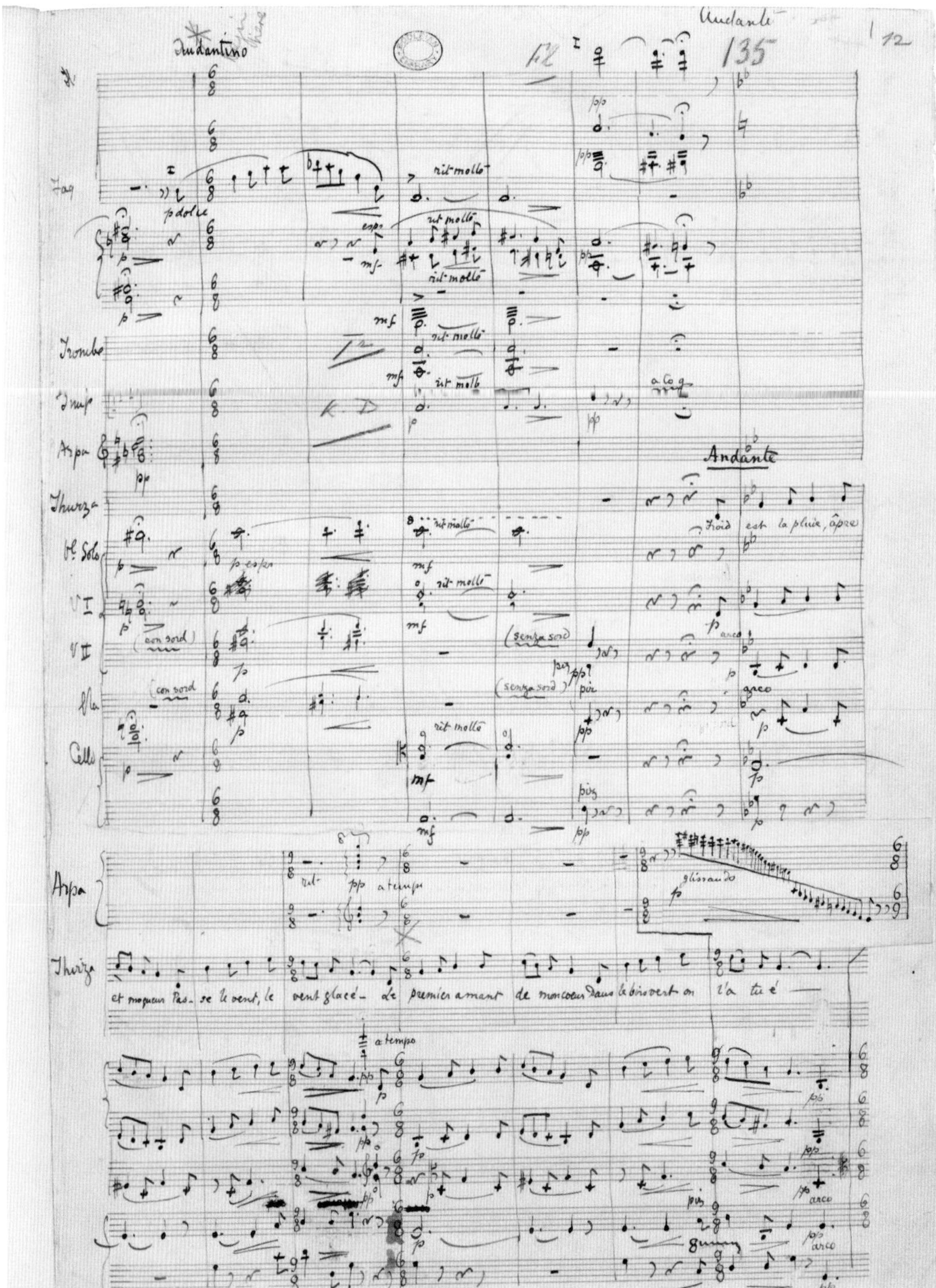

Andantino
12
135
Andante
Fag
p dolce
espr.
rit. molto
mf
Trombe
Timp
pp
Arpa
Thirza
Froid est la pluie, âpre
Vl. Solo
p espr.
VI
VII
con sord
senza sord
pizz
arco
Vla
Cello
glissando
a tempo
et moqueur passe le vent, le vent glacé — Le premier amant de mon coeur dans le bois vert on l'a tué

Ethel Smyth 1858–1944

The opera *The Wreckers* (1902–4) and the suffragette anthem 'The March of the Women' (1910) are probably the two pieces for which Ethel Smyth is best known today. In many ways, they reflect her colourful and unorthodox life – one lived very much on her own terms. *The Wreckers* is a tale of eighteenth-century Cornish lovers who attempt to stop the practice of wrecking – luring ships by false signals onto a rocky shore and plundering their cargo. The couple are discovered and sentenced to death. 'The March of the Women' was written in the two years Smyth spent away from her musical career to campaign for women's suffrage with Emmeline Pankhurst's militant wing of the movement, the Women's Social and Political Union.

Although set in her native country and employing English folk music, *The Wreckers* has a French libretto written by Henry Brewster, the man with whom Smyth spent much of her life from the early 1880s until his death in 1908, although they maintained separate households in separate countries – Smyth in England and Brewster in Italy. Brewster was the husband of Julia Herzogenberg, whose sister Lisl had shared Smyth's life while she was a music student in Leipzig. To add to the complex circle of relations, Smyth's teacher in Leipzig was Heinrich von Herzogenberg, Lisl's husband. According to Smyth's own account, she felt her most passionate engagements to be with women, and she was open about her attraction to them; but Henry Brewster provided a stable foundation, seemingly without jealousy, throughout her somewhat tumultuous and unpredictable emotional life.

The page opposite is from her own corrected autograph score for 'Froid [*sic*] est la pluie' from act I of *The Wreckers*, and the scoring, which includes trombone, harp and flute, gives a sense of the orchestral colour for which she was known. The opera was first performed in Leipzig and Prague in 1906, but was refused by Covent Garden in London until a wealthy American friend provided the backing for a private production conducted by Thomas Beecham (still relatively early in his career) in 1909. Beecham was an admirer

Ethel Smyth, 'Froid [*sic*] est la pluie' from *The Wreckers*

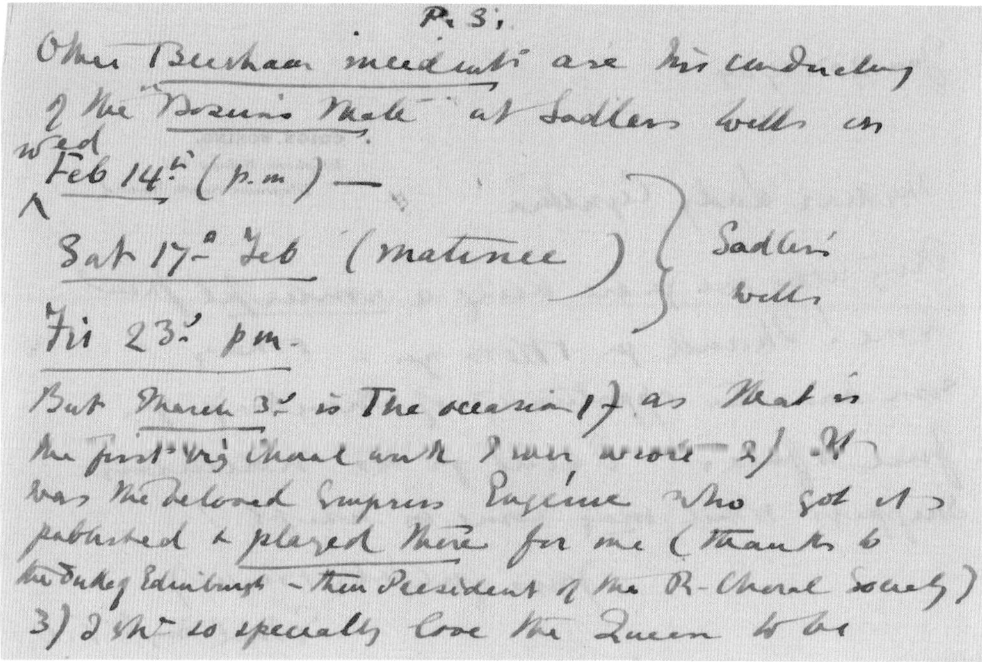

P. 3,

Other Beecham incidents are his conducting of the "Bosun's Mate" at Sadlers Wells on wed Feb 14th (p.m) —

Sat 17th Feb (matinee) } Sadler's Wells

Fri 23rd pm.

But March 3rd is The occasion 1) as that is the first big Choral work I ever wrote — 2) It was the beloved Empress Eugénie who got it published & played there for me (thanks to the Duke of Edinburgh — then President of the R. Choral Society) 3) I shd so specially love the Queen to be

Ethel Smyth, letter concerning her seventy-fifth birthday celebrations

of Smyth's music, and when he was engaged to conduct at Covent Garden in 1910, he included *The Wreckers* in the programme.

Open, adventurous and jolly, Smyth attracted a wide network of friendship and support, especially from women. Her close ties with Mrs Pankhurst led not only to her sabbatical working for women's suffrage and 'The March of the Women', but also to direct action in the form of window smashing and a short term in Holloway prison. She wrote a number of works promoting women's emancipation, including *Female Pipings in Eden* (1933) which included a literary portrait of Pankhurst. In a reply to Lady Cynthia Colville, lady-in-waiting to Queen Mary, she writes:

> I do hope she'll [the Queen] read my "Emmeline Pankhurst" for I expect H[er]. M[ajesty]. has no idea, really, what a magnificent woman she was. A great many people hadn't, of course.

Lady Colville's own letter had been sent to convey the queen's enjoyment of Smyth's *Mass* (1891), which was performed as part of the extensive musical celebrations for her seventy-fifth birthday. Opposite is Smyth's own letter to Lady Colville from 25 January 1934, laying out the planned programme, which included concerts conducted by (now Sir) Thomas Beecham:

> Other Beecham incidents are his conducting
> of the [opera] "Bosun's Mate" at Sadler's Wells on
> Wed. Feb. 14th (p.m.) –
> Sat. 17th Feb (matinee) } Sadler's Wells
> Fri 23rd pm.
> But March 3rd is The occasion 1) as that is the first big Choral
> work I ever wrote 2) It was the beloved Empress Eugénie who
> got it published and played there for me (thanks to the duke of
> Edinburgh – then President of the R[oyal] Choral Society)
> 3) I shd so specially love the Queen to be there when I conduct the
> March of the Women (as grand finale!)

The queen, the duke of Edinburgh, Princess Eugénie, Sir Thomas Beecham – for all Smyth's radicalism and sense of musical neglect, her circle of establishment acquaintance was nevertheless impressive.

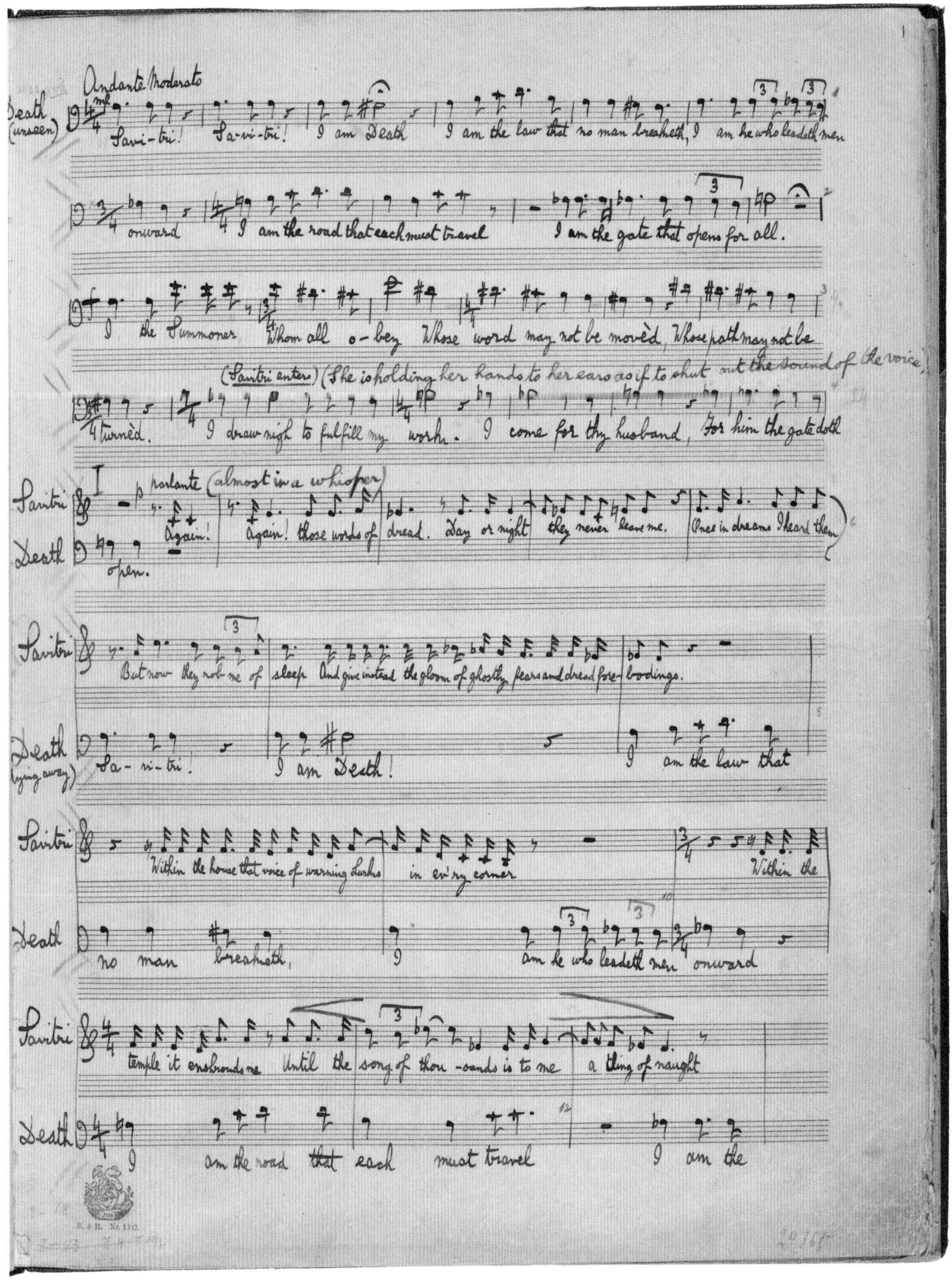Andante Moderato
Death (unseen)
Savi-tri! Sa-vi-tri! I am Death I am the law that no man breaketh, I am he who leadeth men
onward I am the road that each must travel I am the gate that opens for all.
I the Summoner Whom all o-bey Whose word may not be movèd, Whose path may not be
(Savitri enters) (She is holding her hands to her ears as if to shut out the sound of the voice)
turnèd. I draw nigh to fulfill my work. I come for thy husband, For him the gate doth
Savitri
parlante (almost in a whisper)
Again! Again! those words of dread. Day or night they never leave me. Once in dreams I heard them
Death
open.
Savitri
But now they rob me of sleep And give instead the gloom of ghostly fears and dread fore-bodings.
Death (dying away)
Sa-vi-tri! I am Death! I am the law that
Savitri
Within the house that voice of warning lurks in ev'ry corner Within the
Death
no man breaketh, I am he who leadeth men onward
Savitri
temple it enshrouds me Until the song of thou-sands is to me a thing of naught
Death
I am the road that each must travel I am the

Gustav Holst 1874–1934

Unlike his friend, Ralph Vaughan Williams, who was a relatively late musical bloomer, Gustav Holst came from a family of musicians and was earning money as an organist and choirmaster by the time he was seventeen. His first operetta was performed when he was nineteen, and its success persuaded his father to fund Gustav's studies at the Royal College of Music in London.

Although music was always the centre of his life, Holst had wide political and intellectual interests. He joined the Kelmscott House – home of William Morris – Socialist Club and was the conductor of the Hammersmith Socialist Choir; the slow movement of his *Symphony in F*: 'The Cotswolds' (1900) is an elegy in memory of Morris. For much of his life, however, he was a music teacher in London, making a living as a schoolmaster in private schools while also teaching at the Passmore Edwards Settlement and Morley College for working men and women.

Holst had become interested in Hindu mysticism and spirituality in his early twenties, learning Sanskrit so that he could study texts in the original language. In 1906 he completed a three-act opera, *Sita*, based on his own translation of the Ramayana, and it was followed by *Three Vedic Hymns*, again from his translations of the Rig Veda.

The pages shown here are from Holst's second Sanskrit opera, *Sāvitri*, op. 25, completed in 1908 and first performed at the London School of Opera in 1916. Once again with a libretto from Holst's own translation, this time from the Mahābhārata, *Sāvitri* is a one-act chamber piece with a running time (as the score records) of about thirty minutes. An allegory of the power of love to overcome death, the opera concerns the encounter of a faithful wife, Sāvitri, who outsmarts the character of Death, who has come for her husband Satyavān, a woodsman. She persuades Death that he can take Satyavān if he will also grant her one desire – which is that she is to

left and overleaf Gustav Holst, notes to Sanskrit opera, *Sāvitri*, 1908

have her own life in all its fullness. Death agrees, only for Sāvitri to claim that her own happiness is impossible without Satyavān by her side.

In his 'NOTE' preceding the score, Holst lays out his ideal conditions for performance, which include an open-air setting, a small orchestra and four-part female chorus, both hidden from the audience. Death, 'a tall vigorous man with shaven head', 'may be surrounded by a dull red glow whenever it can be arranged quietly and unostentatiously but this is by no means essential'.

The guard book in which the score is kept also contains a letter from Holst, dated 4 July 1928 and sent from St Paul's Girls' School, where he was director of music, which explains how the Library came to acquire the music. In 1925, Sir Michael Sadler, first chairman of the newly established Friends of the Bodleian, wrote to a number of living writers and composers, inviting them to contribute autograph material to bolster the Library's modern collections. It was a successful campaign. Holst replies to say he is honoured by the request and regrets only that he cannot send a later work, adding, 'Perhaps you would allow me to do so in the future.' He was as good as his word: in 1931 he donated the score of *A Choral Fantasia*, a setting of words by Robert Bridges, and now kept in the Library as MS. Don. c. 21.

NOTE. This piece is intended for performance in the open air or else in a small building.

No curtain is required.

The orchestra consists of two string quartets, a contra bass, two flutes and an English Horn.

There is also a hidden (of female voices) chorus in four parts.

They are to sing throughout to the sound of 'u' in 'sun'.

Conductor, chorus and orchestra are to be invisible to the audience.

When performed out of doors, there should be a long avenue or path through a wood in the centre of the scene.

Death (who first appears at the further end of this path) is to be represented as a tall vigorous man with shaven head, dressed in a long robe.

He may be surrounded by a dull red glow whenever it can be arranged quietly and unostentatiously but this is by no means essential.

→ 2

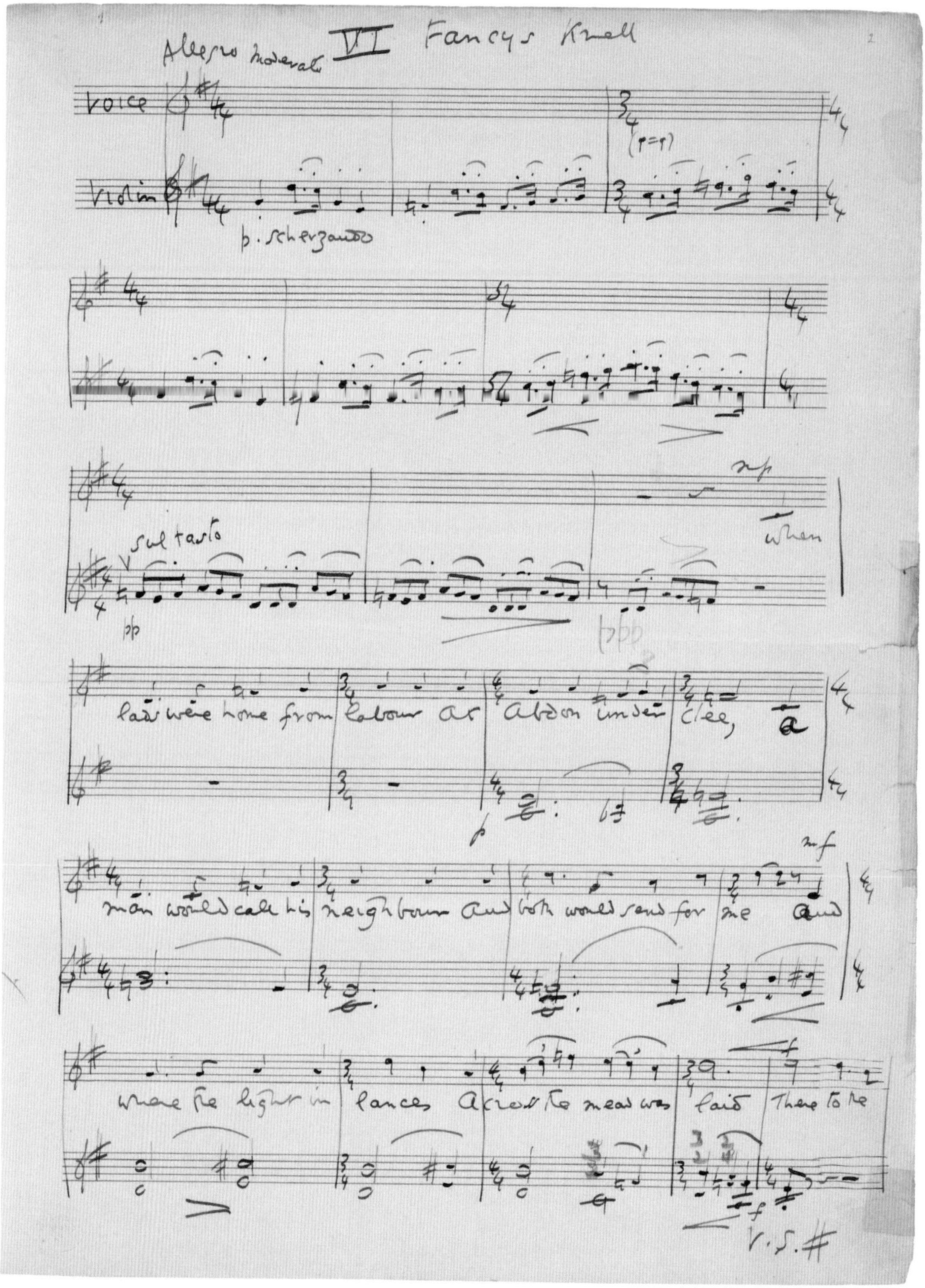
Allegro moderato
VI Fancy's Knell
Voice
Violin
p. scherzando
sul tasto
pp
ppp
mp
When
lads were home from labour at Abdon under Clee, a
man would call his neighbour and both would send for me and
mf
where the light in lances across the mead was laid There to the
f
V.S.

Ralph Vaughan Williams 1872–1958

For all his success in large-scale composition, it is perhaps in the art of song that the music of Ralph Vaughan Williams is still most loved. It was with songs such as 'Linden Lea' (1901; his earliest published work) and his setting of Robert Louis Stevenson's *Songs of Travel* (1904) that he first made his name. In 1904 he became the editor of *The English Hymnal*, revising many old harmonies and writing new tunes, and its publication in 1906 cemented his reputation and gave him enormous – and lasting – influence on generations of singers. The hymnal moved the Church of England decisively away from the Victorian sentiments of *Hymns Ancient and Modern* into a new world of musical sophistication.

Much of the music is strongly evocative of the English landscape; indeed, in some ways it shaped the way that landscape could be viewed. Vaughan Williams was a collector and admirer of folk-songs. For libretti, he often employed contemporary poetry, more than once mining A.E. Housman's collection, *A Shropshire Lad*. 'Fancy's Knell', shown here, is one of a set of songs (originally nine, but later published as eight) for voice and violin composed in 1927 from Housman's text:

> When lads were home from labour
> At Abdon under Clee,
> A man would call his neighbour
> And both would send for me.
> And where the light in lances
> Across the mead was laid,
> There to the dances
> I fetched my flute and played.

As the page makes clear, the violin accompaniment, in the lower of each pair of lines of music, is written as a jaunty, almost Celtic folk-song rhythm, while the voice, when it enters, has longer, more wistful lines.

Ralph Vaughan Williams, 'Fancy's Knell', 1927

16th. I find it very easy to work up here – & as we are having grand hospitality the going is cheap! 8

Incidentally we have been discussing plans & have decided that (i) we must get our papers in order, which means quota & Cuba (ii) we must therefore be in the centre of things & must live in New York – so we shall be hopping it round Manhattan soon. I think it's wise, don't you, in these days, when one must be on the spot.

Auden has been in Hollywood & has made some excellent contacts for him & me (& Christopher Isherwood who is on contract there now) to do a musical film. His agent is Mrs. Edna SCHLEY [10480 Troon Avenue, Los Angeles, (Ardmore: 86201)] and the man he is in contact with is Mr. McKenna, M.G.M Story department. Could you tell this to Schulhoff & get him to follow it up with Abe Meyer of MCA? I feel there's something there.

Do let me have a line here. We don't go east till Thursday.

All the best,
yours.
Ben

greetings from
Auden & Peter.

Benjamin Britten 1913–1976
Peter Pears 1910–1986

For almost forty years, Benjamin Britten and Peter Pears shared a personal partnership that was the foundation of a remarkable musical collaboration. Pears's voice was the inspiration for much of Britten's composition; Britten, in turn, was Pears's most sympathetic piano accompanist. By the time of his death in 1976, Britten was a Companion of Honour, had been awarded the Order of Merit and was the first British composer to be made a life peer, and Pears had been knighted. For two openly gay men to be honoured in this way, when homosexuality was illegal in the United Kingdom until 1967, was a recognition of their international importance in music.

The two men met in April 1937, sorting the papers of a mutual friend who had been killed in an accident. By the following year they were sharing a flat, and together left England for North America in May 1939. The next three years, spent mainly in the United States, cemented their relationship but drew much subsequent criticism that they had deserted Britain and avoided the war. Both Britten and Pears were pacifists and conscientious objectors (Pears had Quaker ancestry), but they were also hoping to reach a more adventurous and appreciative musical audience. Their friends W.H. Auden and Christopher Isherwood were already trying their luck across the Atlantic.

Britten and Pears were staying with Auden in Williamsburg, Massachusetts, in September 1940 when Britten wrote the letter shown opposite to Ralph Hawkes of Boosey & Hawkes, his music publisher. For much of their time in the United States, the couple lived as guests of American supporters, and particularly at the home of Dr William Mayer and his wife Elizabeth, in Amityville, New York, whom Pears had met four years earlier. Britten notes, 'as we are having grand hospitality the going is cheap!' But they needed to earn a living and thought they 'must be on the spot', which would entail a shift to Manhattan. For a short period that winter they moved to Brooklyn and a shared house with Auden and others;

Benjamin Britten, letter to Ralph Hawkes, 1940

but the arrangement was not a success, and they carried on to California, where Britten hoped he might get work in Hollywood:

> Auden has been in Hollywood & has made some excellent contacts for him and me (& Christopher Isherwood who is on contract there now) to do a musical film.

Auden and Britten had earlier collaborated on two striking British documentary films, *Coal Face* (1935) and *Night Mail* (1936), but nothing seems to have come of this Hollywood venture.

The letter also mentions the need 'to get our papers in order, which means quota & Cuba'. The influx of Jewish refugees from Germany was causing the United States to impose restrictions on how many immigrants it would accept from Europe. Movement within the Americas, however, was still allowed, and the pianist Paul Wittgenstein, for whom Britten wrote a new work, was attempting to secure a visa by that route. Britten and Pears were clearly thinking to try the same approach.

For all the initial excitement, the possibilities offered by America could not overcome the draw of Britten's Suffolk roots, and he and Pears returned to settle in Aldeburgh in 1942. The war over, in 1946 Ralph Hawkes proposed a return to the States for a performance by the English soprano Maggie Teyte of Britten's song cycle *Les illuminations*, along with a Britten–Pears recital. The two men independently wrote to Hawkes to decline the invitation, as Pears's reply shown opposite notes:

> Ben is writing to you at this moment too, and our letters may contain a good deal of similar material, but we have in fact quite individually had the same reactions – In the first place, I am not at all keen on singing in America as such – I had enough of it before to know their standards of artistic judgments, exacting in some ways and quite naïve and absurd in others.

The decision was coloured by their recent return from a successful concert tour in Belgium and the Netherlands. For the foreseeable future, they determined to turn their attention to Europe.

Peter Pears, letter to Ralph Hawkes, 1940

persuade us to go. Ben is writing to you at this moment too, and your letters may contain a good deal of similar material, but we have in fact quite individually had the same reactions – In the first place, I am not at all keen on singing in America as such – I had enough of it before to know their standards of artistic judgments, exacting in some ways and quite naive and absurd in others – I feel very much more drawn to and

WRITERS FOR CHILDREN

Ch. Ch. Nov. 2/96 22

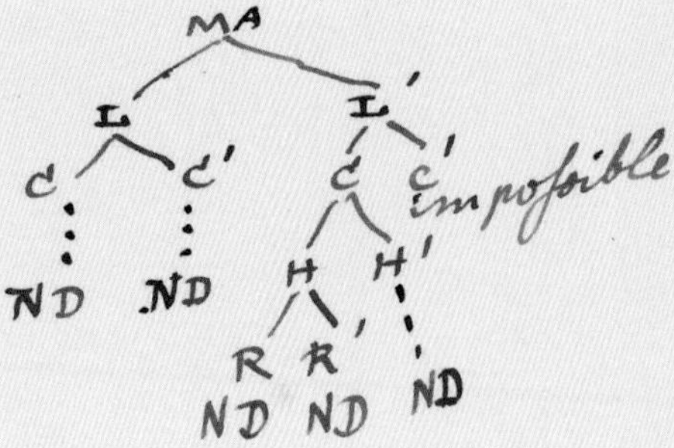

My dear Wilson,

Did you intend the diagram, here copied, as your Solution of the "Pork-Chops"? If so, I fear I must plead inability to understand! I presume the dots mean serieses of Premisses: but *what* Premisses I haven't the least idea. Would you give me the reference-numbers for the Soriteses by which you prove your Conclusion? Truly yours,

C.L.D.

Ch. Ch. Oxford 42

Dec. 20/96

My dear Wilson,

In a certain Library,

(1) All the old books are Greek;

(2) All the quartos are bound;

(3) None of the poets are old quartos.

Let a = bound; b = Greek; c = old;

d = poetry; e = quartos.

Would you favour me with your opinion as to what conclusions, if any, can be drawn from these data?

Very truly yours,

C. L. Dodgson.

CE ~ ABD'

or D ~ either C'E' or BE' or AC'

or D ~ either C'E' or B or A

Lewis Carroll 1832–1898
John Tenniel 1820–1914

Literature for children can often be read on a variety of levels, and perhaps nowhere more so than in the Alice stories of Lewis Carroll. Adult admirers poring over *Alice's Adventures in Wonderland* (1865) and *Through the Looking-Glass, and What Alice Found There* (1871) have discovered within them a wealth of puzzles, paradoxes and metaphysical conundrums that form a hidden system worlds away from a childish entertainment. The existence of this second level of reading may be unsurprising, given that Lewis Carroll was the pen name of Charles Lutwidge Dodgson, mathematics fellow at Christ Church, Oxford, and a specialist in symbolic logic. Indeed, even his pseudonym was a playful game: he left out his surname, Latinised his first name – Charles to Carolus – and anglicized, via Latin, his Germanic second – Lutwidge to Ludovicus to Lewis. A swift reversal of order, and the shy don had disappeared, leaving behind only a smile.

Dodgson was a talented mathematician and logician. The notes shown opposite are part of his professional correspondence with his brilliant colleague John Cook Wilson, Wykeham Professor of Logic at Oxford from 1889. Wilson acted as sounding board and tester for the problems that were to make up Dodgson's planned three volumes on *Symbolic Logic* (part I, 1896; part II, posthumous). An elementary book, *The Game of Logic*, to teach children how to enjoy and solve logical puzzles, had been published by Dodgson a decade earlier. Dodgson sent Wilson the sample exercises he'd created to illustrate a range of logical systems and techniques, and Wilson would try to solve them, spotting the errors, pointing out places where the text was unclear, and making suggestions of his own. Wilson was also cast in the role of straight man, since Dodgson, in the long tradition of logical problems that dates back to the Greeks, tried to keep his readers' interest by concocting a variety of off-beat illustrations. Several letters, like the first shown opposite, consider 'The Pork-Chops Problem',

Lewis Carroll, logic problems for John Cook Wilson, 1896

for example. The second note preserves Wilson's proposed solution to another donnish scenario: we can see his superscript letters identifying the key premises in the problem, and his symbolic formulation of it in the lower left corner.

Lewis Carroll was as serious about his fiction as Charles Dodgson was about his mathematics, and the illustrations for the Alice text were as important to him as the examples illustrating his academic work. As it turned out, just as John Cook Wilson would be a critical collaborator for *Symbolic Logic*, so John Tenniel, celebrated political cartoonist for *Punch*, was an inspired choice for *Alice*. The relationship between text and image has become so close that it is impossible to think of Dodgson's stories without their accompanying Tenniel illustrations.

The pages shown here are part of a letter from Tenniel to 'Dear Mr Dodgson' dated 8 March 1865. Carroll has evidently queried the placing of one of the drawings and, although Tenniel cannot see the problem himself, he is happy for it to be moved. The innovative layout of the book, with text and images intertwined on the pages, was one of its most striking features. At this point, the text of the book is clearly still in flux, since Tenniel asks if he can borrow 'A Mad Tea-Party' for a day or two, so he can refine his illustration: 'There is much more in it than my copy contains.' Everyone familiar with the book will recognize the subjects Tenniel has chosen to depict: 'The Hatter' and 'The March Hare and The Hatter, putting the Dormouse into the tea-pot'. 'We now want an intermediate one,' he says, 'but I don't think "Twinkle twinkle" will do, as it comes close upon the first subject , ie, in my copy.' Here again, Tenniel draws attention to the fact that he is working from an unfinished text, but, as a political cartoonist, tight deadlines must have been his bread and butter.

In 1880 Dodgson discovered that his identity as Lewis Carroll had been unmasked by overzealous cross-referencing in the Bodleian's catalogue of printed books, and applied to the Library curators to have the link removed. They refused.

John Tenniel, letter to Charles Dodgson concerning the illustrations to *Alice's Adventures in Wonderland*

104c

Could you manage to let me have the text of "A mad Tea-party" for a day or two? There is much more in it than my copy contains.
The subjects I have selected from it are – The Hatter asking the riddle; which will do equally well for any other question that he may ask; and can go anywhere: – and – The March Hare and the Hatter, putting the Dormouse into the tea-pot.
We now want an intermediate

104d

one, but I don't think "Twinkle twinkle" will do, as it comes close upon the first subject, i.e. in my copy.

In great haste
Yours very sincerely
J Tenniel

P.S. I am very glad you like the new pictures.

WELL HALL,
ELTHAM,
KENT.

30 June 1910

Dear Miss Sharp,

I am sorry I cannot sign the enclosed Memorial as it does not embody my views. I am for adult Suffrage, but primarily my political interest is all for Socialism, and I do not wish Socialism to be endangered by an extension of the franchise to a class of women mainly Conservative.

Yours sincerely -

E. Nesbit Bland

E. Nesbit 1858–1924

Edith Nesbit was the author of a number of classic children's stories, including *The Railway Children*, *The Phoenix and the Carpet* and *Five Children and It*. She created a rich seam of adventure, magic and utopian fantasy not so far, perhaps, from her own life story. Edith abandoned her fiancé in favour of Hubert Bland, one of the founders of the socialist Fabian Society. Politically aware, she also joined the Fabians and became an 'advanced woman', cutting her hair and abandoning restrictive corsets for flowing Liberty print dresses. She was advanced, too, in having to be the breadwinner of the family: the success of her writing paid the bills.

Like Beatrice and Sidney Webb, Edith and Hubert were known as a radical couple. So it was not surprising that Evelyn Sharp, of the suffragette Women's Social and Political Union (WSPU), wrote to ask for Edith's support for the Conciliation Bill currently going through Parliament. The Bill proposed that women be given the vote on the same terms as men – meaning that all those who owned or rented property to the value of £10 or more would be eligible. This property qualification, as it was known, disenfranchised about 40 per cent of adult males, and many who supported women's suffrage thought that agreeing the same for women was not the way forward.

In her reply, signed 'E. Nesbit Bland', Edith makes her views most definitely known. She supports adult suffrage but cannot add her name here because it would enfranchise only the better-off women in society – those, she assumes, who would be more likely to vote Conservative and endanger the advancement of socialism.

The Conciliation Bill was successfully introduced into Parliament as a private member's bill in May 1910. Edith's letter shown here, dated 13 June, reflects the WSPU working behind the scenes to amass support that might persuade Asquith's Liberal government to turn it into law. They were not successful.

E. Nesbit, letter to Evelyn Sharp, 1910

19

16, Durham Villas, Campden Hill. W.

12th August, 1907.

Dear Robinson

The Water-Rat put out a neat little brown paw, & gave Toady a big hoist & a pull, over the edge of the hole, & there was Mr. Toad at last, standing safe & sound in the hall, covered with mud, & with the water streaming off him, but pleased & happy at being in a friend's house at last after so many perilous adventures. "O Ratty!" he cried, "I've been having such times, you can't think! Such dangers, such escapes, and all through my own cleverness! Been in prison – got out of it! Been thrown into a canal – swam ashore! Stole a horse – sold him for a pocketful of money! O I _am_ a

Kenneth Grahame 1859–1932
Alan Bennett 1934–

Tracking a process of transformation is always absorbing, as stories from *The Ugly Duckling* to *The Very Hungry Caterpillar* bear witness. The Bodleian is fortunate that important donations from two authors, Kenneth Grahame and Alan Bennett, make it possible to follow the development of a much-loved classic, *The Wind in the Willows*, from a series of letters written to keep a promise, to a brilliant Christmas show for children at the National Theatre in London.

For much of his life, Kenneth Grahame combined a responsible position at the Bank of England alongside some success as a writer, and it was not until he was forty years old that he married Elspeth Thomson. A year later their only child, Alastair – known as Mouse – was born prematurely. Mouse was not physically strong, but Grahame was a devoted father, and the two especially enjoyed sharing the bedtime stories that Grahame wove around animals of his son's choosing. When, in May 1907, Mouse was to travel to the seaside resort of Littlehampton for a restorative holiday with his governess, he agreed to go only on condition that Daddy would continue the stories in regular letters. Miss Stott, the governess who read the instalments aloud to Mouse, kept the letters safe, and passed them to Elspeth, who preserved the continuing tale about a mole and a water rat, a badger and a toad.

The letters are initially addressed to 'My dearest Mouse', but part-way through the summer, Alastair decided he would like to be known as Michael Robinson – a change reflected in the salutation of the letter shown here. The letter gets straight down to business, taking up the story *in medias res* – and indeed Grahame often didn't bother with a valediction, simply ending on that enticing phrase, 'To be continued'. At the point where we join the story, Toad has escaped from prison by disguising himself as a washerwoman and, with the help of a bargee and his horse, has made his way back to his friends on the riverbank. Ratty – surely the

Kenneth Grahame, letter to his son, 'Robinson', 1907

kindest of the four – takes him in, wet and muddy as he is, only for Toad, characteristically, to relate his adventures not as a series of disastrous scrapes of his own making, but as a triumphant tale of his particular cleverness in overcoming adversity.

Reworked in the novel, the episode appears under the ironic title (taken from a poem by Tennyson, *The Princess: Home they Brought her Warrior Dead*), 'Like Summer Tempests came his Tears'. The narrative is slightly expanded and the language adapted for an audience somewhat older than Mouse had been. The character of Toad is also slightly heightened, his boasting even more exaggerated. But the relationship of the two versions is instantly recognizable and they are essentially the same.

Kenneth Grahame himself had not been able to afford to study at Oxford University, although he went to school in the city, and Mouse was, for two years until his early death in 1920, an Oxford undergraduate. They are buried together in Oxford's Holywell Cemetery. Grahame's affection for the city was shown in an extraordinarily generous bequest of his residuary estate, including all the royalties from his works, to be used for the benefit of the Bodleian Library, subject only to Elspeth's life interest. She was especially fond of *The Wind in the Willows* manuscript and kept it, along with the collection of letters to Mouse, for ten years after Grahame's death. Finally, however, in 1943, she presented both to the Library, which bound *The Wind in the Willows* in two distinctive blue leather volumes, with a gold scallop shell decoration, part of the Grahame family crest.

The material in the letters forms about a third of the final text, which was published in 1908, with illustrations by E.H. Shepard added in the 1931 edition. *The Wind in the Willows* was not immediately successful with the critics, who found the animal protagonists rather avant-garde (the *Times Literary Supplement* of 22 October 1908 commented, 'as a contribution to natural history the work is negligible'), but the reading public had other ideas. Shepard's illustrations were a definite addition to the book's charm. He later illustrated another children's classic, A.A. Milne's *Winnie-the-Pooh* (1926), and the triangle was completed when Milne, captivated by Grahame's tale, turned part of it into a play for children, *Toad of Toad Hall* (1929).

Kenneth Grahame, *The Wind in the Willows*

'Like Summer Tempests came his Tears'

The Rat put out a neat little brown paw, gripped Toad firmly by the scruff of the neck, & gave a great hoist & a pull; & the water-logged Toad came up slowly but surely over the edge of the hole, till at last he stood safe & sound in the hall, streaked with mud & weed to be sure, & with the water streaming off him, but happy & high-spirited as of old, now that he ~~stood~~ found himself once more in the house of a friend, & dodgings & evasions were over, & he could lay aside a disguise that was unworthy of his position & wanted such a lot of living up to.

"O Ratty!" he cried. "I've been ~~having~~ through such times since I saw you last, you can't think! Such trials, such sufferings, & all so nobly borne! Then such escapes, such disguises, such subterfuges, & all so cleverly planned & carried out! Been in prison — got out of it, of course! Been thrown into a canal — swam ashore! Stole a horse — sold him for a large sum of money! 130

The continuing appeal of the four friends and their triumph over the Wild Wooders was confirmed by Alan Bennett's adaptation of the book as a Christmas production for the National Theatre in London in December 1990. Just as Grahame donated the copyright in his works to the Library, Bennett has given his literary papers, as an 'obligation paid' for receiving a free education from the state. His working notes for the theatre programme show him posing to himself some interesting questions about the characterization of Toad. 'There is something of [Oscar] Wilde in Toad', he writes, 'and not only in his trial and disgrace. Toad like Wilde is not an ordinary individual':

> It occurred to me when I had read the book that Grahame meant Toad to be Jewish. Grahame had endowed him with all the faults that genteel Edwardian anti-semitism attributed to nouveaux-riche Jews – he was loud, he showed off, he had too much money for his own good and he had no sense of social responsibility.

This early typescript draft of Bennett's script, with handwritten alterations, has reached the same episode as the letters and the novel, with the heading: 'Toad arrives Back/Like Summer tempests came his tears'. Bennett has kept some of the distinctive phrasing from the book, but has exaggerated the character even further, with Toad's disguise as the washerwoman providing the children in the audience with a definite touch of the pantomime dame. For the adults, however, his 'frock' offers the possibility of cross-dressing, which Ratty, sending Toad upstairs for 'a choice of tweeds', clearly finds distinctly uncomfortable. There are perhaps elements in Bennett's reading of the riverbank that would have surprised Kenneth Grahame.

Alan Bennett, draft play script of *The Wind in the Willows*

~~Toad Arrives Back/Like Summer tempests came his tears.~~

Toad — OhRatty.How good it is to see you,you dear old thing.

Rat — Toad.What are you dressed in ? Is it..is it..a <u>frock</u>?

Toad — Oh this? Yes.It's rather becoming,don't you think ?

Rat — ~~Dear oh dear~~.Toad.Toad. What has happened to you?

Toad — ~~Now don't start~~ Now don't start shaking your head at me so soon, Ratty. ~~I've not been back five minutes before you're~~

I've not been back two minutes and you're already wanting to tell me off. When you hear what I've been through I think you'll change your tune – the trials & hardships, the suffering and the hunger – oh the <u>hunger</u> – but all of it Ratty so nobly borne, so patiently endured. And then, triumph out of tragedy, escapes, disguises – cleverly planned, impeccably executed. I humbugged everybody. ~~Even~~ When you hear it, Ratty, even you will have to agree I am a very smart Toad.

~~a smart Toad~~.

Enter Badger,very unkempt,having been up all night on patrol.

Badger — Is that Toad ?

Welcome home,Toad.Alas,what am I saying ? Home indeed.Oh unhappy Toad.This is a poor homecoming.

Shaking his head Badger goes and sits at the table and eats a porkpie.

Toad — What on earth's the matter with him. Unhappy Toad ? Why,I've never felt more cheerful in my life..

Rat — ~~Take~~ Don't say anything,not just yet.He's always rather low and despondent when he,s wanting his ~~victuals~~ dinner

Toad — I thought you,d all be so pleased to see me. I'm very pleased to see you.

Rat — I would be more pleased to see you,Toad if you were dressed in something a little more fitting. The first thing to do is to go upstairs and take off that female garment and get into something decent. Look in my wardrobe and you''ll find a choice of tweeds.

Toad — But..

have sailed my little ship to Riga and laid her up for the winter. the end of October I hope to be in England for a week or two, when I shall look for Evelyn Mansions. Till then, Good luck,

Yacht RACUNDRA,
At anchor in Hapsal Roads,
ESTHONIA.
September 10.1922.

Your tarry-handed friend,

a.R.

My dear Ric,

The WORM arrived in time to be the first book planted in the bookshelves of RACUNDRA. That was a month ago. I was sleeping on board surrounded by devilish carpenters driving them with cozening bribes and foul language. Finally I kicked them out, and we put to sea unfinished. In the intervals of strife I read the WORM. We put to sea, and sailed from Riga to the Island of Runo, from there to Reval, from Reval to Helsingfors in Finland, from Helsingfors in a hairy storm back to Reval, from Reval to Baltic Port in a calm, thence against contrary winds to Spithamn, thence to Ramsholm, then (great triumph of navigation) against a violent wind through the intricate channel of Nucke and Worms Island (observe the name) to Hapsal, and here we lie awaiting a northerly wind to hurry southwa before winter.

I need not tell you how enormously I rejoiced in the WORM. I may be a bad book or a good one. I am no judge, because I am its predestined reader. I kept recognising landmarks with exultation as I read. The belly traverse on Castle Crag Borrowdale appeared again all glorious in my mind during a certain chapter, and throug odd memories of old exercise books and theatrical designs carried

Arthur Ransome 1884–1967

Anchored in the Lake District after a life of adventure around the world, tubby retired pirate Captain Flint – also known as the Amazons' Uncle Jim – was Arthur Ransome's portrait of himself in his *Swallows and Amazons* stories for children. 'Mixed Moss, by a Rolling Stone' was the memoir keeping the Captain chained to his typewriter and at the mercy of his publisher. And so might readers picture Ransome himself, in his Coniston cottage, faced with nothing more dangerous than a sail across the lake on a stormy day.

But in 1922, when he wrote the letter shown here, Ransome's life was much more piratical. In 1913 he had travelled to Russia to collect folk tales (and escape an unhappy marriage), and had found himself caught up in the Bolshevik Revolution. He got to know many of the actors in the events and became a reporter, sending dispatches back to Britain. He fell in love with Trotsky's secretary, Yevgenia Shelepina. MI6, it's now thought, made contact, and he was recruited to intelligence; whether he fulfilled the same role for the Bolsheviks has also been a matter for speculation.

In 1919, with the war and the revolution over, and now working for *The Manchester Guardian*, Ransome and Yevgenia moved to 'Esthonia' (as he spells it here) and bought a boat. He had learned to sail on Coniston Water as a child, and being afloat was one of the chief pleasures of his life. Having his own boat would restore normality to a topsy-turvy world.

After a couple of false starts, Ransome commissioned a new craft especially suited to Baltic conditions, and on 20 August 1922, *Racundra* set sail. The book he wrote about the voyage, *Racundra's First Cruise*, was published the next year and has become a sailing classic. This letter, to his friend Eric Rücker Eddison, was written on board, 'At anchor in Hapsal Roads', just as the voyage had ended.

Ric (short for Fredericius; Ransome was Boney, from Bonifacius – their childhood nicknames) and Ransome had shared a governess and tutors as

Arthur Ransome, letter to Eric Rücker Eddison, on board *Racundra*, 1922 boys in Leeds. ‘My friendship with Ric, thus begun in the nursery, lasted until he died during the last war’, Ransome wrote in his autobiography. Eddison (a spare-time writer) had sent Ransome his latest book, *The Worm Ouroboros*, a sort of sci-fi fantasy with a background in Norse and Viking mythology. Ransome is fulsome in his praise: ‘What a book … You may write other books but they will not be as good as this one … You are an enviable fellow’. He was not its only admirer: *The Worm* was a great success.

Before he turns to literary criticism, however, the letter is classic Ransome. He describes in detail and with palpable excitement the progress of the voyage:

> We put to sea, and sailed from Riga to the Island of Runo, from there to Reval, from Reval to Helsingfors in Finland, from Helsingfors in a hairy storm back to Reval, from Reval to Baltic Port in a calm, thence against contrary winds to Spithamn, thence to Ramsholm, thence (great triumph of navigation) against a violent wind through the intricate channel of Nucke and Worms Island (observe the name) to Hapsal, and here we lie awaiting a northerly wind to hurry southwards before winter.

He is a journalist, so naturally he has a typewriter on board.

Ransome’s ability to describe in detail and with clarity was one of the elements that made the twelve *Swallows and Amazons* books (published from 1930 to 1947) such a success. He tells a terrific story, but he also shows his readers how to tie a bowline and how to go about on a windy day without cracking your head on the boom. Ransome had returned to his beloved Coniston, where many of the books are set; but his sailing protagonists – Swallows, Amazons, Ds and the Coot Club – also find themselves on the Norfolk Broads, the North Sea and even the South China Sea. His own maps, illustrations and diagrams, drawn in the style of Captain Nancy Blackett, add to the pleasures of the text.

Arthur Ransome, letter on sailing to R.S. Blaker, 1940

book and one that will stand a
lot of re-readings.

I have never been to Japan
though I've been through the
Formosa Channel, going up to
Chefoo. Taku Bar (in a
little steamship).

I wish you lived a little
nearer these parts and could
come over for a sail and a
talk.

Yours sincerely,

Arthur Ransome

The Pilot had duodenal ulcers. You
seem to know all about them.

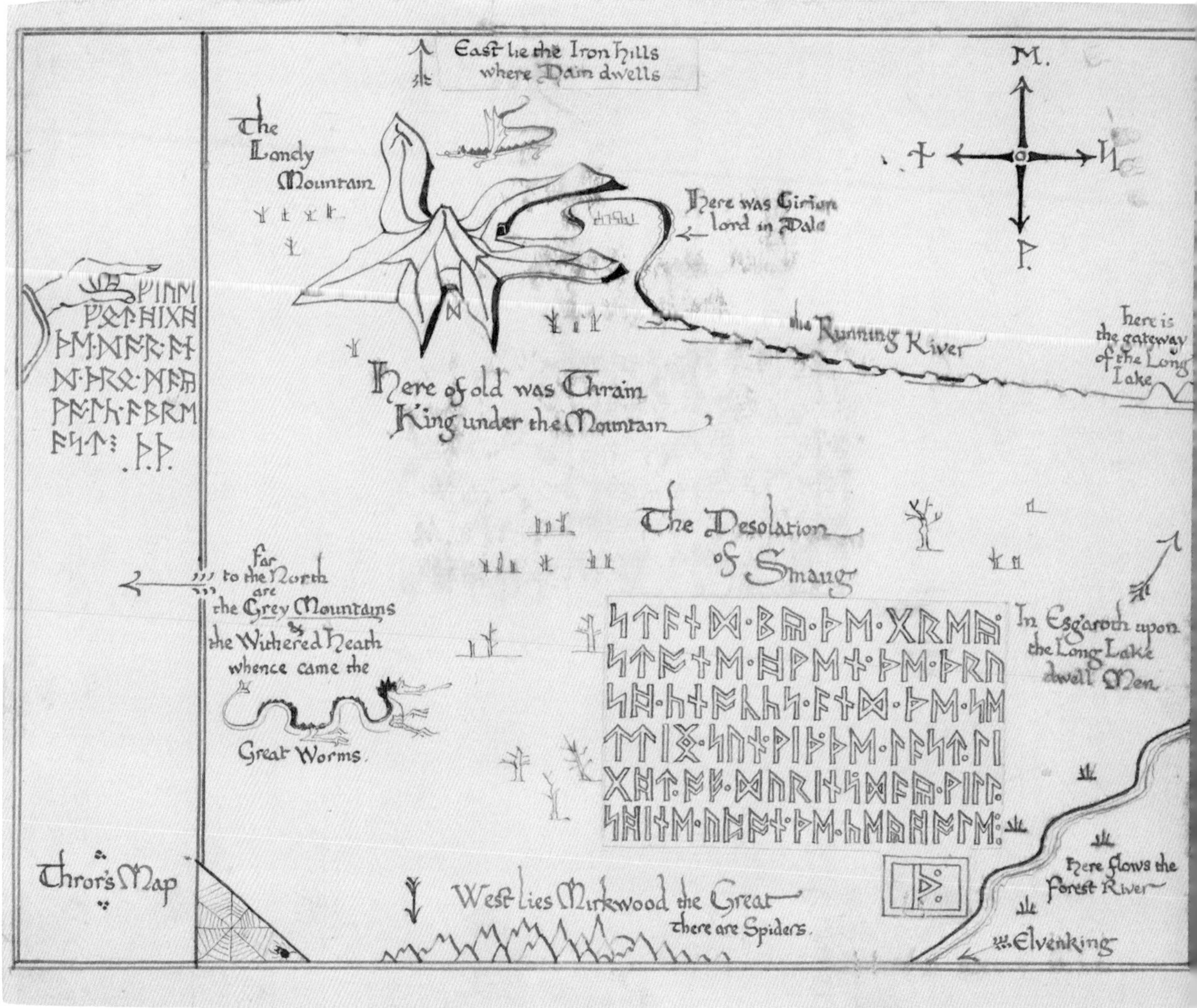
East lie the Iron Hills
where Dáin dwells
The Lonely Mountain
Here was Girion lord in Dale
Running River
Here is the gateway of the Long Lake
Here of old was Thrain
King under the Mountain
The Desolation of Smaug
Far to the North are the Grey Mountains & the Withered Heath whence came the Great Worms
In Esgaroth upon the Long Lake dwell Men
Here flows the Forest River
Elvenking
West lies Mirkwood the Great
there are Spiders
Thror's Map

J.R.R. Tolkien 1892–1973

In his day job, John Ronald Reuel Tolkien was a Germanic philologist: he studied the historical development of and connections between a particular group of northern European languages. He was successively Rawlinson and Bosworth Professor of Anglo-Saxon and Merton Professor of English Language and Literature at Oxford University. So it's not surprising that the languages he devised for his characters in Middle Earth were not so far from the Old and Middle English languages he taught undergraduates every day.

Runic letters, which Tolkien has adapted here, were a series of related alphabets used by the Germanic languages from about the second century onwards. Tolkien presses them into service as part of a map drawn by him for *The Hobbit* (1937), precursor of his *Lord of the Rings* trilogy. The map, drawn by Thrór, leader of the dwarves, was rescued by the wizard Gandalf and used by Thrór's grandson, Thorin Oakenshield, in his recovery of the dwarves' lands. For the story, Tolkien created 'moon runes', which could only be read by moonlight, when the moon was in the same quarter and in the same season as when they were written. He planned the runes to be printed in reverse on the back of the map, so that the reader would have to look through the page to see them. This proved too much for the publisher, so they were simply added to the front of the map, with a medieval-style pointing hand. Tolkien has used a runic alphabet, but the language they spell out is English, and they give instructions for the journey. In accordance with dwarvish convention, the map is orientated so that east is upward: the runes on the compass in the right-hand corner read E S W N.

According to Tolkien's own account, in a letter to W.H. Auden, it was during a bored moment marking examination papers that *The Hobbit* sprang to life: 'On a blank leaf I scrawled: "In a hole in the ground there lived a hobbit". I did not and do not know why.'

J.R.R. Tolkien, Thrór's Map from *The Hobbit*

Now
You Are 10

Quentin Blake 1932–

> Thank you for the invitation to your party. I can come if I get my homework done in time.
> Congratulations on your success. We are all agreed that you are a phenomenon.
> With love from
> Your friend
> Quentin

So reads the message from children's author and illustrator Quentin Blake on the reverse of his drawing, shown here. Blake is replying to an invitation from Sebastian Walker to a party to celebrate the tenth anniversary of the founding in 1978 of Walker Books, the first British publisher and bookseller dealing specifically in books for children. Walker Books is still going strong today.

Colourful and slightly anarchic, in Blake's customary style, the drawing fizzes with energy and fun. The Walker Books mascot-logo, a bear with a candle, is depicted hand in hand with their founder. But the drawing also nods to famous children's books of the past: in this case, the 1927 collection of verse, *Now We Are Six*, by A.A. Milne and E.H. Shepard, writer and illustrator, respectively, of another charismatic bear, Winnie-the-Pooh.

In addition to his own creations, Blake has collaborated with some of the best-known contemporary children's authors, such as Roald Dahl, Michael Rosen and Joan Aiken, as well as illustrating classics such as Hilaire Belloc's *Cautionary Verses*.

The card is part of the Bodleian's Archive of Iona and Peter Opie. Iona and Peter Opie were visionary collectors of children's literature and materials associated with it, from the seventeenth century onwards. They presented their collection to the Library in 1988.

Quentin Blake, reply to party invitation from Sebastian Walker, 1988

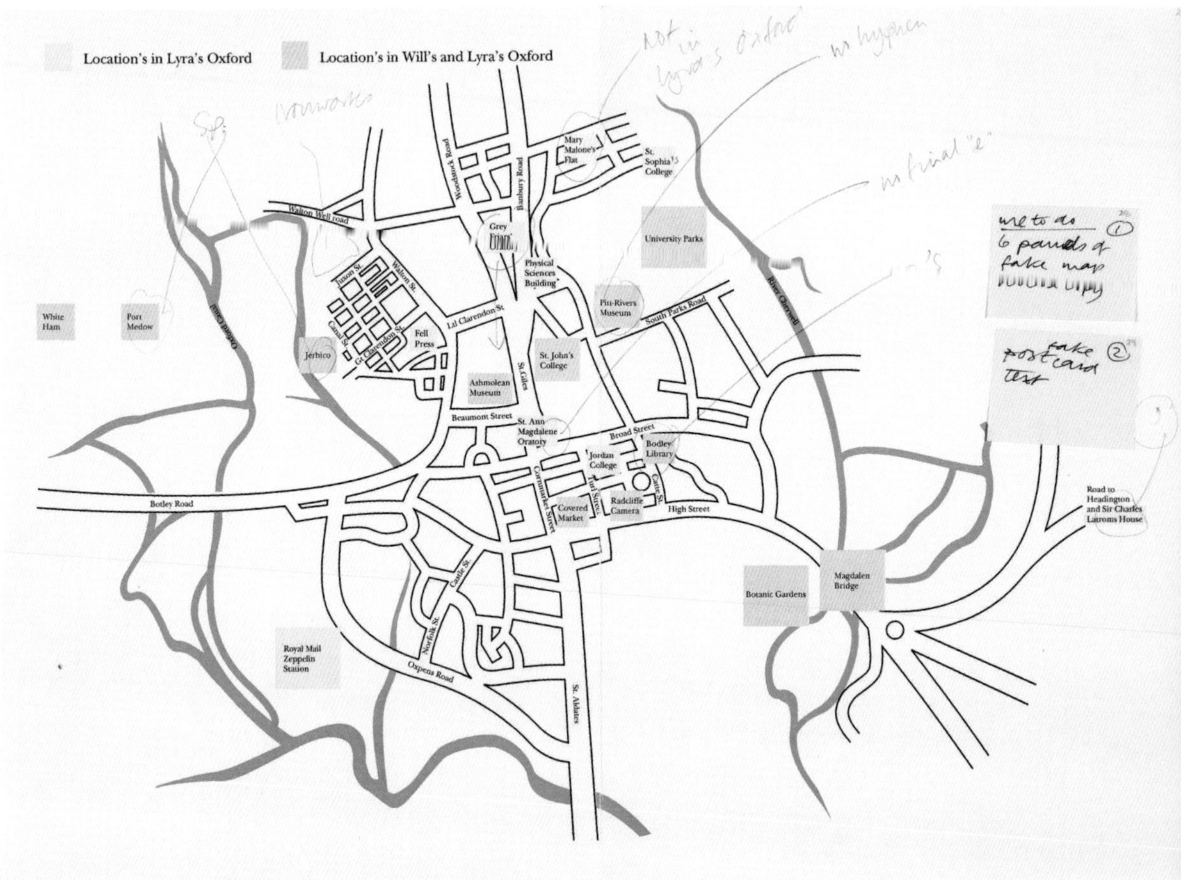
Location's in Lyra's Oxford
Location's in Will's and Lyra's Oxford
Walton Well road
Woodstock Road
Banbury Road
Mary Malone's Flat
St. Sophia's College
Grey
University Parks
Physical Sciences Building
Jaxon St.
Walton St.
Pitt-Rivers Museum
South Parks Road
River Cherwell
White Ham
Port Medow
Oxford Canal
Lil Clarendon St
Fell Press
Canal St.
Gt Clarendon St.
Jerbico
St. John's College
St. Giles
Ashmolean Museum
Beaumont Street
St. Ann Magdalene Oratory
Broad Street
Bodley Library
Jordan College
Cornmarket Street
Turl Street
Catte St.
Radcliffe Camera
Botley Road
Covered Market
High Street
Road to Headington and Sir Charles Latroms House
Magdalen Bridge
Botanic Gardens
Castle St.
Norfolk St.
Royal Mail Zeppelin Station
Oxpens Road
St. Aldates
not in Lyra's Oxford
no hyphen
no final "e"
use to do 6 panels of fake map
fake postcard text

Philip Pullman 1946–

INCLUDES FOLDOUT MAP AND OTHER MATTER
NEVER BEFORE SEEN IN THIS WORLD

Much of children's literature includes the kinds of thing that would make all reading a lot more fun. In their advertisement quoted above, the publishers of Philip Pullman's novella *Lyra's Oxford* (2003) promise a map. The final production is full of hand-drawn, quirky illustrations; but in the draft shown here Pullman has started with a conventional Oxford map and made careful alterations. Lyra's Oxford is and is not like the 'real' thing – a parallel time and space. The Covered Market is in its usual place, but Exeter College has become Jordan, where Lyra lives, and the Royal Mail sorting office has become the Zeppelin Station. Pullman has corrected the printout by hand ('Bodley Library' altered to 'Bodley's'), including a sticky note reminding himself: 'me to do'.

Pullman is probably best known for the *His Dark Materials* trilogy – *Northern Lights* (1995), *The Subtle Knife* (1997), *The Amber Spyglass* (2000) – which begins the story of Lyra Belacqua and her pine marten daemon Pantalaimon. Two years after the setting of *Spyglass*, *Lyra's Oxford* takes the story forward.

Overleaf is part of the draft of the story itself. Pullman is writing in ball-point pen on narrow feint loose leaf paper. He writes only on the front (or recto) page, using the back of the sheet ('verso') for running comments on the material opposite. On these pages he has crossed out everything he's written, while asking himself some key questions about the plot – 'why?', 'who?', 'how?' – and working out the story in more detail: 'The witch wants to kill Lyra … But the birds save Lyra and thus she sees that Oxford itself is protecting her.'

left Philip Pullman, map of Lyra's Oxford
overleaf Philip Pullman, draft of *Lyra's Oxford* (2003)

Why?
- Revenge — her son was killed in Bolvangar (?)
- religion

The witch wants to kill Lyra

so

she sends her daemon with a false message seeming to ask for help but in fact drawing her into a trap

who? — the father of her son her old lover the alch

where

someone will kill her.

how?

But

the birds save Lyra and thus she sees that Oxford itself is protecting her

Why doesn't the witch herself just shoot an arrow at Lyra? Why the trap?

came up cleanly and she got her shoulder under him and stoutly, stumbling, clumsy, she carried the swan, his wings trailing, ~~all the way~~ a few yards to the end of the street, ~~to~~ where the black water of the canal gleamed beyond the pavement.

And above, wheeling high and skimming low with that mighty creak as their wings beat, the other swans ~~swept~~ hurtled past so close that Lyra felt the rush of air —

And then she was at the edge of the water, and she bent down, trembling with the weight of him, and let him slide out of her arms and back to his own element. He shook his wings, beat them hard so that he stood up in the water, and paddled away. He was unhurt.

But the witch . . .

She was crawling towards Lyra, crawling like a broken lizard, and there were sparks around her — real sparks — as her knife grated on the stone; and her eyes seemed to flash as the sparks did but with hatred. Her daemon, with no strength left to fly, crawled ~~close~~ after her, trying to haul himself up to her body for warmth and comfort; they were dying.

"Lyra whispered "Why?"

~~And the witch muttered hoarsely: "Bolvangar."~~

~~"But . . ." Lyra couldn't understand.~~

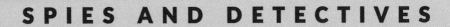

SPIES AND DETECTIVES

1520

TELEGRAMS:
CROWBOROUGH.
NAT. TEL. No. 77.

WINDLESHAM,
CROWBOROUGH,
SUSSEX.

My dear Ward

Several men will dine with me at 7, Metropole Hotel, June 24th, Friday, going over afterwards to see "The Speckled Band". Will you come? I hope so.

Yours very ty

Arthur Conan Doyle.

Arthur Conan Doyle 1859–1930

In 1893 Sherlock Holmes fell to his death at the Reichenbach Falls. His creator, Sir Arthur Conan Doyle, had tired of the fame of his brilliant detective and determined that he would live no more. Conan Doyle felt, in modern terms, typecast by his association with 221B Baker Street, and so he conjured up Professor Moriarty to fill the role of the great detective's arch enemy. Cornered at the edge of the falls, Moriarty plunges to his doom; but he takes Holmes over with him.

Conan Doyle breathed a sigh of relief. He lived a busy and successful dual life as a medical practitioner in London and a writer of gripping adventure stories and thrillers, with a line in social radicalism. Holmes had been a marvellous idea, but he had outgrown his ulster and deerstalker; his creator had other, more serious, stories he wanted to tell and his detective was in the way. Over the Falls – their realism founded on the year Conan Doyle had spent at school in Austria – he must go.

The readers of *The Strand Magazine*'s Christmas number, however, had different ideas. They thought *The Adventure of the Final Problem* an unwelcome sort of present, and they made their unhappiness felt. Faced with a mutiny on the part of his public, Conan Doyle was eventually forced to relent. In *The Adventure of the Empty House*, Dr Watson discovers that his old friend had not perished after all, and the two are reunited for further adventures.

The short letter shown here marks another stage in Holmes's career. In 1909 Conan Doyle had leased the Adelphi Theatre in London for a production of a play he had adapted from one of his novels. When theatres had to close, in mourning for the death of King Edward VII, he was forced to think again. Holmes had already been brought successfully to the stage by the American actor William Gillette; Conan Doyle decided it was time for the detective to tread the boards again:

Arthur Conan Doyle, invitation to dinner, 1910

> I shut myself up and devoted my whole mind to making a sensational Sherlock Holmes drama. I wrote it in a week and called it *The Speckled Band* after the short story of that name. I do not think I exaggerate if I say that within a fortnight of the one play shutting down I had a company working upon the rehearsals of a second one, which had been written in the interval. It was a considerable success.

It was indeed. Opening on 4 June 1910, the play ran for 169 performances before touring in the United Kingdom and Europe. During the run, Conan Doyle invited groups of friends to dine with him before going off to see the play. This invitation, to Ebenezer Ward, founder of Ward, Lock & Co., who had published two of his full length Holmes stories, *A Study in Scarlet* (1887) and *The Sign of the Four* (1890), is sent from Conan Doyle's home in Sussex. The length of their friendship is shown in the salutation, 'My dear Ward'. Ward is asked to dinner at the smart Hotel Metropole in Northumberland Avenue, from where the party could make the easy ten-minute walk to the Adelphi in The Strand. The valediction, 'Yours very ly' – probably a contraction of 'Yours very truly' – is one he often used in correspondence.

Despite the play's success, Conan Doyle was critical of his work. He thought he had made the villain too interesting, in order to provide Holmes with a worthy opponent, and his verdict on the ending was 'terrible'. Worse, the production's real snake – the 'speckled band' of the title – of which he was rather proud, was reported in one review as 'a palpably artificial serpent'.

Holmes kills the snake: *The Speckled Band*

"HOLMES LASHED FURIOUSLY."

smell grew stronger. For half an hour I sat with straining ears. Then suddenly another sound became audible—a very gentle, soothing sound, like that of a small jet of steam escaping continually from a kettle. The instant that we heard it, Holmes sprang from the bed, struck a match, and lashed furiously with his cane at the bell-pull.

"You see it, Watson?" he yelled. "You see it?"

But I saw nothing. At the moment when Holmes struck the light I heard a low, clear whistle, but the sudden glare flashing into my weary eyes made it impossible for me to tell what it was at which my friend lashed so savagely. I could, however, see that his face was deadly pale, and filled with horror and loathing.

He had ceased to strike, and was gazing up at the ventilator, when suddenly there broke from the silence of the night the most horrible cry to which I have ever listened. It swelled up louder and louder, a hoarse yell of pain and fear and anger all mingled in the one dreadful shriek. They say that away down in the village, and even in the distant parsonage, that cry raised the sleepers from their beds. It struck cold to our hearts, and I stood gazing at Holmes, and he at me, until the last echoes of it had died away into the silence from which it rose.

"What can it mean?" I gasped.

"It means that it is all over," Holmes answered. "And perhaps, after all, it is for the best. Take your pistol, and we shall enter Dr. Roylott's room."

With a grave face he lit the lamp, and led the way down the corridor. Twice he struck at the chamber door without any reply from within. Then he turned the handle and entered, I at his heels, with the cocked pistol in my hand.

It was a singular sight which met our eyes. On the table stood a dark lantern with the shutter half open, throwing a brilliant beam of light upon the iron safe, the door of which was ajar. Beside this table, on the wooden chair, sat Dr. Grimesby Roylott, clad in a long grey dressing-gown, his bare ankles protruding beneath, and his feet thrust into red heelless Turkish slippers. Across his lap lay the short stock with the long lash which we had noticed during the day. His chin was cocked upwards, and his eyes were fixed in a dreadful rigid stare at the corner of the ceiling. Round his brow he had a peculiar yellow band, with brownish

Dorothy L. Sayers 1893–1957

The Detection Club still exists. It was founded around 1930, somewhat on the lines of the earlier Crimes Club, which numbered Conan Doyle as a member, to discuss 'clues and corpses', as Dorothy Sayers says here, and provide congenial company for those engaged in the essentially solitary act of writing. Along with Sayers, founder members included Agatha Christie and Ronald Knox, author of the famous 'Ten Commandments of Detective Fiction'.

Sayers – honorary secretary at this point – was an enthusiastic participant. Members had to undergo a pseudo-serious initiation rite, and meetings were always attended by Eric, a skull. Although the group initially met at the home of Anthony Berkeley, another founder member, they eventually hired a clubroom in Gerrard Street in central London, where they would repair after dining in one of the nearby Soho restaurants. Sayers's note here is to Edmund Crispin who had just been inducted into the membership. Crispin was the pen name of Bruce Montgomery, whose detective creation, Gervase Fen, was an unconventional Oxford professor.

Sayers herself is best known for eleven novels featuring the aristocratic polymath Lord Peter Wimsey, his manservant Bunter, and detective novelist and Wimsey's eventual wife, Harriet Vane. Sayers, a clergyman's daughter, had won a scholarship to Somerville College, Oxford, where she specialized in medieval languages. Harriet Vane, too, was an alumna of the fictional Shrewsbury College, which was the setting of the 1935 novel *Gaudy Night*. Wimsey himself was a Balliol man.

Although she was president of the Detection Club from 1949 to 1957, Sayers had stopped writing detective fiction a decade earlier. Her interest had shifted back to her undergraduate studies in languages and the religion of her vicarage upbringing. She embarked on a translation of Dante's *Inferno*, and wrote *The Man Who Would be King*, a radio play

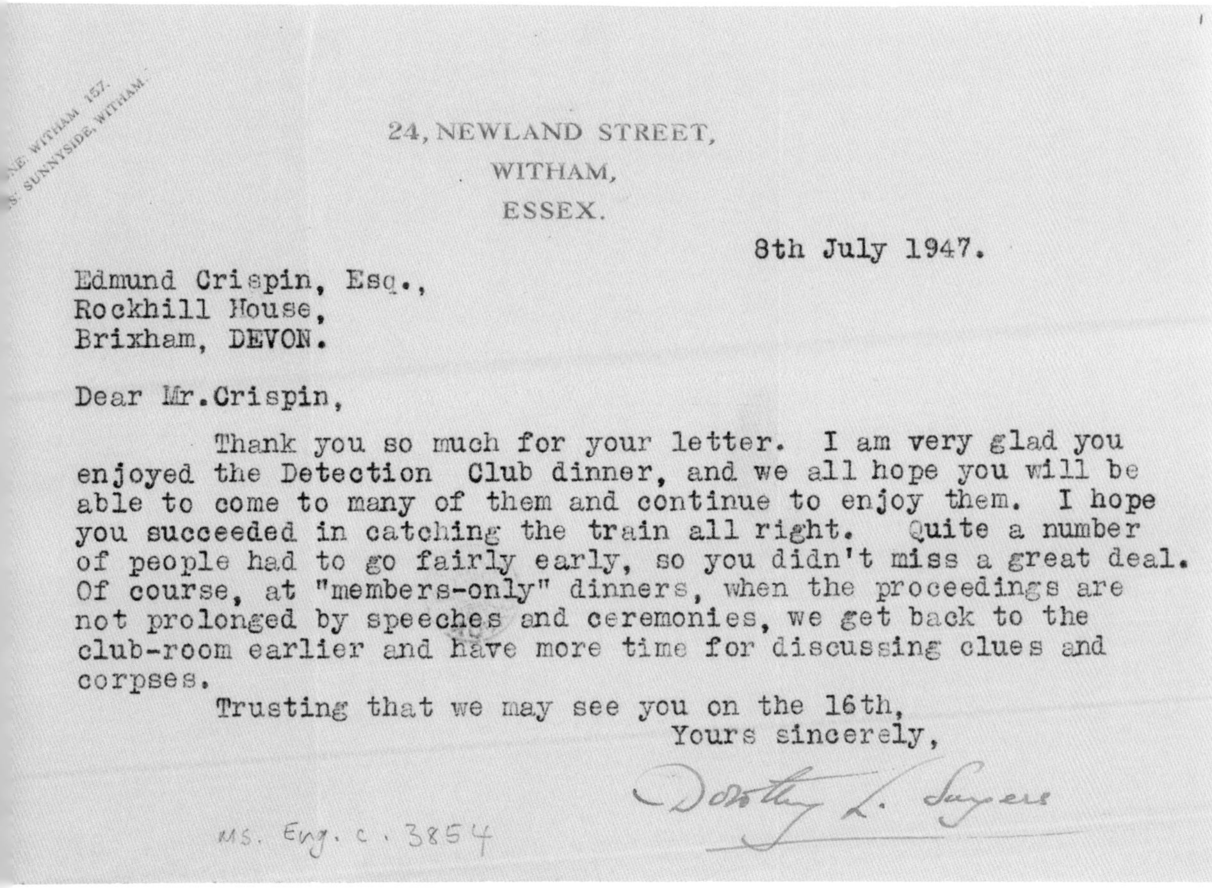

NE. WITHAM 157.
S. SUNNYSIDE, WITHAM.

24, NEWLAND STREET,
WITHAM,
ESSEX.

8th July 1947.

Edmund Crispin, Esq.,
Rockhill House,
Brixham, DEVON.

Dear Mr.Crispin,

Thank you so much for your letter. I am very glad you enjoyed the Detection Club dinner, and we all hope you will be able to come to many of them and continue to enjoy them. I hope you succeeded in catching the train all right. Quite a number of people had to go fairly early, so you didn't miss a great deal. Of course, at "members-only" dinners, when the proceedings are not prolonged by speeches and ceremonies, we get back to the club-room earlier and have more time for discussing clues and corpses.

Trusting that we may see you on the 16th,

Yours sincerely,

Dorothy L. Sayers

Dorothy L. Sayers, letter to Edmund Crispin, 1947

about the life of Jesus Christ. By the time of this note, however, she was living unhappily in Essex and, whatever her feelings about Wimsey, the Detection Club may have provided a much-needed change of scene.

Agatha Christie 1890–1976

Lady Mallowan, the signatory of the letter shown here, was the wife of a celebrated archaeologist, Sir Max Mallowan. She had been born Agatha Miller and published romantic novels as Mary Westmacott, but it is by the name she took on her first marriage, Agatha Christie, that she is famous in detective fiction. Christie is said to be the bestselling novelist of all time, having sold more than one billion books in English and a further billion in translations into more than one hundred languages. One of her plays, *The Mousetrap*, is the longest-running in history. Two of her detective creations, the self-important dandy Hercule Poirot and the deceptively self-effacing elderly spinster Miss Jane Marple, are synonymous with the Christie name; but she created several other serial sleuths, including the husband and wife crime-solving duo, Tommy and Tuppence Beresford. Among the Golden Age 'queens of crime', Christie is surely empress.

Christie writes here to Edmund Crispin, another writer with more than one name. In an earlier letter she begins, 'Dear Edmund Crispin, or B[ruce] M[ontgomery] – Because I know you in Devon as well as at the Detection Club'. Christie was the president of the club, founded for writers of detective fiction, from 1958 to 1976, having been a founder member when it began, around 1930. She knew Crispin 'in Devon' because she owned a holiday home, Greenway House, near Dartmouth, but this letter is sent from Wallingford, near Oxford, where she lived with Sir Max, who became a fellow of All Souls College, from 1934 to her death in 1976.

Crispin was a regular reviewer of crime fiction for *The Sunday Times*, and the review referred to here (published ten days previously on 20 September 1970) is of Christie's *Passenger to Frankfurt*. Advertised by her publishers as her eightieth book, written for her eightieth birthday, and celebrating her fiftieth year as a novelist, *Passenger to Frankfurt* was unusual in being a sort of spy thriller, dealing with the problems of the post-war generation. Not exactly what Christie readers had come to expect, the book was not as well received by all reviewers – which may have prompted this grateful note, although it was not the first time she had written to thank Crispin for a positive notice. Nevertheless, it had the largest first printing of any of her novels – 58,000 copies – and soon sold out.

In the letter shown here, sympathizing with Crispin's impending operation, Christie offers a medical experience of her own. Rather nicely, the mistress of suspense reveals herself unwilling to stand 'the Cat and Mouse strain' of having nine teeth out in instalments – preferring instead to have the job done 'in one complete sweep'. 'I refused forcibly', she says, and there is something about the character of her handwriting that makes that statement particularly believable – to this reader at least.

Many of Christie's books have Near and Middle Eastern locations, and a number are sited at or around archaeological digs. She had a genuine interest in her husband's work and accompanied him abroad on many occasions. They had met at a dig at Ur of the Chaldees, introduced by her friends the archaeologists Leonard and Katharine Woolley. She listed among her likes travel and 'strange foods', and was happy to rough it. During the day, she would help with the sorting of finds, and in the evenings, as the archaeologists sat around and discussed the progress of the work, she joined them to knit, while silently working out the plot of the next book. By the time she came to the writing, she worked quickly, having already planned the story in her head. After *The Mysterious Affair at Styles* (1920), she produced at least a book a year.

overleaf Agatha Christie, letter to Edmund Crispin, 1970

Sept 30th

WALLINGFORD 2248.

WINTERBROOK HOUSE,
WALLINGFORD,
BERKS.

Dear Edmund

I just have to write & say you really did me proud in the way of a review of my book — Particularly delighted with the "slips down like a draught of cold water on a hot day" idea — Just what I'd like it to be —

Do hope your hand

operation will go well –
It's always beastly looking
forward to things –
I had 9 teeth out once
in one complete sweep –
They suggested my having
out 2 at a time – & come
back in intervals – but I
refused forcibly – Couldn't
have stood the cat & mouse
strain –
Good luck to you –
And thanks to all. Yours ever
Agatha Mallowan

Raymond Chandler 1888–1959

If the first thing that Raymond Chandler did each morning was not to put a fresh sheet of paper in the typewriter, then surely, after a drink and a cigarette, it ran a close third. Much of Chandler's life was spent in front of the keyboard – so that, although the Bodleian has many boxes of the Chandler archive, very little of it reveals his own handwriting. Often, to friends and colleagues, he even typed his signature: 'RAY'.

Influenced by the hard-boiled realism of Dashiell Hammett – best known today for *The Maltese Falcon* – Chandler revolutionized the detective novel. His now much-imitated style was as far away from the cosy country house, with suspects gathered in the library, as it was possible to be. It was a style he parodied in his essay 'The Simple Art of Murder'. Instead, Chandler took contemporary American life and turned it into classic tales of unlikely heroism and integrity: in his famous phrase, 'Down these mean streets a man must go who is not himself mean.'

For much of his life Chandler lived in California and for a time he worked as a writer in Hollywood. His screenplays for the director Billy Wilder, *Double Indemnity* and *The Blue Dahlia*, are distinctive and memorable; both were nominated for Academy Awards. His own detective, Philip Marlowe, was most famously portrayed on screen by Humphrey Bogart, who played him – tough, smart, but with a sensitive soul – in an adaptation of *The Big Sleep*. But Chandler himself said that he always had a rather more suave and intellectual incarnation of Marlowe in mind, and his first choice for the part would have been Cary Grant. It's Marlowe's decency that comes over on the page – someone trying hard to do the right thing, in spite of the world around him.

The wise-cracking, tough guy settings of Chandler's novels belie his English public school education at Dulwich College in south London.

Raymond Chandler, working notebook: 'Similes – including "comparisons"'

Similes – including comparisons

As rare as a fat postman ([illegible]) (not [illegible])
As hard as a park bench L S
As dull as a football interview L.S.
As clean as Aunt Harriet's guest room (used?)
As systematic as a madam counting the take.
As busy as a dirty joke in a sorority house.
As gaudy as a chiropractor's chart L.S.
Lower than a badger's balls (!!) Vulgar. belly used L.S.
No more charm than a washtub (used?) L.S.
Lonely as the caboose of a fifty car freight.
No more personality than a paper cup. (Used?) L S
About as French as a doughnut (i.e. not French at all)
His face was long enough to wrap twice around his neck, L S
As generous as a trade rat
As graceful as a Chopin ending L S
Like the little dog that runs around and yaps after the big dog.
Too weak to lift a Scotchman's tip.
Longer than a round trip to Siam. ~~Still~~ L S
Take your ears out of the way and I'll leave – to [illegible]
As soothing as a piano salesman. L S?
As exclusive as a mail box L.S.
As lonely as a lighthouse. L S
As much sex appeal as a turtle. L.S.
As unforgettable as the eyes of a [illegible] dog. L.S.
A nose like a strap-hanger's elbow L.S.

Born in Chicago, he barely knew his alcoholic father, but moved with his mother to her family home in Ireland and then to London. His education continued with a year in Paris, Munich and Freiburg, where he polished his languages with a view to taking the Civil Service exams. He came third out of 800 candidates, and top in classics; but after six months at the Admiralty he left to try his hand at teaching and writing, without a great deal of success. In 1912 he returned to the United States, settling in San Francisco and qualifying as a book-keeper. In the First World War he fought in France with the Canadian Army, was wounded and shipped back to the States where he found some success as an oil company executive, until his own difficulties with alcohol got him the sack. Needing money – he was by now married – he started to write crime stories, but it wasn't until 1939, when he was fifty, that his first full-length novel, *The Big Sleep*, made him an overnight literary success.

Chandler was a thinker about writing. In the pages from a loose-leaf notebook shown here, he jots down ideas and stores up possibilities for current and future work. It's divided into sections headed 'Similes', 'Gags', 'Titles', 'Style', 'Notions' (this section is empty) and 'Grab Bag'. Chandler had trained as an accountant after all, and his papers (with their flimsy typewritten carbon copies of correspondence) reveal order and organization. On the page of 'Similes' illustrated, he also notes where the idea was used, annotating the entry with the initials of the book where it appears: 'LS' for *The Little Sister* (1949), for instance, or 'LG' for *The Long Goodbye* (1953). Chandler himself was rather genteel: one of the entries on this page reads 'Lower than a badger's balls (!!)' – which he has glossed with the comment 'vulgar', and added instead the word 'belly'. Sure enough, the phrase appears in chapter twenty-two of *The Little Sister*, but in its more refined form.

The page from the section on 'Style' (fol. 51r) begins with some handwritten ideas for phrasing. Reversing the conventional trope 'pale and interesting', Chandler gives us 'His face had an uninteresting pallor', which he did indeed use, as noted, in *The Long Goodbye*. Further down the page, he reverts to his typewriter and thoughts about the American use of language. Brought up in England, and having studied languages in Europe,

left Raymond Chandler, working notebook: section headings
right Raymond Chandler, working notebook: 'Style'

Chandler was aware of 'American' as having its own distinctive form, and was an admirer of the democratic directness of the best American idiom:

> The fascination of the American language is that it is not, like other vernaculars, a language of limited thought but a mood language, proper to supreme court justices, full professors as well as to cops, sports writers and truck drivers. It is the shirt sleeve language of intellectuals not the fumbling solecism of the plumber's helper.

The popularity of Chandler's fiction, and its influence in the cinema, meant that he not only described the American language; he shaped its idiom as well.

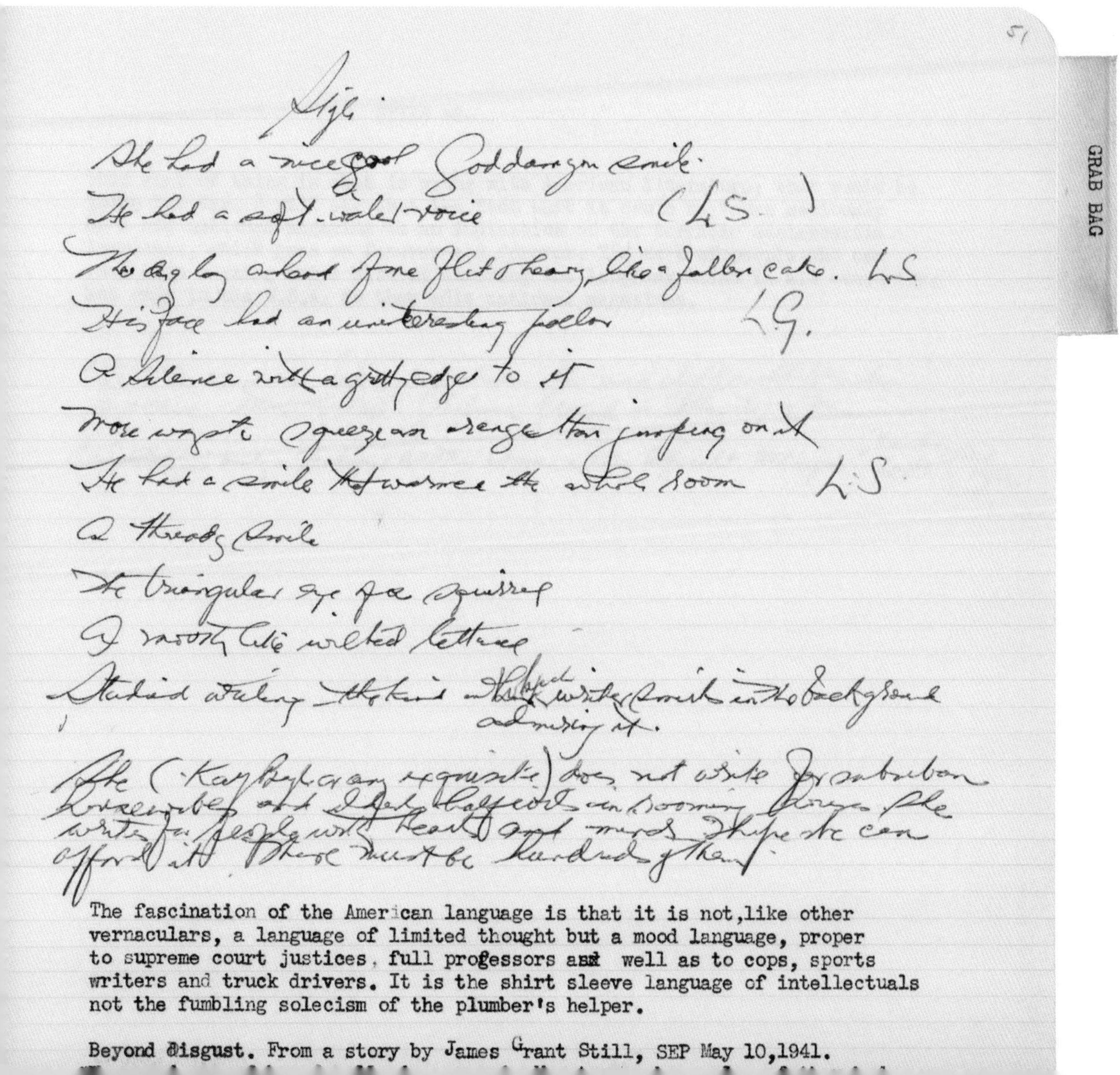
51

GRAB BAG

Style

She had a nice good Goddam grin smile.
He had a soft-walled voice (L.S.)
The dog lay ahead of me flat & heavy, like a fallen cake. L.S
His face had an uninteresting pallor L.G.
A silence with a gritty edge to it
More wrapt. Squeeze an orange than jumping on it
He had a smile that warmed the whole room L.S
A thready smile
The triangular eye of a squirrel
As smooth like wilted lettuce
Studied writing that kind with a hard writer's smirk in the background admiring it.

She (Kay Boyle, crazy exquisite) does not write for suburban housewives and elderly halfwits in rooming houses. She writes for people with hearts and minds. I hope we can afford it. There must be hundreds of them.

The fascination of the American language is that it is not,like other vernaculars, a language of limited thought but a mood language, proper to supreme court justices, full professors and well as to cops, sports writers and truck drivers. It is the shirt sleeve language of intellectuals not the fumbling solecism of the plumber's helper.

Beyond Disgust. From a story by James Grant Still, SEP May 10,1941.

THE BOOK COLLECTOR

A QUARTERLY JOURNAL INCORPORATING BOOK HANDBOOK

9 GREAT JAMES STREET LONDON WC1 · CHANCERY 8075

as from: Kemsley House,
W.C.1.

24th June, 1952.

Percy Muir, Esq.,
Messrs. Elkin Mathews,
Takeley,
Bishops Stortford,
Herts.

My dear Percy,

Yes, the next meeting is on 9th July and I count on your presence. You were much missed last time.

The sales of "The Book Collector" are a considerable improvement on the first issue and 1,400 have already gone which is admirable.

I managed to get a 'puff' into "Atticus" on Sunday, as a result of which a fascinating letter has come in suggesting very plausibly that the imaginary portrait was not of Dr. Johnson at all. I am sending you copies of the correspondence. It looks as if a first-class hare has been started.

I have decided gingerly to re-enter the Original Thought market via your good offices, so if from time to time you have any 'musts', please let me know and I will be a probable buyer on your say-so.

I hear that Chatsworth is going to have to produce very considerable death duties. I assume you have absolute priority on any parts of the library that may have to be sold?

Yours ever

Ian

Ian Fleming 1908–1964

Like many children with a brilliant and admired sibling, Ian Fleming didn't quite measure up to his elder brother, Peter. His career at Eton had been unremarkable, and it was clear that he wasn't cut out for either Oxford or Sandhurst. For a time, he bummed around Austria learning to ski and climb; he failed the Civil Service exam; he tried his hand at journalism. Eventually, he followed his wealthy family into banking: he was bored sick.

Like many of his generation, however, Fleming was saved by the war. With family contacts and a knowledge of French and German, he was invited to join Naval Intelligence as assistant to the director. Ironically, administration proved to be his hidden talent and he prospered; in 1941–2 he helped plan the Allied response, codenamed Operation Goldeneye, should Spain join or be invaded by Germany and the Axis Powers.

The war over, he joined the Kemsley Newspapers Group as foreign manager, negotiating his contract to work only nine months of each year. The rest of the time he spent in Jamaica, in the house he had built, Goldeneye. The combination suited him. In Jamaica he began to write, and in 1953 *Casino Royale*, his first James Bond adventure, was an immediate success. From then on, he wrote a novel a year at Goldeneye.

Like his hero, Fleming was at home with the rich; but, unlike Bond, physical action was not his forte. Alongside the publication of *Casino Royale*, in 1952 he founded a quarterly journal, *The Book Collector*, devoted to a subject close to his heart. This letter illustrates his immersion in the detail of its production, as he writes to the influential antiquarian bookseller Percy Muir, a founder member of its board of directors.

Like Bond, Fleming was not a man to do his own office typing. However, rather than Moneypenny, his secretaries were a Miss Chamberlin and a Miss Howe.

Ian Fleming, letter to Percy Muir, 1952

Even so, Dorothy L. Sayers in her fiction can be seen as something of an intellectual snob, Ngaio Marsh as a social snob and Josephine Tey as a class snob in ~~their~~ her character's attitudes to their servants and

in her fiction Dorothy L. Sayers can be seen as something of an intellectual snob, Ngaio Marsh as a social snob and Josephine Tey as a class snob in her characters' attitudes to their servants and

is necessarily there but it is so muted that it is sometime difficult, reading an Agatha Christie, to remember exactl how the victim died. Parents might well complain if thei adolescent son were continually reading Agatha Christi when it was time he turned to the books set for his nex examination, but they would be extremely unlikely t complain that he was immured in nothing but horro and violent death. But the allegation of snobbery is reiter ated, particularly with regard to the women writers of th 1930s, and what I think many people forget is that thos writers were producing for an age in which social division were clearly understood and generally accepted since the seemed an immutable part of the natural order. And w have to remember that the detective novelists of the thir ties had been bred to a standard of ethics and manners i public and private life which today might well be seen a elitist. Even so/there are risible passages which are difficul to read without embarrassment, including the unfortunat tendency of Ngaio Marsh's suspects to say what a comfor it is to be interrogated by a gent. I wonder what they woul have made of the Continental Op.

This acceptance of class distinction was not confine to novelists. I have a number of volumes of the successfu plays of the Thirties, and almost without exception drama tists were writing for the middle class, about the middl class and were themselves middle class. This was, of course decades before, on 8 May 1956, the English Stage Compan produced John Osborne's iconoclastic play *Look Back i Anger.* Servants do appear in the inter-war plays, but usu ally to provide what is seen as the necessary comic relief Popular literature, whether detective stories or not, ac

P.D. James 1920–2014

Writers of detective stories are often connoisseurs of the genre. This was certainly true of Phyllis Dorothy (P.D.) James, a page from whose *Talking about Detective Fiction*, published by the Bodleian Library in 2009, is shown here. In the book, she looks back to the 1920s and 1930s, the so-called Golden Age of Detection, which was dominated by the success of a remarkable generation of women writers including Margery Allingham and, of course, Agatha Christie.

Elegant and well spoken, P.D. James carried on their legacy in many ways. Almost all her books are built around the enigmatic, intellectual, poetry-writing policeman Adam Dalgliesh of Scotland Yard. Dalgliesh is reminiscent of earlier protagonists such as Ngaio Marsh's Roderick Alleyn or even Dorothy L. Sayers's Lord Peter Wimsey, with a closed community of suspects in an often remarkable setting. But the books are tougher than they first appear. James's difficult early childhood and marriage, followed by work in criminal justice at the Home Office, gave her – and the novels – an underlying steel and an awareness of the darker side of life. The demands of work and family meant that her first book was not published until 1962, and it was not until 1979 that she could retire from the Civil Service and write full time.

The illustrated page is from a proof copy of the book – that is, the trial run printed before the final version, where mistakes can still be caught and corrected by author and publisher. Of course, this means it is important that the typesetter is sure what the alteration is meant to be. James has made additions to this page in black ink in a somewhat wispy hand. Her note refers to three of the greatest of the Golden Age 'queens of crime':

> Dorothy L. Sayers in her fiction can be seen as something of an intellectual snob, Ngaio Marsh as a social snob and Josephine Tey as a class snob in her characters' attitudes to their servants.

P.D. James, corrected proof of *Talking about Detective Fiction*, 2009

Deborah Susman, the Bodleian Library Publishing editor seeing the book through publication, was clearly uncertain that James's handwriting would be completely legible to whomever was to make the final corrections to the digital file before it went to press. Throughout this proof copy she has rewritten the alterations more clearly, in red ink, alongside the original. But, as we can see from the alterations even to the new red text, she had not always managed to read James's writing either, and she has had to correct herself too.

The document here illustrates another change for historians of the twentieth-century novel, as opposed to those of earlier writers. Whereas Dickens and Collins had sent their handwritten text directly to the publisher, Raymond Chandler used a typewriter and P.D. James employed an assistant working at a computer keyboard. What we can glimpse of their own script is in the margins of typescript or printout. Indeed, the Library's dossier for James includes hard copies of emails exchanged with Bodleian Library Publishing, rather than the handwritten notes that passed between, say, John Murray and Jane Austen.

Born in Oxford, and a resident there in the latter part of her life, P.D. James was a great supporter of the Bodleian. She donated the royalties from the sale of this book to the Library.

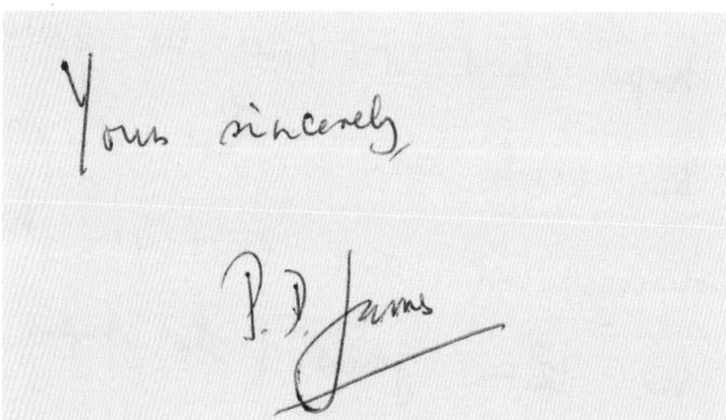

above P.D. James, signature
right P.D. James in the Divinity School, Bodleian Library, Oxford

And then there was Karla, ~~he said~~ said Smiley, and the enigma which ~~Smiley~~ had never been resolved.

Guillam had even asked him: 'What's it all about with Karla? What's the story?'

This was not the first time Karla's shadow had fallen between them ~~since Ascot~~ since Ascot, but it was the first time that Smiley had ~~consented to recognise its~~ acknowledged its ~~existence~~ existence to Guillam. They had spoken of him ~~already in connection with~~ while discussing Voroslov, otherwise Academician Vladimir Alexeyevitsc Krajn, on the journey back to London; ~~a discussion~~ an exchange which, by the time the orange daylight of the City rose ahead of them, had taken on, for Guillam at least, something of the unsettling quality of the revelations of the previous night. ~~but Karla belonged apparently~~

How could Guillam be certain, ~~Smiley~~ he had asked from the recesses of his (voluminous) greatcoat, ~~as they drove home,~~ that the Voroslo he remembered from his days in the Middle East was the Voroslov alias Krajn whom Irene had mentioned in her letter?

Guillam's answer was conclusive. The Foreign Office bulletin of Diplomatic Staff in London supplied not only a short biography but a photograph:

'The biography may have been Krajn but the photo graph was brother Voroslov.'

The biography, he added, was extremely meagre, and gave almost nothing beyond a couple of obscure academic appointments out in the sticks of Central Russia. Krajn was described as single, he had a flat in Knights-

John le Carré 1931–2020

When spies write about spying, they don't do it as themselves. So when David Cornwell, who had worked in intelligence since his National Service after the Second World War, published *Call for the Dead* in 1961, he had to find a new identity: John le Carré was born.

George Smiley – the sort of man you wouldn't notice on the street – was an unlikely hero. Quiet, ordinary, serially betrayed by his flamboyant wife Anne, Smiley was as far from a shaken martini as it was possible to be; his was the *intelligence* in MI6. Le Carré fashioned a world away from casinos and dinner jackets, with hole-in-the-corner meetings and squalid hotels. Acres of boredom relieved only by moments of sheer terror.

Like Holmes and Moriarty, Smiley is brought into relief by his Soviet counterpart, Karla. Set against the reality of the Cold War, a trilogy of books from the 1970s charted their long-distance duel. The page shown here is from an early version of the first book in the series, *Tinker, Tailor, Soldier, Spy* (1974). Le Carré began the book in longhand, but then worked on a succession of typescript drafts made by a secretary. The development of his thinking is recorded in alterations made in two different colours. Sometimes the original is good after all: 'since Ascot' is crossed out in blue, then rewritten above in red.

Given his position, le Carré was not allowed to publish without the approval of the secret service: they agreed, he said, because they regarded it as 'sheer fiction from start to finish'. Nevertheless, the books' distinctive vocabulary of spying – lamplighters, the Circus, housekeepers, and the rest – was taken up as truth and adopted, so he said, by his colleagues in the secret world.

John le Carré, working typescript of *Tinker, Tailor, Soldier, Spy* (1974)

FAMILIES

Dr Herschel respectfully presents his Duty to The Duke of Kent, and acknowledges the receipt of a letter which his Royal Highness has transmitted to him from the Earl of Buchan. It contains a very ingenious account of the Solar eclipse which according to the Nautical Almanac will happen in the year 1816. He is in hopes that His Royal Highness, in addition to his condescending goodness will also transmit the inclosed answer to the Earl.

Slough
Decr 5. 1814.

William Herschel 1738–1822
Caroline Herschel 1750–1848
John Herschel 1792–1871

Brother and sister, William and Caroline Herschel stood at the forefront of nineteenth-century European astronomy, together forming a team that is estimated to have doubled contemporary knowledge of the universe. Two of the ten children of a military bandsman from Hanover, they began their working lives as musicians. William (anglicized from Wilhelm) moved to England in 1757 to play the violin in Charles Avison's Newcastle orchestra. Professional commitments led him to settle in Bath, where he began to pursue a serious interest in astronomy. In 1772 he sent for his younger sister Caroline to come and run his household, sing for his musical events and help him in his scientific work.

Caroline had been denied formal schooling, and childhood typhus had restricted the vision of one eye and stunted her growth, so that she stood only four foot three inches tall; but the move to England was transformative in giving her success as a musician and widening her education. William realized that advances in astronomy would require better telescopes, and he set out to produce them, with Caroline and their brother Alexander working to his designs. William and Caroline worked at a systematic mapping of the night sky, which led to numerous discoveries of new nebulae, comets, asteroids, binary and multiple stars, planetary moons and sunspots. In 1781 William discovered the planet Uranus, which he initially named after King George III. This was the first addition to the solar system since antiquity and it led to William being appointed the king's astronomer and a household move to Datchett, near Windsor Castle.

William's discoveries (which included infrared radiation) became known throughout Europe, but Caroline's own work, and her skill as an observer, were also recognized. In 1787 the king gave her an annual salary of £50, making her the first modern European woman to be paid for scientific work and the first to hold a government post. After William's

William Herschel to the duke of Kent, 1814

marriage to a wealthy widow in 1788, Caroline's work became more independent, and she began to be better known in her own right, in particular for her discoveries of comets and nebulae, as well as her thorough revision of John Flamsteed's comprehensive star catalogue, the *Historia coelestis Britannica*.

William was one of the founders, in 1820, of the Astronomical Society of London, which became the Royal Astronomical Society in 1831. Caroline was made an honorary member of the society (jointly with Mary Somerville) in 1835, having been awarded its Gold Medal for her scientific work in 1828 – the first and only woman to be so honoured until Vera Rubin in 1996. When William died, Caroline moved back to Hanover where, on her ninety-sixth birthday, she was given the Prussian Gold Medal for Science, brought to her by the greatest German scientist of the day, Alexander von Humboldt.

In the two short notes on astronomical affairs shown here, William's royal and aristocratic connections are clear, as he uses the duke of Kent as a postman to reach the earl of Buchan on the matter of a solar eclipse. Caroline, meanwhile, writes with humour to Dr James Lind, scientist and physician to the king at Windsor, of their shared interest:

> I know you are almost as fond of a comet as I am myself, therefore it is high time to point out a spot where you may see one.

Caroline regretted her decision to leave England after her brother's death, since it separated her from her much-loved nephew, his son John – who was also a notable astronomer. His work, like that of his father and aunt, extended the size and range of telescopes, using bigger and better instruments to take over William and Caroline's cataloguing of double and multiple stars and nebulae, and for which he won the Royal Astronomical Society's Gold Medal in 1836.

But astronomy was only one string to John's bow. He excelled in a number of branches of science, including mathematics (he was a friend of Charles Babbage), chemistry, meteorology and physics, as well as writing on the philosophy of science. To the recent invention of photography,

Caroline Herschel to James Lind, 1795

Nov.r 9, 1795.

Dear Sir,

I know you are almost as fond of a comet as I am myself, therefore it is high time to point out a spot where you may see one. Saturday night Nov.r 7 I found a telescopic Comet near γ Cygni, which according to my brother's description is about 5' dia.m and ~~is~~ just ~~seen with~~ (perceptible to) the naked eye. Nov.r 7 at 0h 33' Sid. time its RA was 20h 3' 48" PD 49° 17' 18"
Nov.r 8 at 0h 31' RA — 19 48 23 51 21 45
You will see by these two observations that it has moved about 3° 3/4 ‡ per day, and that it makes its way to the sun passing between the neck of the Swan and the constellation Lyre.

With my love & Comps.ts to Mrs Lind
I remain
Dear Sir
your Obed.t humble
Servant
C. Herschel.

‡ I know not if my brother is of the same opinion, but its rate of going must be there about.

he made crucial advances in the new science of photochemistry and experimented with photosensitivity. He coined the now standard terms 'positive', 'negative', 'snapshot' and 'photographer'.

In 1836, while working in the Cape of southern Africa, he met Julia Margaret Cameron, and they became lifelong friends. He encouraged her interest in photography and explained his new processes to her. When Cameron moved to the Isle of Wight in England after her husband's death, a gift of photographic equipment from her daughter allowed her to set up her first studio, in a hen house, in 1863. Here, over the next couple of years, Cameron took the series of photographs that made her name, including the portrait of John Herschel shown here. In her memoir, *Annals of my Glass House* (1874), she wrote:

> When I have such men before my camera, my whole soul has endeavoured to do its duty towards them in recording faithfully the greatness of the inner as well as the features of the outer man.

Among Herschel's numerous publications, his *Preliminary Discourse on the Study of Natural Philosophy* (1830) was perhaps his most important, influencing Charles Darwin and John Stuart Mill (who wrote on logic as well as philosophy), among others. Knighted in 1838 and showered with scientific honours, he was held in such admiration and affection by his contemporaries that his achievements were recognized by his burial in Westminster Abbey, next to Sir Isaac Newton.

Julia Margaret Cameron, portrait of Sir John Herschel

Frances Nelson 1761–1831
Horatio Nelson 1758–1805

The Bodleian collection includes the handwriting of Emma, Lady Hamilton; but Nelson's famous – infamous in its day – affair with her should not lead us to forget his marriage to Frances Woolward, Lady Nelson. Despite her years of public humiliation, which she bore with dignity and forbearance, Frances remained devoted to her husband to the end of her life.

They met in 1785 when Nelson was commander of the frigate *Boreas*, on station in the West Indies, protecting British and American trade. The daughter of a judge and niece of a wealthy planter on the island of Nevis, Frances was a widow with a small son. Pretty, charming and sophisticated, Frances was regarded by local opinion as rather a good catch for the clergyman's son from Norfolk. In his element at sea, Nelson was always rather lost and needy on land. They were married on the island in March 1787, with Nelson's friend and fellow frigate captain Prince William Henry (later King William IV) as best man. Three months later, *Boreas* returned to England, with Frances and her son following in a merchant ship – the symbolism of their separation setting something of a pattern for the rest of their lives.

Royal Navy captains were employed only when they were needed, and the five years of relative peace that followed the Nelsons' marriage saw Horatio and Frances, with no children of their own, living on half-pay in his father's chilly Norfolk rectory. But the approach of war with France provided Nelson with a new command, and he set off for the Mediterranean in 1793, where his tactical brilliance and willingness to bend the rules began to make his name. He lost the sight of his right eye at the Siege of Calvi in 1794, and at the battle of Santa Cruz de Tenerife in July 1797 a musket ball so shattered his right arm that it was immediately amputated above the elbow.

Nelson returned to Frances to convalesce, and ironically this was probably the happiest time of their married life. They bought a house near Ipswich and spent time at the spa town of Bath, from where on

6 September 1797 Frances wrote this letter to William Suckling, Nelson's maternal uncle, who had written to invite them to stay with his family in London. Frances replies with thanks, but her 'Dear Husband' must still have his arm dressed by a surgeon every day. They propose to take a house in London until the surgeon is no longer needed, after which they will spend time with the Sucklings.

His spirits are very good,

> although he suffers a great deal of Pain. The arm is taken off very high near the shoulder – Opium procures him rest – and last night he was pretty quiet. The Corporation have handsomely congratulated him on his safe arrival – Such a letter from Lord Hood – it does him honor, and I have forgot the ill treatment of former years – which My good Man received from him.

In her fluent, open hand she signs herself at the bottom of the page 'Frances H[erbert] Nelson', adding on the opposite page a postscript, 'I heard not long back from Mrs Wigley' – Suckling's married daughter.

In later years, Nelson became as proficient writing with his left hand as he had been with his right, but here, barely two months after the amputation, he is still practising with his pen:

> Pray remember me most kindly to Mr Rumsey H. Nelson.

By the following April, Nelson had returned to sea, and in September he met the British minister at Naples, Sir William Hamilton, and his enticing wife, Emma. His fellow officers found the two sides of Nelson's character – warm and generous to his shipmates but cold and heartless to his wife – incomprehensible and embarrassing. At five foot four, with the sight of only one eye and a single arm, and regularly in poor health, he was not an obvious Casanova; but heroism was clearly a powerful aphrodisiac.

overleaf Lord and Lady Nelson, letter to William Suckling, 1797

good –

although he suffers a great deal of Pain
the Arm is taken off every Night near
the Shoulder – Opium procures him
rest – and last Night he was pretty
The Corporation have handsomely Con
=gratulated him on his safe Arriv
such a letter from Lord Hood – it d
him honor, and I have forgot the
illtreatment of former Years – whic
My good Man received from Him
every thing which concerns My Hu
-band I know you feel interested
therefore – shall not make any excu
for what I have told you – Mrs Suck
will excuse My writing – but mak
My best thanks – My Husband Love
to you and Mrs Suckling – Mr Nelso
desires to be kindly remembered
you Mrs S – and family – Yr sincer

Frances H Nelson –

29

I heard not long back from
Mrs. Wigley —

pray remember me most kindly to
Mrs. Rumsey   H Nelson

Nelson lost his arm 3 July 97

Mary Wollstonecraft 1759–1797
William Godwin 1756–1836
Mary Shelley 1797–1851
Percy Bysshe Shelley 1792–1822

Mary Wollstonecraft and William Godwin lived only a short walk from one another near the Euston Road in London, and in the days before a regular postal service, family members and servants were often employed to carry their frequent correspondence. Both radicals with unconventional opinions, they continued their independent existence even after their marriage in March 1797.

They had first met in 1791, at a dinner given by their publisher Joseph Johnson for another member of his stable, Thomas Paine, author of *Common Sense* and *Rights of Man*, and godfather of the American and French revolutions. Godwin was a radical anarchist, novelist and philosopher; Wollstonecraft had already published her *Thoughts on the Education of Daughters* (1787) and *A Vindication of the Rights of Men* (1790). But at this first meeting Godwin was not impressed, and shortly afterwards Wollstonecraft travelled to Paris to observe revolutionary France for herself. When she returned, they met again, and in the fourteen months from July 1796 to September 1797 became correspondents, friends, lovers, spouses and, finally, parents of a daughter, Mary.

Wollstonecraft already had an illegitimate daughter, Fanny Imlay, from a relationship with an American she had known in France, and her feminist views, set out in *A Vindication of the Rights of Woman* (1792), regarded marriage as a form of legalized servitude; but to have two illegitimate children would have put her so far outside the boundaries of society that when she discovered she was pregnant once again, she agreed to Godwin's proposal, with the understanding that they would live apart.

The 160 notes and letters they exchanged in this time were carefully preserved, ordered and numbered by Godwin. They paint a vivid picture of a relationship of intellectual sympathy, but also full of sparks, misunderstandings and emotional vulnerability. The letters, and Godwin's

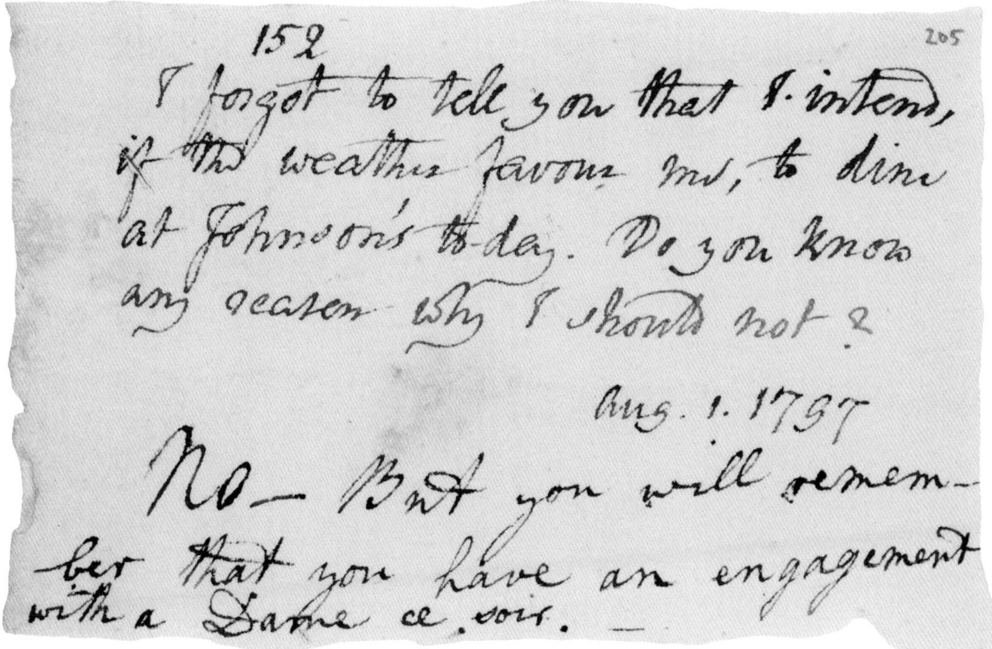

152 205

I forgot to tell you that I intend, if the weather favours me, to dine at Johnson's to-day. Do you know any reason why I should not?

Aug. 1. 1797

No – But you will remember that you have an engagement with a Dame ce soir. –

Mary Wollstonecraft and William Godwin, correspondence, 1797

diary, which the Bodleian also preserves, map their busy, independent social lives, although they often returned to see each other (and to make love, as recorded in the diary's code) in the evenings. In the note shown here, Godwin writes to say he will dine with Johnson, their publisher, unless Wollstonecraft objects. She has sent it back with a subscription:

> No – But you will remember that you have an engagement with a Dame ce soir.

The final three notes, all sent on 30 August 1797, keep Godwin updated on the progress of her labour, attended by the midwife, Mrs Blenkinsop. She is bored with the wait for 'the animal', as she calls the baby, and wishes him to send her the newspaper or a novel to while away the time. Mary was indeed born that day, but Wollstonecraft contracted puerperal fever – the most common cause of death for women until the advent of penicillin – and died on 10 September.

Godwin married again, and Mary had an unhappy upbringing with her stepmother and four siblings. Not yet seventeen, she eloped to France with the poet Shelley, early in the morning of 28 July 1814. Two years later, on holiday in a rainy Geneva, their neighbour, Lord Byron, suggested entertaining themselves by writing ghost stories. *Frankenstein* was born.

Mary wrote her draft in two notebooks, between August 1816 and April 1817. Scholars were at one point sceptical that Mary rather than Percy could have been the author of the novel; but the manuscript shows clearly that the main text is in Mary's hand, with alterations and annotations by Percy.

The page opposite is from the first notebook, volume I, chapter 6.

> When I found so astonishing a power placed within my hands, I hesitated a long time concerning the manner in which I should employ it. Although I possessed the capacity of bestowing animation, yet to prepare a frame for the reception of it, with all its intricacies of fibres, muscles and veins, still remained a work of inconceivable difficulty and labour.

Her mother's daughter, Mary Shelley was well aware of the struggle, as well as the joy, of creation.

Mary Shelley (annotated by Percy Bysshe Shelley), manuscript of *Frankenstein*, 1816–17

Chapter 6.

When I found ~~the~~ so astonishing a power
placed ~~in~~ within my hands, I hesitated a long time
concerning the ~~use~~ the manner in which I should ~~make~~ employ it.
Although I ~~conceived myself capable of~~ possessed
the capacity of bestowing animation, yet
~~my~~ to ~~create~~ prepare a ~~creature~~ frame for the ~~idea of it~~ reception of it with all its intri
cacies of fibres muscles & veins ~~must be~~
~~a~~ work of inconceivable labour [2] & diffi [1]
culty. I doubted at first whether I should
attempt the creation of a ~~creature~~ being
like ~~unto~~ myself or one of simpler
organization; ~~&~~ but my imagination
was too much exalted by my first success
to permit me to doubt of my ~~capacity~~
ability to ~~create a creature~~ give life to an animal as complex
and wonderful as man. ~~yet~~ but ~~when~~
~~when~~ & ~~looked around for my materials~~ considered
~~they~~ hardly appeared adequate to so arduous
an undertaking; ~~but I did not despair~~ but I doubted not that I should ul-
-timately succeed
I allowed that my first attempts might
be futile, my operations fail & my work
be imperfect, ~~but I looked around on~~
the improvement ~~that~~ which every day
takes place in science and mechanics
~~and in my attempt~~ I was encouraged to hope ~~was so much grander~~
~~and and all although I could not hope~~
~~that~~ my present attempts would ~~at 4~~ ~~a be~~ ~~given~~ lay
at least the foundations of future success

Still remained

The materials
at present within my command

I prepared myself
for a multitude
of reverses, my
operations ~~might~~
be baffled ~~an~~
incessantly, & at
last my work be
but imperfect,
yet, when I con
sidered

A narrative of George and Sarah Green of the parish of Grasmere addressed to a friend. A.D. 1808

You remember a single cottage at the foot of Blintern Gill, it is the only dwelling on the western side of the upper reaches of the Vale of Easedale and close under the mountain, a little stream runs over rocks and stones beside the garden wall, after tumbling down the Crags. I am sure you recollect the spot, if not, you remember George and Sarah Green who dwelt there. They left their home to go to Langdale on the afternoon of Saturday 19th March last. It was a

William Wordsworth 1770–1850
Dorothy Wordsworth 1771–1855

The resistance of the earth to human control, if not human destruction, is a matter for much current debate, as an era of thinking that Man had triumphed over Nature is giving way to a renewed understanding of the consequences of human intervention and the power of untamed natural forces. In their different ways, the documents shown here, by brother and sister writers William and Dorothy Wordsworth, are responses to the uncontrollable power of the natural world.

The first, opposite,

> A narrative of George and Sarah Green of the parish of Grasmere addressed to a friend A.D. 1808

is a memoir by Dorothy of an event that struck their close-knit community at Grasmere in 1808, when George and Sarah Green were killed in a snowstorm above Langdale, leaving eight orphaned children, six of them under eleven years old. In an age with few organized forms of social welfare, this was a tragedy that needed immediate action, if the children were to survive. The neighbourhood rallied round with a public subscription, and with marked success, since all survived to old age.

Dorothy's account of the event is determinedly unemotive and unemotional, concentrating on the search for the Greens when they did not return and on practical efforts to help the children when their parents were found dead. Her telling is deliberately plain and straightforward, with no attempt to imagine herself in the children's shoes or claim to understand their feelings; her testament to the tragedy is in her use of detail:

> You remember a single cottage at the foot of Blintern Gill, it is the only dwelling on the western side of the upper reaches of the Vale of Easdale and close under the mountain a little stream runs over rocks and stones beside the garden wall after tumbling down the Crags.

Dorothy Wordsworth, 'A narrative of George and Sarah Green'

Dorothy did not intend the account to be published in case it brought notoriety to the family, although it was privately circulated among the Wordsworths' circle. Indeed, William wrote a testy letter to another Lake District writer, John Pagen White, refusing him permission to publish the memoir, which was finally edited only in 1936.

Dorothy's literary response contrasts strongly with that of William, who wrote a ballad about the ghastly night and the terror that the parents would have felt, confronted by the implacable fells. In his telling, the children left behind are consoled by the assurances of religion and the hope of heaven, rather than by the practical efforts of neighbours.

The sonnet opposite, dated and signed by Wordsworth at Rydal Mount, the home he shared with Dorothy and his wife Mary from 1813, is a response to a much earlier and less local natural disaster. In 1607 a tidal wave in the river Severn had undermined the foundations of the medieval church of St Mary in Cardiff. Over the course of the next century, the church collapsed; but a campaign in the 1840s led to the construction of a replacement, with land donated by the marquis of Bute and money from public subscription. Wordsworth's sonnet was part of the fundraising appeal.

When Severn's sweeping flood had overthrown
  St Mary's Church, the preacher then would cry
'Thus, Christian people, God his might had shown,
  That ye to him your love may testify;
Haste, and rebuild the Pile …
  That in its beauty Cardiff may rejoice!

William Wordsworth, sonnet on the collapse of St Mary's, Cardiff

When Severn's sweeping flood had overthrown
St Mary's Church, the preacher then would cry
"Thus, Christian people, God his might had shown,
That ye to him your love may testify;
Haste, and rebuild the Pile."—But not a stone
Resumed its place. Age after age went by
And Heaven still lacked its due, though piety
In secret did, *we trust*, her loss bemoan.
But now her spirit hath put forth its claim
In power, and Poesy would lend her voice—
Let the new Church be worthy of its aim,
That in its beauty *Cardiff* may rejoice!
Oh! in the past if cause there was for shame,
Let not our times halt in their better choice.

Wm Wordsworth.

Rydal Mount,
23d. Jany. 1842.

Eng Chang

Eng and Chang 1811–1874

Eng and Chang were the original 'Siamese twins'. Born in Siam (now Thailand), at the age of seventeen they travelled to the United States with a Scottish merchant, Robert Hunter, and an American sea captain, Abel Coffin, who saw them as a money-making proposition. For several years, they toured the United States and Europe before eventually breaking with Hunter and Coffin and setting up in business for themselves. Their self-presentation was much more Western: they appeared in a formal setting, dressed in European clothes, answering audience questions in English and billing themselves 'The Siamese Twins'. They were so famous that until recently the term was applied to all conjoined twins.

Far from being simply freak show performers, the brothers were a social and financial success. They bought a North Carolina plantation, lived in some style and adopted the Western surname Bunker. They married sisters, Sarah and Adelaide Yates, and divided their time equally between two separate family homes on their property. With twenty-one children, they needed the space.

Joined fairly minimally at the breastbone, today the twins would probably be relatively easily separated, but at the time an operation was ruled out as being too dangerous. Their health was good until Chang suffered a stroke in 1870, dying four years later after a bout of bronchitis. Although himself still healthy, Eng died within hours of his brother.

The Library's 'Signature of the Siamese Twins', as it is described in a contemporary annotation, probably dates from a visit to Britain in 1830–31, before they had adopted their surname. It's not obvious if one twin wrote for both or if each wrote his name separately. The singular form, 'Signature', suggests they were thought of as one entity, and the document is alphabetized in its protective guard book under 'S' for Siamese. It's an early celebrity autograph of two men who made the most of the hand life had dealt them.

Signature of Eng and Chang, the 'Siamese twins'

dem edlen Künstler der, umgeben von dem Baalsdienst einer
falschen Kunst, durch Genius und
Studium es vermocht hat den Dienst
der wahren Kunst, wie ein anderer
Elias, treu zu bewahren, und unser
Ohr, aus dem Taumel eines gedan-
kenlosen Tönegetändels, wieder
an den reinen Ton nachahmender
Empfindung und gesetzmäßiger Harmo-
nie zu gewöhnen, – dem großen
Meister der alles sanfte Gesäusel
wie allen mächtigen Sturm der
Elemente an dem ruhigen Faden
seines Gedankens vor uns auf-
rollt – zur dankbaren Erinnerung
geschrieben

von

Albert.

Buckingham Palace.
April 24. 1847. —

Queen Victoria 1819–1901
Prince Albert 1819–1861

Victoria and Albert – first cousins – met on her seventeenth birthday in April 1836. By the time of Albert's second visit to England in October 1839, Victoria had become queen, and so it was she who proposed marriage to him. His premature death at the age of forty-two left her bereft: she wore mourning black until her own death forty years later.

Music was one of the bonds that held them together. Both were accomplished amateur pianists and singers, and Albert also wrote songs and choral music. Of their first meeting, Victoria wrote in her Journal:

> he sang to me some of his own compositions, which are beautiful and he has a very fine voice. I also sang for him.

They accompanied one another on the piano, as well as playing duets.

Albert was a particular supporter of the young German composer Felix Mendelssohn Bartholdy, whom the couple were excited to meet in London in 1842, when Mendelssohn acted as postman for a letter from Albert's cousin, the king of Prussia. The friendship prospered, as Mendelssohn made regular visits to England. On Friday 23 April 1847 (St George's Day), the couple attended the second performance of Mendelssohn's new oratorio *Elijah*, given by the Sacred Harmonic Society at Exeter Hall in the Strand, with the composer himself conducting.

Writing from Buckingham Palace the next day, Albert sent Mendelssohn his own copy of the programme, bound in royal blue shot silk with gold-tooled decoration, with an inscription in German in appreciation of the evening. The prince writes two different scripts, depending on whether he is writing English (for the place and date) or his native German. This was the common educated script of the time in Germany, but it can be hard for modern readers to decipher. Albert addresses Mendelssohn as a noble artist ('dem edlen Künstler') and

Prince Albert to Felix Mendelssohn Bartholdy, 1847

compares him to Elijah in preserving the worship of true art rather than the false worship of Baal ('umgeben von dem Baalsdienst einer falschen Kunst … hat den Dienst der wahren Kunst, wie ein anderer Elias, treu zu bewahren'):

> zur dankbaren Erinnerung geschrieben, von Albert
> [written in grateful reminiscence, by Albert].

As he often did, Mendelssohn sent a piece of music in reply, arranging one of his *Songs without Words*, Op. 85 no. 6, for the couple to play as a piano duet; the copy survives today in the Royal Collection. He died later that year, aged only thirty-eight.

After Albert's death in 1861, the queen commissioned the Scottish lawyer and writer Theodore Martin to produce a *Life of the Prince Consort*. She interviewed him for the job in 1866 and liked what she saw: 'very pleasing, clever, quiet and *sympathique*'. The finished work appeared in five volumes between 1875 and 1880. Although Martin tried hard for independence, and the volumes were well received, the queen was a controlling influence throughout their production. Some of her interventions can be seen in the page opposite, which comes from a set of proof sheets from the first volume.

Victoria is anxious to make it clear that the delay in her marrying Albert had not been because she had thoughts of another candidate:

> All that the Queen had heard of the Prince was most favourable; and, to use her own words, 'she never had an idea, if she married at all, of any one else'. Still Her Majesty [altered from 'she'] desired delay, and she had expressed this wish so strongly in writing to King Leopold, that he apparently deemed it prudent to place the prospects of a union before the Prince under a more unpromising aspect than was altogether justified by Her Majesty's language. The Prince could not otherwise have come to England, as he did, under the mistaken impression that the Queen 'wished the affair to be considered as broken off, and that for four years she could think of no marriage'.

Martin was knighted for his work in 1880.

Queen Victoria's corrections to the proof sheets of Theodore Martin, *Life of the Prince Consort*

well probably as to close the life of dazzling and continuous excitement, which the Queen has herself pronounced to be 'detrimental to all natural feelings and affections,' those who had her welfare most at heart were anxious to secure for her without longer delay a husband's guidance and support. This, however, was no simple matter. All that the Queen had heard of the Prince was most favourable, and her own inclination towards him remained unchanged. Still she desired delay, and expressed this wish strongly in writing to King Leopold, that he apparently deemed

Early Years, p. 200.

Letter to King Leopold, 15th July, 1839.

and, to use her own words, "She never had an idea of her marrying at all of any ..."

Her Majesty's reasons for desiring this delay need not be dwelt upon, as they were destined very soon to give way before the irresistible feeling inspired by the Prince, when they again met. On the 10th of October, 1839, he arrived with his brother at Windsor Castle. 'The three years,' says General Grey, 'which had passed since the Princes were last in England had greatly improved their personal appearance. Tall and manly as they both were, Prince Albert was eminently handsome. But there was also in his countenance a gentleness of expression, and peculiar sweetness in his smile, with a look of deep thought and high intelligence in his clear blue eye and expansive forehead, that added a charm to the impression he produced in those who saw him, far beyond that derived from mere beauty or regularity of features.' On the second day after their arrival, the Prince informs his friend Prince von Löwenstein, 'the most friendly demonstrations were directed towards him,' and on the same day the impression produced on the Queen is thus conveyed in a letter to her uncle: 'Albert's beauty is most striking, and he is most amiable and unaffected—in short, very *fascinating*.' 'The young men are very amiable delightful companions, and I am very happy to have them here.'

Early Years, p. 223.

Early Years, p. 246.

Reading these lines the King must have felt disposed to exclaim, like Prospero at Miranda's burst of admiration when she first sees Ferdinand,[1]

> It goes on, I see,
> As my soul prompts it.

While, for example, the Queen was looking eagerly forward to the arrival of the Prince in England, the following description of him reached her, as she informs her uncle in a letter of the 1st of October, 1839, from her cousin, Count (afterwards Prince), Alexander Mensdorff, a very correct observer

[1] I might call him
A thing divine, for nothing natural
I ever saw so noble.—*Tempest*, act i. sc. 2.

it prudent to place ~~Her Majesty~~ the prospects of a union before the Prince under a more unpromising aspect, than was altogether justified by Her Majesty's language. The Prince could not otherwise have come to England as he did, under the mistaken impression that the Queen "wished the affair to be considered as broken off, & that for four years she could think of no marriage."

See his letter to Prince Löwenstein, Early Years, p. 246.

Requirements for India.

✓ ~~Write the two High Commissioners~~

~~Inoculations~~

Sell spare clothes

~~Get clothes ready.~~

✓ ~~Prepare lecture on authors & civilisation~~

~~Correct Bunyan proofs if ready.~~

~~Complete Will.~~

~~Arrange about G.'s house.~~

~~Visit Aunt Belle if possible.~~

✓ ~~Write Lanhams at Lyndhurst.~~ ✓

~~Write Macmillan for names of 3 representatives~~

✗✓ ~~See Mr Barker re itinerary~~ ✓

✗✓ ~~Ask Mr B. about food coupons for airports.~~

~~Visit children unless they come to London.~~

~~Arrange for travellers cheques~~

~~Prepare Librarians lecture for Nov. 17.~~

~~Get Navy spun with shoes soled if necessary.~~

✓ ~~Ask Agatha re evening dress etc.~~

~~See about cleaning of navy & white spotted suit.~~

~~Buy tropical corselets~~

✓ ~~Fetch nylon nightdresses~~ (over)

[illegible] ✓ ~~get food coupons from airport.~~

Vera Brittain 1893–1970
Shirley Williams 1930–2021

Mother and daughter, the writer Vera Brittain and the politician Shirley Williams, were both committed to radical causes. This didn't necessarily make for an easy relationship. In her autobiography, *Climbing the Bookshelves* (2009), Williams recalls her closeness to her gentle father, the political scientist and philosopher Sir George Catlin, and her distance for many years from her mother. 'As a child,' she wrote, 'I realised that her deepest commitment was to writing.'

Although the writing was often in the form of novels, Brittain's subjects were never frivolous; their themes were her own great concerns, feminism and pacifism. She had grown up in a well-to-do, conservative household, but by the time she went off to Somerville College, Oxford, in 1914, she had already rejected the traditional gender roles assumed by her parents. At the end of her first year, with grim news from the war, she volunteered as a VAD (Voluntary Aid Detachment) nurse and was sent to care for returning soldiers in London.

Brittain was very close to her brother, Edward, and his friends Roland Leighton, Victor Richardson and Geoffrey Thurlow. All four had joined up, and she and Roland had become engaged during his first leave from the Western Front in 1915. One by one, the four young men were killed: Roland by a sniper in December 1915; Geoffrey a year after having been wounded in 1916; Edward, wounded at the Battle of the Somme, at Asiago in 1918; and Victor from his wounds at Vimy Ridge.

Brittain never really recovered from the shock; but she returned to Somerville and formed an important friendship with a fellow student, the writer Winifred Holtby. After Oxford, they made a living as writers of fiction and journalism, joined with social activism, but Holtby's early death in 1935 was another serious blow. By then, however, Brittain had married Catlin, given birth to her two children, John and Shirley, and published the memoir for which she is most famous, *Testament of Youth*

Vera Brittain, 'to do' list for trip to India, 1949

(1933). The book relives the intensity of wartime experience and honours the sacrifice of a lost generation, while revealing the roots of her own pacifist convictions. It was an instant best-seller and is still in print.

In 1949 Brittain was invited to be a delegate at the World Pacifist Meeting in India. The page illustrated overleaf is her preparatory 'to do' list, 'Requirements for India', from her account of the trip, written up in a series of reporter's notebooks that the Bodleian holds. The range of tasks, almost all of which she has successfully crossed off, gives a vivid sense of her varied life:

> Write the two High Commissioners …
> Prepare lecture on authors and civilisation
> Correct Bunyan proofs if ready …
> Ask Mr B about food coupons for airports …
> Visit children unless they come to London
> Get Navy open-work shoes soled if necessary …
> Buy tropical corselets.

The question of food coupons is repeated – a reminder of the complications of travel while Britain was still under rationing.

George Catlin stood unsuccessfully as a Labour Party candidate in 1931 and 1935; his daughter Shirley was a Labour member of parliament (MP) from 1964 until 1979, including a spell as Secretary of State for Education. She lost her seat when the Conservatives won the May 1979 general election. In the letter of 10 June shown here, she replies to the writer and former *Observer* journalist Anthony Sampson, who had written to express his sympathy:

> I guess I feel rather relieved about being out of Parliament – perhaps the obverse of whatever makes you feel apprehensive. I began to feel a bit ground down with responsibility!

She was not, however, at a loose end: 'you can get me at PSI' (the Policy Studies Institute, a left-wing think tank). Williams was not out for long. Disillusioned with the Labour Party, she was one of the Gang of Four that

Shirley Williams, letter to Anthony Sampson, 1979

broke away to form the Social Democratic Party in 1981, becoming its first MP at the Crosby by-election later that year. She was made a member of the House of Lords in 1993.

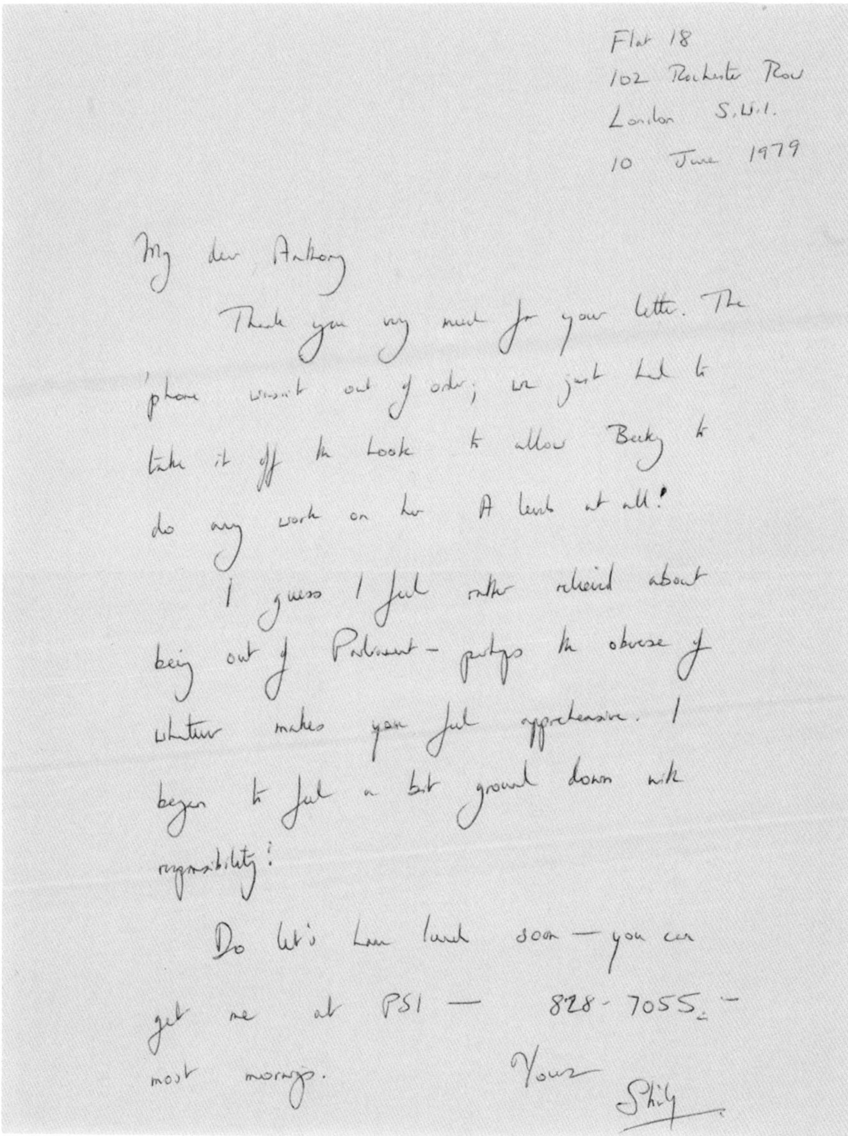

Flat 18
102 Rochester Row
London S.W.1.
10 June 1979

My dear Anthony

Thank you very much for your letter. The 'phone wasn't out of order; we just had to take it off the hook to allow Becky to do any work on her A levels at all!

I guess I feel rather relieved about being out of Parliament – perhaps the obverse of whatever makes you feel apprehensive. I began to feel a bit ground down with responsibility!

Do let's have lunch soon — you can get me at PSI — 828-7055 — most mornings.

Yours

Shirley

SCRIBES AND CALLIGRAPHERS

cwæð him eftsona simon ioh
16 Dicit ei iterum simon iohannis
lufast tu me cwæð him gee driht ðu wast
diligis me aitilli etiam dne tu scis
ðætte ic lufo ðec cwæð him foed lombor
quia amo te. Dicit ei pasce agnos
mine cwæð him ðriddan siðe simō ioh
17 meos. Dicit ei tertio simon iohan
lufast me gunrotad pet
nis amas me contristatus est pe
forðon cwæð him ðriddan lufast me
trus quia dixit ei tertio amas me
& cwæð him driht ðu alle wast ðu
et dicit ei dne tu omnia scis quia
ic lufige ðec cwæð him foed sceap mine
amo te. Dicit ei pasce oues meas.
soð soðlice icsecga ðe miððy ðu wære
18 Amen amen dico tibi cum esses
gingra ðu gyrdest ðe & ðu gonga
iunior cingebas te et ambulabas
hwider ðu walde miððy soðlice ðu bist aldig
ubi uolebas. Cum autem senueris
aðenest honda ðine & oðer ðec
extendes manus tuas et alius te
gyrdeð & lædeð hider ðu nelt ðas
19 cinget et ducet quo non uis. Hoc
soðlice cwæð getacnade on hwelcum
autem dixit significans qua
deaðe geberhtnad wære god
morte clarificaturus esset dm.
& ðis miððy cwæð cwæð him gefolgiga
Et hoc cum dixisset dicit ei seque
re me.

Se min bruche gebidde fore owun ðe ðas boc gloesde. Færmen ðæm preoste æt harawu

Macregol d. 822
Owun 10th century
Farmon 10th century

This spectacular copy of the Christian Gospels was decorated – so the reader is told by a note at the end of the book, asking for prayers – by a certain Macregol, who was also one of its two scribes. He was almost certainly the same Macregol who was bishop and abbot of Birr in County Offaly, Ireland, and who was renowned for his scribal ability.

The Latin text of the Gospels (here, John 21:16–19) is written in a large, clear, formal script known as semi-uncial. The letters that begin each verse are highlighted in alternating red and yellow ochre, and outlined with dots of the opposite colour. There was not yet an agreed system of numbering the chapters and verses of the Bible (the marginal numbers here were added much later), but the coloured initials enable readers to see their way from one sentence to the next. The text begins:

> *Dicit ei iterum simon iohannis Diligis me*
> *ait illi Etiam Domine tu scis quia amo te*
> [He said to him again, 'Simon son of John, do you love me?'
> He said to him, 'Indeed Lord, you know that I love you.']

Macregol is not the only scribe on the page. By the later tenth century, the book had found its way to England, where an Old English translation-gloss was added between the lines of the Latin. Along with the Lindisfarne Gospels, this is the earliest rendering of the Gospels into English. On this page from the end of the text, below the decorative border, the glossing scribes identify themselves as Owun ('oƿun') and Farmon ('færmen'), working 'æt hara ƿuda' – Harewood, though whether Harewood in Hereford or in Yorkshire is not known. Owun and Farmon each write different Old English dialects.

We know nothing more until 1665, when the book was owned by John Rushworth, formerly deputy clerk to the House of Commons. He gave it to the Bodleian Library perhaps in 1681.

The Macregol Gospels

qua vorax flamma pascitur. Si quis autem habet in conscientia sua zizania quae inimicus homo dormiente patre familias superseminavit, haec ignis exuret, haec vorabit incendium, et omnia sanctorum oculis eorum supplicia monstrabuntur. qui autem auro et argento et lapide pretioso edificaverit super fundamentum domini fenum, ligna, stipulam, ignis pabulum sempiterni. Porro qui volunt supplicia aliquando finiri, et licet post multa tempora, tamen habere terminum tormenta, his utuntur testimoniis. Cum intraverit plenitudo gentium, tunc omnis Israel salvus fiet. Et iterum. Conclusit deus omnia sub peccato, ut omnibus misereatur. Et in alio loco scriptum est. Iram domini sustinebo. loquitur quoniam peccavi ei, donec iudicet causam meam, et auferat iudicium meum, et educat in lucem. Et rursum. Benedicam te domine quoniam iratus es mihi, avertisti faciem tuam a me, et misertus es mei. Dominus quoque loquitur ad peccatores. Cum ira furoris mei fuerit, rursum sanabo. Et hoc est quod in alio loco dicitur. Quam grandis multitudo bonitatis tuae domine, quam abscondisti timentibus te. Quae omnia replicant, affirmare cupientes post cruciatus atque tormenta futura refrigeria, quae nunc abscondita sunt ab his quibus timor utilis est, ut dum supplicia reformidant, peccare desistant. Quod nos dei solius debemus scientiae derelinquere, cuius non solum misericordiae, sed et tormenta in pondere sunt, et novit quem quomodo aut quamdiu debeat iudicare.

Solumque dicamus, quod humanae convenit fragilitati. Domine ne in furore tuo arguas me, neque in ira tua corripias me. Et sicut diaboli et omnium negatorum atque impiorum qui dixerunt in corde suo non est deus, credimus eterna tormenta, sic peccatorum atque impiorum et tamen christianorum quorum opera igni probanda sunt atque purganda, moderatam arbitramur et mixtam clementiae sententiam iudicis.

EXPLICIT LIBER BEATI IHERONIMI SUPER YSAIAM.

Hugo Pictor fl. late 11th century

To describe oneself as a painter and decorator had different connotations in the late eleventh century. Hugo, the artist-decorator and one of the four scribes of this fine copy of Jerome's commentary on Isaiah, writes this phrase, 'pictor et illuminator', alongside the self-portrait he added at the end of the text.

This is not the only manuscript Hugo is known to have written. He seems to have been working in Normandy (possibly at Jumièges), producing books for abbeys there and in England after the Conquest of 1066. This book was already part of Exeter Cathedral library when Osbern was bishop (1072–1103). Exeter was Thomas Bodley's hometown and his brother Lawrence was a canon of the cathedral. Storage conditions for its manuscript books were poor – the effects of damp are still evident in the purple-pink mould affecting the parchment. The cathedral gave most of its collection to the new Library as a foundation gift in 1602.

This copy of the text also has illustrations by Hugo, which include depictions of Isaiah, Jerome and the woman for whom the commentary was composed, Eustochium. Despite portraying himself with a monastic tonsure, Hugo may not in fact have been a monk – merely someone with literate, clerkly status. He appears to be left-handed; but like his green hair, this may not be intended as an accurate record of reality. But it is certainly true that scribes worked at slanted writing desks, dipped their quill pens into horn inkwells, and held down the springy parchment with a penknife, as Hugo does here.

Tiny as he is, and modest as it may seem, the figure makes a dramatic statement, if we remember that it is probably the earliest self-portrait in Western art since classical times.

Hugo Pictor, Jerome's commentary on Isaiah

Iam librarius hoc & ipse dicat.
Ohe iam satis est ohe libellę.

M·VAL·MARTIALIS EPIGRAMMATON LIB·V· AD CAESARĒ GERMANICUM

HOC TIBI PALLADIAE SEU COLLIBUS UTERIS ALBAE
Cæsar. & hinc triuiam: prospicis inde thetim
Seu tua ueridicæ discunt responsa sorores:
Plana suburbani qua cadit unda freti.
Seu plac& æneæ nutrix: seu filia solis:
Siue salutiferis candidus anxur aquis.
Mittimus o rex felix tutela salusq;:
Sospite quo gratū credimus ēē iouem.
Tu tantū accipias: ego te legisse putabo.
Et tumidus falsa credulitatē fruar.

Bartolomeo Sanvito 1433–1511

It's an interesting quirk of history that the invention in Europe of the movable-type printing press, around 1450, came at the same time as a new flourishing of the art of the scribe. The elaborate and entwined Gothic scripts of the fourteenth and fifteenth centuries, often grimly illegible to modern eyes, gave way to a revival in the Italian humanist period of an older and clearer mode of writing. As part of the modernization of his empire, the ninth-century ruler Charlemagne had ordered the adoption of a new, legible script based on Roman models. 'Caroline minuscule' (from Carolus, his name in Latin) became standard across Europe. Its rebirth in these humanist hands was to have lasting ramifications: not only was it taken up by the earliest printers for their own fonts, but its virtues of neatness and clarity mean it is still in use today.

The separated letters of Caroline minuscule make it relatively slow to write, so the succeeding generation of humanist scribes developed a faster, cursive form, known as italic. Sanvito was one of the greatest exponents of the new writing, with a career that moved from his native Padua to Venice and Rome, working for the most influential men of the time and alongside some of the best miniature painters. Renaissance scholars looked to reinstate the literature of the Greeks and Romans in the canon of knowledge, and they made or commissioned copies of ancient texts in these new scripts derived from those of an earlier age. True to this humanist enterprise, most of Sanvito's surviving works are copies of classical texts, such as the *Epigrams* of the Roman poet Martial, dating from the early 1460s, shown here. Although we cannot be sure whether Sanvito himself was responsible for the striking initial, the rest of the page is his. The main text is in a delicate and beautifully balanced italic, while the multicoloured headings are a revival of the square capitals familiar from Roman inscriptions on stone.

Bartolomeo Sanvito, Martial's *Epigrams*

Esther Inglis 1570/71–1624

Esther Inglis was probably taught to write by her mother, who was also a skilled calligrapher. Her Huguenot parents had come to London as religious refugees from Catholic France, moving to Edinburgh when Esther was small and adopting Inglis as an anglicized version of their name, Langlois or Anglois.

Inglis is not the only woman calligrapher of the time whose work survives, but her combination of quality and quantity make her remarkable. At least fifty-nine of the books she wrote survive, dating between 1586 and 1624. Most are dedicated to the rich and famous, perhaps from commissions or perhaps 'on spec': Inglis wrote to make a living. This copy of the *Proverbs of Solomon* in French (one of three versions she produced, along with another three in English), is dedicated to Robert Devereux, second earl of Essex (1566–1601), and was:

> *Escrites en diverses sortes de lettres par Esther Anglois Françoise*
> *A Lislebourg En Escosse 1599*[.]
> [Written in various sorts of letters by the Frenchwoman Esther Inglis
> at Edinburgh in Scotland 1599.]

She wasn't joking. Each chapter of the book is executed in a different type of script, from elegant italic to letters written in an extraordinary cursive loopy chain made up of hundreds of tiny dots – a sort of *pointilliste* alphabet. The scripts were not her own invention; she used pattern books by recognized master calligraphers.

Everything on the page shown here is the work of Inglis herself, from the patterned border, which appears on every page, to her self-portrait, which is found in similar form in many of her productions. She is pictured, pen in hand, having just written out her Christian motto –

De l'Eternel le bien	[From the Eternal [God] comes good
De moi le mal, ou rien[.]	From me comes evil, or nothing.]

Esther Inglis, *Proverbs of Solomon*

– poignant, in the light of the beauty of her creation. The precision and uniformity of her handiwork was as evident in her needlework as her calligraphy. Many of her books (though not this one) have textile covers that she made herself.

Ditchling 19 Decr. mcmxli.

Dear

This is to wish you a happy Xmas and to thank you for many little kindnesses wh. from time to time you most thoughtfully have done me — your last kind letter ✱ (of 23.XI.41) refers to my "new theory of lettering": I don't know what that refers to [I'm trying to write a Book — perhaps it will be in it] — & to let you know that there's life in the Old Dog yet

with very kind regards Yrs. E.J.

{✱ wh. is one of them}

Edward Johnston 1872–1944

The visionary designer William Morris had pioneered a new interest in calligraphy as part of his campaign to promote all things made by hand. Edward Johnston had been making his own 'parchments' even as a child in Scotland, before he encountered the Arts and Crafts movement and Morris's own attempts to produce illuminated manuscripts in the medieval style. Still, he was lucky, given his inexperience, to be put in charge of a new lettering class at the Central School of Arts and Crafts in London while still in his twenties. The influence of the class and Johnston's teaching reverberates today.

At the British Museum, Johnston studied the script of ancient and medieval manuscripts, under the tutelage of Sydney Cockerell, the charismatic director of the Fitzwilliam Museum in Cambridge; but he developed a style that was all his own. His comprehensive handbook *Writing & Illuminating & Lettering* (1906) was inspirational in combining both the study of ancient script (palaeography) and its revival in modern practice.

From his study of the historical development of script, Johnston formed a preference for italic, written with a broad-edged nib, such as the AF monogram opposite; the remainder of the page is in his spiky and characterful narrow italic. The letter was sent from his home at Ditchling in Sussex on 19 December 1941 (mcmxli) to A[lfred] F[airbank], a leading light of the next generation. Johnston refers to another book he is trying to write – one begun in the 1920s, in fact – but his creativity was not to be so easily captured in words; it remained unfinished at his death.

Ironically, Johnston is now best known for a typeface rather than a written script. Rather against his usual run of work, he was commissioned by Frank Pick to produce an alphabet to be used in the London Underground. The clear and simple design he produced in 1916 is still part of the brand recognition of London's transport.

Edward Johnston, letter to Alfred Fairbank, 1941

POSTSCRIPT

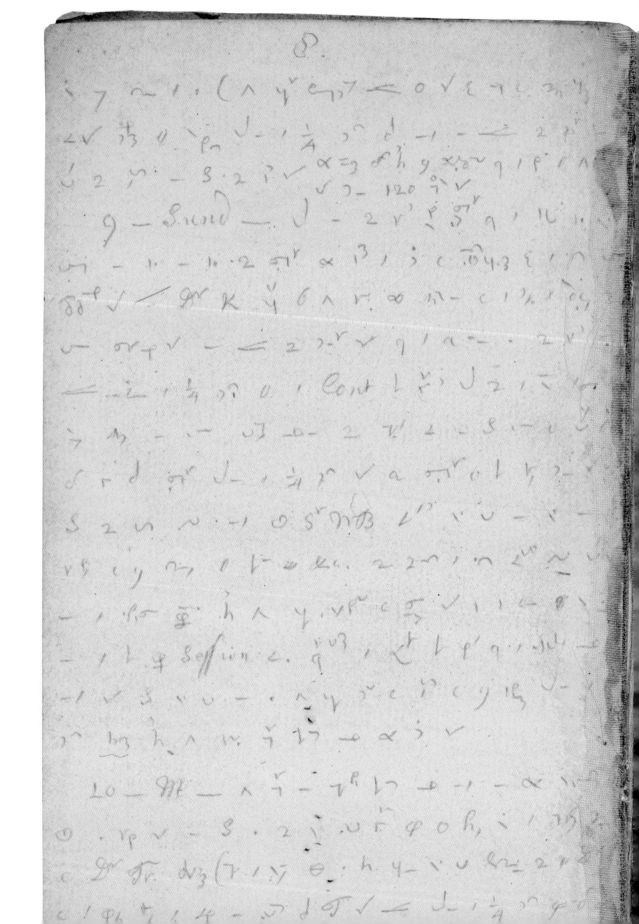

[illegible]

[illegible] 120 [illegible]

9 — Second — [illegible]

[illegible] Cont [illegible]

[illegible]

[illegible] Session [illegible]

[illegible]

10 — M — [illegible]

[illegible]

Samuel Pepys 1633–1703

Just as many letters end with an autograph 'P.S.', so this book cannot close without a nod to one of the best-known writers by hand, Samuel Pepys. His famous diary covers less than ten years of his life (1 January 1660 to 31 May 1669), but its combination of sex, gossip and literary verve have entranced generations of readers. What is less well known is that Pepys recorded his entries in a form of shorthand invented by Thomas Shelton (1600–*c*.1650), so it was not until 1841 that a deciphered edition was printed.

The diary is now held in Pepys's old Cambridge college, Magdalene; but the Bodleian preserves his Admiralty papers, including a second diary, also written in shorthand, kept by Pepys during a visit to Tangier and Spain in 1683–4. Although the latter part of the trip was a holiday, the beginning most definitely was not. Tangier had been acquired as a colony by Charles II as part of the dowry of his wife, Catherine of Braganza. Pepys, whose working life was largely spent as a naval official, was appointed to the committee overseeing Tangier in 1662 – a position he held until 1679. For the king, what had at first seemed a lucrative acquisition, by 1683 had become a problem. He sent Lord Dartmouth with a fleet of ships to evacuate the colonial inhabitants, with Pepys as his secretary in charge of assigning compensation. The delicacy of the task was perhaps what prompted Pepys to revive his diary-keeping habit.

He wrote on small, narrow pages, ideal for slipping into a pocket. In all honesty, this Second Diary, as it is known, is not a patch on the first for pacy interest, but some of the details resonate – his concern for music, for example, or for his own health (he's a martyr to mosquitoes). And on a few occasions, such as this entry for 8 September, the old Pepys shines through, where he ends the day (third line down)

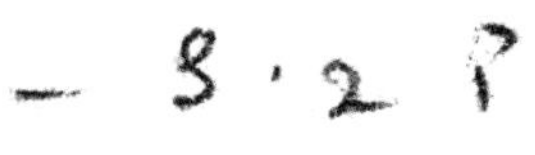 '... and so to bed'.

Samuel Pepys, diary from Tangier, 1683

FURTHER READING

Introduction

J.W. von Goethe and F.H. Jacobi, *Briefwechsel Zwischen Goethe und F. H. Jacobi*, Weidmann, Leipzig, 1846, no. 119

Marcus Tullius Cicero, *Letters to Atticus*, ed. and transl. E.O. Winstedt, Loeb Classical Library, 3 vols, Heinemann, London, 1912–28

A.N.L. Munby, *The Cult of the Autograph Letter in England*, Athlone Press, London, 1962

David Ganz, '"Mind in Character": Ancient and Medieval Ideas about the Status of the Autograph as an Expression of Personality' in *Of the Making of Books: Medieval Manuscripts, Their Scribes and Readers. Essays Presented to M.B. Parkes*, eds P.R. Robinson and Rivkah Zim, Scolar, Aldershot, 1997, pp. 280–99

Walter Benjamin, 'The Work of Art in the Age of Mechanical Reproduction', in his *Illuminations*, ed. with an introduction by Hannah Arendt, transl. by Harry Zorn, Pimlico Press, London, 1999, pp. 211–44

P.J. Parsons, *City of the Sharp-Nosed Fish: Greek lives in Roman Egypt*, Weidenfeld & Nicolson, London, 2007

Jewish Treasures from Oxford Libraries, eds Rebecca Abrams and César Merchán-Hamann, Bodleian Library, Oxford, 2020

The Tudor Court

Lucy Wooding, *Tudor England: A History*, Yale University Press, New Haven, CT, 2022

Some of the papers of Henry VII are online via the National Archives website https://www.nationalarchives.gov.uk/help-with-your-research/research-guides/letters-papers-henry-viii/

Thomas Cranmer, Edmund Bonner and Henry VIII, *The Institution of a Christian Man: The Bishops' Book (1537); The King's Book (1543); Bishop Bonner's Book (1555)*, ed. G.L. Bray, James Clarke and Co., Cambridge, 2019

Thomas Cromwell is currently best known via the trilogy of *Wolf Hall* novels by Hilary Mantel; the National Archive has a blog post about the sources and accuracy of her interpretation: https://blog.nationalarchives.gov.uk/wolf-hall-national-archives/

G.R. Elton, *England Under the Tudors*, foreword by Diarmaid MacCulloch, Routledge, London, 2018

Chapter 4 of Aysha Pollnitz, *Princely Education in Early Modern Britain*, Cambridge University Press, Cambridge, 2015, considers Edward VI's education

Peter Beal and Grace Ioppolo (eds), *Elizabeth I and the Culture of Writing*, British Library, London, 2007; Elizabeth's book, MS. Cherry 36, is fully digitalized at: https://digital.bodleian.ox.ac.uk/objects/e3609380-b56e-4bde-9636-85736559db52/

Marc Shell, *Elizabeth's Glass: With 'The Glass of the Sinful Soul' (1544) by Elizabeth I and 'Epistle Dedicatory' & 'Conclusion' (1548) by John Bale*, University of Nebraska Press, Lincoln, NB, 1993

Doran, Susan (ed.), *Elizabeth and Mary: Royal Cousins, Rival Queens*, ed. Susan Doran, British Library, London, 2021

Poets and Novelists

Helen Gardner, *John Donne's Holograph of 'A letter to the Lady Carey and Mrs Essex Riche'*, Scolar Mansell in conjuction with the Bodleian Library, Oxford, 1972

R.W. Chapman, *The Watsons: A Fragment*, Athlone Press, London, and Dover, NH, 1985

Jane Austen's *Volume the First* is digitized at: https://digital.bodleian.ox.ac.uk/objects/9e416479-53f1-480f-ac97-de44dd5e7e59/

Austen's surviving letters are digitized at:
https://www.e-enlightenment.com/letterbook/collections/austjaEE

Elizabeth Gaskell, *The Life of Charlotte Brontë*, ed. Elisabeth Jay, Penguin, London, 1997

The Letters of Mrs. Gaskell, eds J.A.V. Chapple and Arthur Pollard, Manchester University Press, Manchester, 1966

The Letters of Charlotte Brontë: with a Selection of Letters by Family and Friends, ed. Margaret Smith, 3 vols, Oxford University Press, Oxford, 1995–2004

Andrew Thompson (ed.), 'A George Eliot Holograph Notebook: An edition (MS. Don g. 8) held at the Bodleian Library, Oxford', *George Eliot – George Henry Lewes Studies*, no. 50/51, 2006, pp. 1–109

Malcolm Pasley, *Catalogue of the Kafka Centenary Exhibition, 1983*, Bodleian Library, Oxford, 1983

T.S. Eliot, *The Rock: A Pageant Play*, Faber & Faber, London, 1934

T.S. Eliot, *Collected Poems, 1909–1935*, Faber & Faber, London, 1954

Scientists

Newton's papers are collected at:
https://www.lib.cam.ac.uk/collections/departments/manuscripts-university-archives/significant-archival-collections/papers-sir

John T. Young, 'Isaac Newton's Alchemical Notes in the Royal Society', *Notes & Records of the Royal Society of London*, vol. 60, 2006, pp. 25–34

Letters of Edward Jenner, and Other Documents Concerning the Early History of Vaccination, ed. Genevieve Miller, Johns Hopkins Press, Baltimore, MD, 1983

Mary Somerville, *On the Connexion of the Physical Sciences*, 5th edn, London, 1840

Mary Somerville, *The Mechanism of the Heavens*, John Murray, London, 1831

Christopher Hollings, Ursula Martin and Adrian Rice, *Ada Lovelace: The Making of a Computer Scientist*, Bodleian Library, Oxford, 2018

Charles Darwin's Beagle Diary, ed. R.D. Keynes, Cambridge University Press, Cambridge, 2001

Darwin's letters are collected at the Cambridge University Darwin Correspondence Project: https://www.darwinproject.ac.uk/

Robert Fox, 'Einstein in Oxford', *Notes and Records of the Royal Society of London*, vol. 72, 2018, pp. 293–318

Guy Dodson, 'Dorothy Mary Crowfoot Hodgkin, O.M.', *Biographical Memoirs of Fellows of the Royal Society*, Vol. 48, 2002, pp. 179–219

Georgina Ferry, *Dorothy Hodgkin: A Life*, Granta, London, 1998

Conrad Keating, *Great Medical Discoveries: An Oxford Story*, Bodleian Library, Oxford, 2013

Reformers

For a Bodleian blogpost on the Luther autograph, see: https://teachingthecodex.com/2017/10/28/can-i-have-your-autograph-martin-luthers-sprichwortersammlung-oxford-bodleian-library-ms-add-a-92/

Thomas Coram's Foundling Hospital is still pursuing its work: https://coramstory.org.uk/

John Newton and William Cowper, *Olney Hymns*, T. Nelson, London, 1855

John Pinfold, *The Slave Trade Debate: Contemporary Writings For and Against*, Bodleian Library, Oxford, 2007

Florence Nightingale: Letters and Reflections, ed. Rosemary Hartill, Arthur James, Evesham, 1996

Emmeline Pankhurst, *My Own Story*, London, 1914

Susan Pedersen, *Eleanor Rathbone and the Politics of Conscience*, Yale University Press, New Haven, CT, 2004

Friendships of 'Largeness and Freedom': Andrews, Tagore, and Gandhi: An Epistolary Account, 1912–1940, ed. Uma Das Gupta, Oxford University Press, New Delhi, 2018

Friends and Rivals

Charles I and Oliver Cromwell, see: http://www.putneydebates.com/

The papers of both George Washington and Thomas Jefferson are stored (and digitized) by the Library of Congress, Washington, DC:
https://www.loc.gov/collections/george-washington-papers/about-this-collection/
https://www.loc.gov/collections/thomas-jefferson-papers/about-this-collection/

C.R Leslie, *Memoirs of the Life of John Constable: Composed Chiefly of His Letters*, ed. Jonathan Mayne, 3rd edn, Phaidon Press, London, 1995

John Gage (ed.), *The Collected Correspondence of J.M.W. Turner: With an Early Diary and a Memoir by George Jones*, Oxford University Press, Oxford, 1980

John Stuart Mill, *Autobiography*, ed. John Robson, Penguin, London, 1989

John Stuart Mill, 'Walking Tour of Yorkshire and the Lake District', in *The Collected Works of John Stuart Mill Volume 27 – Journals and Debating Speeches Part II*, University of Toronto Press, Toronto, 2000

Jeremy Bentham's 'auto-icon' (his preserved body) is kept at University College, London, which houses a research project on the man and his works:
https://www.ucl.ac.uk/bentham-project/about-jeremy-bentham

Helen Langley (ed.), *Benjamin Disraeli, Earl of Beaconsfield: Scenes from an Extraordinary Life*, Bodleian Library, Oxford, 2003

Benjamin Disraeli Letters: 1860–1864, Volume VIII, ed. M.G. Wiebe, et al., University of Toronto Press, Toronto, 2009

H.C.G. Matthew, *Gladstone 1809–1898, Clarendon Press, Oxford, 1997*

Wilfred Owen, *Poems*, ed. Siegfried Sassoon, Chatto & Windus, London, 1920

Jon Stallworthy, *Anthem for Doomed Youth: Twelve Soldier Poets of the First World War*, Constable, London, 2002

The Henry Moore Foundation is at:
https://henry-moore.org/discover-and-research/discover-henry-moore/

For Barbara Hepworth at Wakefield and St Ives:
https://barbarahepworth.org.uk/

Travellers and Adventurers

For more on Books of Hours in England see Eamon Duffy, *Marking the Hours: English People and their Prayers, 1240–1570*, Yale University Press, New Haven, CT, 2006

England and Russia: Comprising the Voyages of John Tradescant the Elder, Sir Hugh Willoughby, Richard Chancellor, Nelson, and Others, to the White Sea, etc., ed. I. Hamel and trans. J.S. Leigh, R. Bentley, London, 1854

Barrie Juniper and Hanneke Grootenboer, *The Tradescants' Orchard: The Mystery of a Seventeenth-century Painted Fruit Book*, Bodleian Library, Oxford, 2013

'Tradescants' Orchard' is fully digitized at:
https://digital.bodleian.ox.ac.uk/objects/5475fa30-607d-4ca9-b809-213c8c8d1a42/

Mary Kingsley, *West African Studies*, 2nd edn, Macmillan, London, 1901

Mary Kingsley, *Travels in West Africa*, Phoenix, London, 2000

Fridtjof Nansen, *Farthest North: The Voyage and Exploration of the Fram and the Fifteen Month's Expedition by Fridtjof Nansen and Hjalmar Johansen*, Gibson Square, London, 2002

Gertrude Bell, *A Woman in Arabia: The Writings of the Queen of the Desert*, ed. Georgina Howell, Penguin, New York, 2015

T.E. Lawrence, *Seven Pillars of Wisdom: a Triumph: 1919–1920*, privately printed, Oxford, 1922. The manuscript is fully digitized at:
https://digital.bodleian.ox.ac.uk/objects/35b69208-effd-457d-b8ab-22f4b9029b5a/

Patrick Leigh Fermor, *A Time of Gifts: On Foot to Constantinople: From the Hook of Holland to the Middle Danube*, John Murray, London, 1977

Patrick Leigh Fermor, *Mani: Travels in the Southern Peloponnese*, John Murray, London, 1958

Composers

Handel's Conducting Score of 'Messiah': Reproduced in Facsimile from the Manuscript in the Library of St Michael's College, Tenbury Wells, introduction by Watkins Shaw, Scolar Press, London, 1974

Peter Ward Jones, *Mendelssohn: An Exhibition to Celebrate the Life of Felix Mendelssohn Bartholdy (1809–1847), June–August 1997*, Bodleian Library, Oxford, 1997

Peter Ward Jones, *The Mendelssohns on Honeymoon: The 1837 Diary of Felix and Cécile Mendelssohn Bartholdy, Together with Letters to their Families*, Clarendon Press, Oxford, 1997

Ethel Smyth, *Impressions That Remained: Memoirs*, Longmans, Green, London, 1919

Gustav Holst, *Sāvitri*, Eulenberg, London, 1976

Ralph Vaughan Williams, *Along the Field: Eight Housman Songs for Voice and Violin*, Oxford University Press, London, 1954

A.E. Houseman, *A Shropshire Lad*, Tern Press, Market Drayton, 1990

V.P. Stroeher, *My Beloved Man: The Letters of Benjamin Britten and Peter Pears*, eds Nicholas Clark and Jude Brimmer, Boydell Press, Martlesham, 2016

Writers for Children

Lewis Carroll and John Tenniel, *The Annotated Alice: Alice's Adventures in Wonderland and Through the Looking Glass*, ed. Martin Gardner, Penguin, London, 2001

C.L. Dodgson, *Symbolic Logic. Part I. Elementary*, Macmillan, London, 1896

Doris L. Moore, *E. Nesbit: A Biography*, Ernest Benn, London, 1967

Kenneth Grahame, *Paths to the River Bank: The Origins of 'The Wind in the Willows'*, Blandford, London, 1988

Kenneth Grahame, *My Dearest Mouse: 'The Wind in the Willows' Letters*, ed. David Gooderson, Pavilion, London, 1988

Alan Bennett, *The Wind in the Willows*, Faber & Faber, London, 1996

Arthur Ransome, *'Racundra's' First Cruise (Sailing on the Eastern Baltic)*, B.W. Huebsch, New York, 1923

Arthur Ransome, *The Autobiography of Arthur Ransome*, ed. Rupert Hart-Davis, Arthur Ransome Trust, Durham, 2018

Catherine McIlwaine, *Tolkien: Maker of Middle-earth*, Bodleian Library, Oxford, 2018

Quentin Blake: https://www.quentinblake.com/

Philip Pullman, *Lyra's Oxford*, Corgi Childrens, London, 2007

Spies and Detectives

Arthur Conan Doyle, *Memories and Adventures*, Oxford University Press, Oxford, 1989

Arthur Conan Doyle, *Waterloo and The Speckled Band*, Cambridge Scholars Publishing, Newcastle, 2009

A 2020 radio play, *Eric the Skull*, about the founding of the Detection Club, by Simon Brett (himself a member), can be heard at:
https://www.bbc.co.uk/sounds/play/m000j9kf

The Club produced a series of co-authored detective novels, with each member writing a single chapter, e.g., *The Floating Admiral* (Hodder & Stoughton, London, 1931) and *Ask a Policeman* (Arthur Baker, London, 1933)

Agatha Christie, *Passenger to Frankfurt: An Extravaganza*, Crime Club, London, 1970

Raymond Chandler, *The Simple Art of Murder*, Hamish Hamilton, London, 1950

Selected Letters of Raymond Chandler, ed. Frank MacShane, Columbia University Press, New York, 1981

P.D. James, *Talking about Detective Fiction*, Bodleian Library, Oxford, 2009

John le Carré, *Tinker, Tailor, Soldier, Spy*, Hodder & Stoughton, London, 1974

Families

Many of the Herschel family papers are now available online, for example from the Harry Ransom Center, University of Texas:
https://norman.hrc.utexas.edu/fasearch/findingAid.cfm?eadid=00568
the Wellcome Collection, London: https://wellcomecollection.org
and the Royal Museums Greenwich, London https://www.rmg.co.uk/collections

Julia Margaret Cameron, *The Herschel Album: An Album of Photographs Presented to Sir John Herschel*, National Portrait Gallery, London, 1975

Papers relating to Lord and Lady Nelson are kept at the National Maritime Museum (Royal Museums Greenwich):
https://www.rmg.co.uk/collections/archive/search/horatio%20nelson

The Nelson Society is at:
https://nelson-society.com/

Daisy Hay, *The Making of Mary Shelley's* Frankenstein, Bodleian Library, Oxford, 2019

Mary Wollstonecraft Shelley, *The Frankenstein Notebooks*, ed. Charles E. Robinson, Bodleian Library, London, 1996

The Abinger Papers (of the Godwin-Wollstonecraft-Shelley family) are digitized at:
https://digital.bodleian.ox.ac.uk/collections/abinger/

An online exhibition of the Godwin-Wollstonecraft-Shelley family is at: https://wayback.archive-it.org/org-467/20160519085535/http://shelleysghost.bodleian.ox.ac.uk/

Dorothy Wordsworth, *George and Sarah Green: A Narrative*, ed. E. de Selincourt, Clarendon Press, Oxford, 1936

The Letters of William and Dorothy Wordsworth, ed. E. de Selincourt, et al., Clarendon Press, Oxford, 1967–1993

Theodore Martin, *The Life of the Prince Consort*, 5 vols, London, 1875–1880

W.W. Tulloch, *The Story of the Life of the Prince Consort, Revised by the Queen*, London, 1887

Shirley Williams, *Climbing the Bookshelves*, Virago, London, 2009

Vera Brittain, *Testament of Youth: An Autobiographical Study of the Years 1900–1925*, Centenary Edition, Virago, London, 2018

Scribes and Calligraphers

The Macregol Gospels are fully digitized at:
https://digital.bodleian.ox.ac.uk/objects/b708f563-b804-42b5-bd0f-2826dfaeb5cc/

Hugo Pictor and his manuscript is chapter 6 in Christopher Dd Hamel's *Meetings with Remarkable Manuscripts*, Allen Lane, London, 2016

A.C. de la Mare, *Bartolomeo Sanvito: The Life and Work of a Renaissance Scribe*, ed. Laura Nuvoloni, et al., Association Internationale de Bibliophilie, Paris, 2009

Esther Inglis's Les Proverbes de Salomon: A Facsimile, ed. Nicholas Barker, Roxburghe Club, 2012

Edward Johnston, *Writing & Illuminating & Lettering*, The Artistic Crafts Series of Technical Handbooks, Pitman & Sons, London, 1906

Alfred Fairbank, *A Book of Scripts*, Penguin, Harmondsworth, 1968

Calligraphy and Palaeography: Essays Presented to Alfred Fairbank on his 70th birthday, ed. A.S. Osley, Faber & Faber, London, 1965

Postscript

Letters and the Second Diary of Samuel Pepys, ed. R.G. Howarth, J.M. Dent & Sons, London and Toronto, 1933

LIST OF MANUSCRIPTS

COPYRIGHT ACKNOWLEDGEMENTS

p. 70 MS. Kafka 49, fol. 79, The Bodleian Library, University of Oxford / HS.2011.0037.00064, Deutsches Literaturarchiv Marbach. By permission of the Kafka family.

pp. 72, 75 Unpublished material by T.S. Eliot reproduced by permission of Faber and Faber Ltd.

pp. 84, 87 By permission of The Principal and Fellows of Somerville College, Oxford.

pp. 88, 91, 92 Reproduced by permission of Lord Lytton.

p. 94 Reproduced by permission of William H. Darwin.

p. 96 © The Hebrew University of Jerusalem – With permission of the Albert Einstein Archives.

pp. 100, 103 © The Estate of Dorothy Crowfoot Hodgkin.

p. 123 By permission of Helen Pankhurst.

p. 128 By permission of Arun Gandhi.

pp. 142, 145 By permission of the Bentham Project.

p. 150 By permission of the Trustees of the Wilfred Owen Estate.

p. 153 Copyright Siegfried Sassoon by permission of the Estate of George Sassoon.

p. 154 Reproduced by permission of The Henry Moore Foundation - Henry Moore Foundation of Dane Tree House, Perry Green, Much Hadham, Hertfordshire SG10 6EE.

p. 156 Barbara Hepworth © Bowness.

pp. 166, 169 By permission of Peter Covey-Crump.

p. 178 By permission of the Trustees of the Seven Pillars of Wisdom Trust.

p. 180 By permission of the Estate of Patrick Leigh Fermor.

p. 202 'Fancy's Knell' from 'Along The Field', eight Housman songs for voice and violin by Ralph Vaughan Williams © Oxford University Press 1954. Reproduced by permission. All rights reserved.

pp. 204, 207 © Britten Pears Arts.

p. 221 Donated by Alan Bennett (© Forelake Ltd) c/o United Agents LLP.

pp. 222, 225 By permission of the Arthur Ransome Literary Trust.

p. 226 © The Tolkien Estate Limited 1937, 2011.

p. 228 © Sir Quentin Blake, 2023 (drawn in 1988)

pp. 230, 232 By permission of Philip Pullman

p. 236 Special thanks to Richard Doyle, Cathy Beggs, Charles Foley, and the Conan Doyle Estate Ltd. for permission to reprint Sir Arthur Conan Doyle's letter to Ebenezer Ward.

p. 241 By permission of David Higham Associates Ltd.

p. 244 By permission of The Christie Archive Trust.

pp. 247, 248, 249 Copyright © The Estate of Raymond Chandler. Reproduced by permission of the Estate c/o Rogers, Coleridge & White Ltd., 20 Powis Mews, London W11 1JN.

p. 250 Quotes by Ian Fleming, reproduced with the permission of The Ian Fleming Estate, copyright © The Ian Fleming Estate 1942, 1965. www.ianfleming.com

p. 252, 254 copyright © P.D. James, 2010. reproduced by permission of Greene & Heaton Ltd.

p. 256 © The John le Carré Literary Estate, reproduced with permission.

p. 284 Vera Brittain material is included by permission of Mark Bostridge and T.J. Brittain-Catlin, Literary Executors for the Estate of Vera Brittain 1970.

p. 298 By permission of Andrew Johnston.

INDEX

References to images are in **bold** type

This publication has been generously supported by the
Martin J. Gross Family Foundation.

First published in 2023 by the Bodleian Library
Broad Street, Oxford OX1 3BG
www.bodleianshop.co.uk

ISBN: 978 1 85124 595 6

Publisher: Samuel Fanous
Managing Editor: Susie Foster
Editor: Janet Phillips
Picture Editor: Leanda Shrimpton
Designed and typeset by Dot Little at the Bodleian Library in 10.5/15pt Minion
Printed and bound by C&C Offset Printing Co., Ltd on 140 gsm Chinese Golden Sun (white) Woodfree paper

FSC www.fsc.org
MIX
Paper | Supporting responsible forestry
FSC® C008047

British Library Catalogue in Publishing Data
A CIP record of this publication is available from the British Library